CONTENTS

FOREWORD   4

BASICS   6

CAMPAIGN   16

EXTRAS   110

MULTIPLAYER   142

INDEX   208

VERTICAL TAB

The vertical tab on the right-hand margin of each double-page spread is a navigational tool designed to help you find your way around the guide. The top section lists the individual chapters, while the lower section highlights the part of the chapter you are currently reading.

FOLDOUT

The back cover foldout lists all the symbols that appear on maps throughout the guide. Feel free to leave it open so that you have access to this handy key at all times.

FOREWORD

Being ardent fans of the Halo series, this guide has been a labor of love for the Piggyback team. After half a year of research and development, including three intensive months on site at Bungie's offices and many hundreds of hours of play, you might suspect that the editorial team would be looking forward to playing something, *anything*, else. But no: at the time of writing, we're currently enduring a painful period of withdrawal while we wait for our boxed copies of Halo 3 to arrive.

Without wishing to appear unduly arrogant, we're also extremely fond of the book you now hold in your hands. Why? Well…

Quality is everything

We have striven to create a book that we would genuinely like to read, rather than one that would be easy to write.

This is a strategy guide, not an instruction manual

While we're fully aware of the irony inherent in pointing this out in a foreword, we've taken every step to avoid needless preamble. The short Basics chapter that follows this introduction offers a quick, ten-page crash course to help first-time Halo players get up to speed, and that's it – blink, and you'll miss it. From there, we leap directly into the Campaign chapter, just as you most likely will as a player.

Spoilers are the work of the devil

We've gone to great lengths to avoid mentioning even the slightest detail about Halo 3's storyline in the Campaign chapter. Millions of players worldwide, even those who howled with outrage at Halo 2's cliffhanger denouement, have been fidgeting impatiently for three years while waiting to learn how the story ends, and it's not our place to ruin it for them. We've also been very careful to respect the importance of gameplay-related surprises, such as new enemies, weapons, vehicles and equipment, by introducing them only *after* you encounter each during play.

We focus on guidance, tips and finer points that you actually need

You may be surprised to read this here, but a meticulous blow-by-blow account of how to play through Halo 3 on the Normal difficulty level simply isn't necessary - there are plenty of onscreen prompts, visual waypoints and spoken clues that tell you where to go or what to do next. Thing is, though, playing on the default Normal difficulty setting is pretty much a dress rehearsal for the *real* Halo 3. Sure, you'll get to see how the story ends, enjoy plenty of unforgettable sights and sounds, and kill alien adversaries in clever, creative ways… but if you want to experience the true game, you'll need to complete it on Heroic and, eventually, Legendary.

The Heroic difficulty level is where all veteran Halo players and dedicated gamers should start, and is, in Bungie's words, "Halo 3 as it is meant to be played". Legendary comes later. Unlike its equivalent mode in Halo and Halo 2, it has been carefully tuned and refined to remove needlessly cruel difficulty spikes. It's consistently challenging, sometimes maddeningly so, and will push many players to the very limits of their abilities. You may hurl your joypad aside in disgust from time to time, but never so furiously that you can't simply reach over to pick it up and try again. We would speculate that the Gamerscore reward for beating every level on Legendary will be the most gratifying Achievement many Xbox 360 owners will ever unlock.

For that reason, our Campaign chapter is rather unique, as we've divided each double-page spread into two distinct sections. The left-hand page is designed for readers playing through on Easy, Normal and Heroic, and features a detailed map annotated with the positions of weapons, vehicles and points of interactivity, surrounded by bite-sized captions that provide targeted guidance, practical tips, and useful observations. The right-hand page, though, is written specifically for those playing Halo 3 on Legendary, and features exhaustively researched strategies, tactics and techniques for every key battle you fight.

So: while you don't necessarily need a guide to finish Halo 3, you won't truly "beat" Bungie's opus until you complete it on Legendary, and unlock all associated Achievements. And this is where you **will** need our help.

Of course, there's much more to this guide than the Campaign walkthrough. The Extras chapter that follows it is meant to prepare players for life on Heroic and Legendary, and also reveals detailed information on special features that you can read about after you've witnessed the game's ending. We strongly advise — nay, *insist* — that you refrain from reading it until you have finished the Campaign mode for the first time. Last, but by no means least, the guide's closing chapter focuses on Halo 3's magnificent multiplayer mode. It has detailed annotated maps, of course — essential for those seeking to learn the location of principle "power weapons" straight away — but also includes essential tried-and-tested techniques and strategies either contributed by, or approved by, the Halo 3 team.

Finish Halo 3's Campaign mode once, and you'll have seen a mere fraction of what it has to offer. Complete it five times, and you'll still feel that there's much more that you could experiment with... not to mention a multiplayer mode that will keep you playing for years. There's no doubt about it: Halo 3 is a game designed to last. And so, as we hope you'll soon appreciate, is this guide.

The Piggyback Team
September 2007

BASICS

This short opening chapter is designed to introduce you to important Halo 3 concepts, providing both essential practical instructions and an introduction to many key gameplay features. Dedicated Halo players should feel free to skim-read or, indeed, skip it entirely if they wish.

HOW TO PLAY

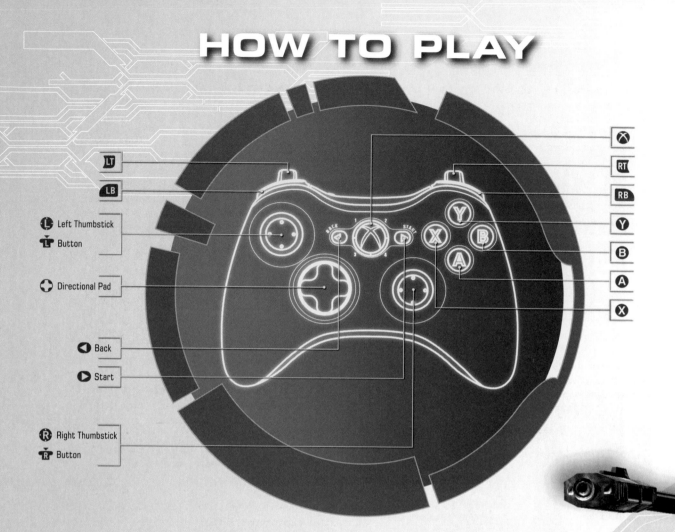

LT
LB
L Left Thumbstick
T Button
Directional Pad
Back
Start
R Right Thumbstick
R Button

X
RT
RB
Y
B
A
X

COMMANDS

The following button configuration applies to Halo 3's default settings, so don't fret if you're a strict southpaw – they can be modified at any time. For further details, please turn to page 9.

COMMAND	IN MENUS	ON FOOT	ABOARD VEHICLES
L	Move cursor	Move forward/backward, strafe left/right	Move forward/backward, strafe (where applicable)
R	-	Look around, aim	Rotate camera/change direction
✛	Move cursor	Up: toggle Flashlight on/off	-
A	Confirm	Jump Skip cinematics	Brake
B	Cancel	Melee attack	-
X	Edit options	Use equipment	-
Y	-	Draw reserve weapon Drop weapon in left hand (when dual wielding)	-
LB	-	Change grenade type Hold to pick up weapon with left hand Reload weapon in left hand	-
RB	-	Hold to pick up weapon with right hand Reload weapon in right hand	Hold: climb aboard/exit vehicle
LT	Select the top menu option	Toss grenade Fire with weapon in left hand (when dual wielding)	Use optional feature (varies with each vehicle type): power slide, speed boost, et al
RT	Select the bottom menu option	Fire with weapon in right hand	Fire (only available with certain vehicles or with turrets) Horn
L (Press)	-	Crouch	-
R (Press)	-	Zoom	-
Start	Enter Settings menu	Enter/exit pause menu	
Back	-		
Xbox	Access/exit Guide menu		

HAL∋3

BASICS
CAMPAIGN
EXTRAS
MULTIPLAYER

HOW TO PLAY
HALO 3 MEDIA
HALO 3 PRIMER

MENUS

This section introduces the most common menus in Halo 3, describing everything first-time players need to know to get started. If you require any further help, or simply crave a hand to hold as you hesitantly behold Halo 3's intuitive user interface for the first time, you can always take the radical step of consulting your Halo 3 game manual...

The Main Menu

To begin a new Campaign, select Start Solo Campaign from the Main Menu. You then must choose a difficulty level from the four available: Easy, Normal, Heroic and Legendary. Normal is the best setting for those playing Halo 3 for the first time. If you find this level (or, perhaps, the demands of regularly walking across the room to retrieve your controller) too challenging, you can always play on Easy until you grow in both confidence and ability. As suggested in the guide introduction, only veterans of Legendary campaigns in Halo and Halo 2 should consider starting on Heroic; everyone, and we mean *everyone*, should leave Legendary alone at first.

The Campaign menu (Fig. 1) enables you to pick specific missions to play once they have been unlocked. This is also where you can launch co-op games. Once in the Campaign Lobby, you are free to choose previously completed levels to play (and individual Rally Point starting positions within those levels), and to adjust the difficulty level. For co-op, you can set up a split-screen game, or meet up with other players on a LAN or via Xbox LIVE (either by hosting them in your party or by joining theirs). You may additionally press ▶ to change certain settings. As soon as you're ready, select Start Game to proceed.

The Pause Menu

Press ▶ at any time during the game to access the pause menu. It features two main pages that you can switch between by moving the stick left or right.

The Game page shows the status of your current mission objectives, which are marked with a tick once completed. From here, you can choose to restart your mission, or revert to the last checkpoint (an extremely useful feature if a battle goes spectacularly awry). The Save and Quit option enables you to quit your game and resume it later from the last-triggered checkpoint.

Most of the options in the Settings page are self-explanatory. However, there are a few options in the Game Controls sub-menu that we should at least briefly explain.

Look Inversion: Determines if you need to move the stick up to look up and down to look down, or vice versa.

Look Sensitivity: The higher this setting, the greater the speed at which you look around. A high sensitivity will not necessarily make you more effective, though. It's best to leave this on the default setting, then adjust it in small increments at a later date if required.

Button Layout: Choose the layout that best suits your needs. Note that the Bumper Jumper setting is interesting for left-handers, as it enables them to have the commands of the most crucial battle moves mapped to triggers and bumpers.

Stick Layout: Controls the functionality of both sticks. Most left-handers will use this option to switch to the Southpaw configuration.

Auto Look Centering: With this option enabled, the camera will automatically return to a forward-facing position as you move. This is useful if you're struggling to control the camera during combat.

Crouch Behavior: Determines if you must hold ✛ to crouch, or instead press it once to toggle between stances.

ONSCREEN DISPLAY

1 Primary Weapon: The weapon currently held in your right hand. The number to the left shows the total ammunition carried or remaining battery power, while the gauge below displays the ammo in the current clip, or a temperature gauge for weapons powered by fuel cells. If this gauge reaches its red extreme, an automatic cooling system will prevent you from firing for a few seconds. When you dual wield (use two weapons simultaneously – see page 14), an additional (and functionally identical) display will appear in the left-hand corner of the screen for the weapon held in the corresponding hand.

2 Reserve Weapon: The secondary weapon you have at your disposal, which will either be holstered or slung over the Master Chief's shoulder. Note that the reserve weapon icon will flash if it is out of ammunition or has a depleted fuel cell.

3 Energy Shield: This gauge shows the status of your shield, with the bar decreasing as the Master Chief is hit by weapons or explosions. Once empty, it will turn red and flash (there's also an alarm that sounds), indicating that any further damage might kill you. If you avoid being hit for a number of seconds, your shield will return to normal working order and the gauge will be refilled.

4 Grenades: You can carry a maximum of two grenades per type; the currently selected model is highlighted. When you're dual wielding, this display will be replaced by information about the weapon held in your left hand (see Primary Weapon).

5 Equipment: You may only hold one piece of equipment at a time; a representative icon will be positioned here when you're carrying an item. Guidance on how to use these gadgets is provided in the Campaign chapter.

6 Crosshair: The crosshair shape varies with each weapon, and its color indicates whether a target is an ally (green) or a foe (red).

7 Onscreen Instructions: Every time you can interact with your environment (for example, to pick up a weapon or to open a door), the button you need to press will appear here.

8 Radar: Also called Motion Tracker, this device reveals the location of all moving or firing entities in your immediate vicinity. The top of the radar corresponds to the direction you're facing. Friendly beings are represented as yellow dots (this includes you, in the center of the circle), while hostiles are red dots. Larger dots signify vehicles. When you have an objective to fulfill, the direction of your target will sometimes be shown as a white triangle

9 Waypoint Indicator: In some instances an icon will indicate the direction of your next destination, as well as how far you need to travel to reach it.

10 Checkpoint: Whenever you cross a new checkpoint, it will be briefly mentioned above the radar. Read the "Halo 3 Primer" section further along in this chapter to learn more about the checkpoint system.

HALO 3 MEDIA

BASICS

CAMPAIGN

EXTRAS

MULTIPLAYER

HOW TO PLAY

HALO 3 MEDIA

HALO 3 PRIMER

Halo 3 isn't just great to play: it's also fun to watch and look at, and the ability to create, share and download custom Game Types and edited maps is endlessly absorbing. In this section, we provide a brief introduction to the File Share and Theater features, and tell you how you can use them to watch, play and distribute film clips, screenshots, custom maps and Game Types.

To visit the Media page (Fig. 1) in Your Settings, simply press ▶ at any time. From here, you have access to several self-explanatory options. Bungie Favorites provides a list of Bungie's recommended files, which are frequently renewed. File Share and Screenshots enable you to manage, amazingly enough, your File Share and your Screenshots.

FILE SHARE

Your File Share is a dedicated online area where you can make files available for other people to download. Each Halo 3 player with an Xbox LIVE Gold Membership has their own File Share space allocated, with no limits on the number of transfers that can take place.

Uploading data to your online File Share is dead easy. All you have to do is enter your File Share menu from Your Settings (see above), and select the files you would like to upload. These files can be:

- Video footage stored while playing Campaign or Multiplayer modes (including Forge sessions).

- Screenshots taken while watching Campaign or Multiplayer game videos in the Theater (more on this below).

- Custom Game Type Variants created in the Custom Games menu (for more information, turn to page 146).

- Maps that you have edited in the Forge (see page 206).

Downloading data from another person's File Share is also a snap. Simply highlight their name from within a game Lobby, then press Ⓐ to display their Player Details, which includes their File Share. You can also press ✖ and browse your Friends and Recent Player lists. If you select someone while Halo 3 is running, you'll see a special File Share entry added to the usual list of options.

Once a file is in your File Share space, you are free to use it as you please, and as many times as you want. You can access your File Share from the Custom Games Lobby to load a map and/or a Game Type Variant; from the Forge Lobby to load a map; or from the Theater Lobby to load entire game films, edited clips or screenshots.

You can also recommend files from your File Share to your friends. Whenever you do so, they'll receive a message taking them directly to the file in question.

THEATER

The Film option enables you to choose the file you want to watch from several categories (Fig. 2), including those in your File Share. Halo 3 automatically records events when you play in Campaign and multiplayer modes, so you can find your prior performances in the Recent Films list. If you'd like to store one of these for future viewing or sharing, simply highlight it and press ⊗, then follow the onscreen prompts.

Once you have chosen a video to play, select Start Film. While watching it, you can press ▶ at any time to pause. From there, you can end the film you're watching, change the usual Settings, and check the commands available in Theater mode (Fig. 3). If you are viewing a video in a group, note that only the Party Leader has access to certain Theater functions.

Camera controls: Use ⓨ to change the camera type (following the selected character, or flying freely around him); move the camera with ⓛ or ⓡ, and LB or RB; note that you can hold LT to increase the speed of movement.

Adjustments: The following commands are handy when taking screenshots. Ⓐ enables you to pause and resume playback, and Ⓑ cycles through the various HUD settings. Use RT to control the playback speed, and press up or down on ⬦ to change player (only available for footage from co-op and multiplayer games).

Advanced controls: Press ⊗ at any time to display the Theater Control Pad, and navigate its options by pressing left or right on ⬦. You can take screenshots by selecting the camera-shaped icon (Fig. 4). Once you have taken a screenshot, you must name it (either manually, or using the Autoname function) before it is saved. The Record Clip option enables you to create a smaller film clip that shows a particular sequence of events. As a rule, most people won't be willing to wade through an entire Campaign level recording to see the funny thing that happens eight minutes in, so it pays to edit your files accordingly.

The Theater can be used to enjoy memorable videos, but it's also a great way to study how others play in multiplayer matches. You can pick up a surprising number of techniques and strategies by watching how your opponents and teammates behave. With the tools at your disposal, including the flying camera and the "change player" feature, there's not a single moment in a match that you won't be able to analyze and learn from.

HALO 3

BASICS
CAMPAIGN
EXTRAS
MULTIPLAYER

HOW TO PLAY
HALO 3 MEDIA
HALO 3 PRIMER

HALO 3 PRIMER:
A GUIDE FOR NEW RECRUITS

If you haven't played a game in the Halo series before, we strongly recommend that you read the following introduction to the key features that set Halo 3 apart from its FPS ("first person shooter") peers. If you *have* previously played a Halo game, but perhaps feel a little rusty after years of inactivity, consider this a brief refresher course. More experienced Halo players can either drum their fingers while we run through these fundamentals, or skip straight ahead to the Campaign chapter on page 16.

So, in brief, Halo 3's Campaign mode isn't a low-rent FPS single-player experience where you listlessly trade shots with cardboard cut-out assailants. It offers variable, sophisticated and – above all – endlessly enjoyable sci-fi combat where, as your opponents generally have greater firepower, you need to be clever and creative to survive. Completing levels is not the only goal – *how* you play them matters just as much. With all the vehicles, weapons and gadgets at your disposal, Bungie's sandbox-style design affords you a remarkable degree of freedom to fight battles in any way you please. There's no real "right" or "wrong" way to approach combat. The point is to freely experiment, and to enjoy doing so.

The first step on this road, then, is to familiarize yourself with a few of the noteworthy features that make Halo 3 and its forebears so very special. So, without further ado...

MOVEMENT

We don't intend to teach you how to play an FPS: we presume throughout the guide (and especially after, in the words of Sergeant-Major Johnson, we "kick off the training wheels" at the end of this short opening chapter) that you can use a dual-stick controller, and have fired a few virtual shots in anger before now. That said, there are a couple of general playing tips that it would be foolish of us not to mention. Firstly, even when playing on the Normal difficulty setting, you'll soon notice that the Covenant troops are shrewd and aggressive. You'll need to learn to use available cover intelligently, taking refuge behind a solid element separating you from your foes every time you're in danger.

Secondly, if you stand stock still and shoot from the hip, you'll be cut to pieces. You should try to keep moving whenever the Master Chief is exposed during combat. It's vital that you strafe to dodge enemy fire while fighting out in the open, and you should always have a rough escape plan in mind. There's no shame in a temporary retreat, especially when it provides valuable time for the Chief's shields to recharge.

SHIELDS

One of the original Halo's many pioneering design features was the Master Chief's energy shield. Capable of withstanding a level of damage linked to the game difficulty setting, it would cut out under extreme fire from enemy weapons, rendering the Chief vulnerable to damage on a secondary health meter. However, and here's the deceptively-simple-yet-very-clever bit, the shield would be fully replenished if the player could avoid damage for a short period of time. This novel revision of the traditional "energy gauge" system encouraged players to use cover intelligently, and treat their smart and sneaky Covenant opponents with respect.

In Halo 2, Bungie dispensed with Health Packs and the visible second energy bar entirely, and it's this system that is used in Halo 3. You can find the shield gauge at the top of the HUD (see page 10). When the Master Chief's shield energy is full, he's (broadly speaking) protected from all but the most dangerous weapons when you play on Normal. The moment the bar is reduced to below a quarter full, and especially when the gauge flashes an insistent, angry red (Fig. 1), it's vital that you take cover.

While the Master Chief can withstand a certain amount of additional damage once his shield fails, this "period of grace" is hard to judge. Through experience you'll gain a better understanding of the punishment he can endure, but it's generally advisable to find a good place to hide when the in-helmet alarm sounds.

WEAPONS

There's a hint of Rock, Paper, Scissors to the balance of Halo 3's subtle, finely tuned weapons system. Every firearm has its place, excelling in certain situations, yet perhaps lacking bite in others. Some are specialist tools (underestimate the slight yet mightily useful Plasma Pistol at your peril), some (such as the Battle Rifle or Carbine), are solid against a wide assortment of foes, while others offer the carefully rationed pleasure of sheer pure brute force: indeed, certain weapons are powerful enough to take down armored vehicles.

On the Normal difficulty level, it's generally the case that some firearms are simply more efficient than others in specific situations, but learning how to make the most of your arsenal is still highly important. You will learn more about the strengths and weaknesses of weapons in the Campaign chapter, but try to bear the following points in mind:

- An extremely cool feature inherited from Halo 2 is dual wielding (Fig. 2). Dual wielding is the practice of holding two one-handed weapons at the same time. If it's possible to dual wield a nearby weapon with the gun held in the Master Chief's right hand, an onscreen prompt will appear at the upper left-hand corner of the screen. Dual wielding has two main applications: it can double your firepower if you carry the same type of firearm in both hands, or it can offer tactical benefits if you handle two weapons of different types. However, you cannot throw grenades while dual wielding; furthermore, any attempt to perform a melee attack will lead you to discard the weapon held in your left hand.

0 2

- The Master Chief can carry a maximum of three weapons at once – one in reserve (holstered or slung over the Chief's shoulders), and up to two "active" weapons if you're dual wielding. A portable turret can count as a third weapon too.

- Frequent reloading is a discipline that you'll need to learn quickly. Ducking back behind cover to change a clip becomes second nature after a while, but you can always tell a fresh-faced Halo 3 recruit by the way that they charge into battle with a practically empty clip, then skitter, slide and squeal like a baby gazelle when they hear the ominous and abrupt report of the "dead man's click". We'd love to think up a clever new mantra or mnemonic to help such individuals, but the timeless "Reload or Die!" pretty much communicates the message perfectly.

- Unlike in Halo 2, you can use **LB** and **RB** to reload each weapon independently, adding a subtle but important strategic layer to dual wielding.

- Many enemies have vulnerable spots, particularly unprotected heads, so learn to pick your shots carefully. If your aim is akin to that of a six-year-old boy taking a restroom break, even lowly Covenant Grunts will struggle to stifle their snickering behind cupped claws. "Spraying and praying" just doesn't cut it in Halo 3.

- It often pays to conserve ammunition. Unless you're in a situation where you have a ready supply of useful weapons, try to save more powerful firearms until they're actually required. You'll find advice on weapon usage throughout the Campaign chapter. By walking over the same type of weapon as the one that you are carrying, you will automatically collect new ammunition if it's possible to do so. However, certain weapons (particularly the Plasma Pistol and Plasma Rifle) are powered by built-in fuel cells, and cannot be recharged.

0 3

- A melee attack is often a viciously efficient way to finish off an opponent (Fig. 3). Hits from behind are instantly lethal against a wide range of enemies – such "stealth" kills may even slay a fully armored Brute.

GRENADES

Another defining feature of the Halo series is the inclusion of a dedicated button for throwing grenades, which clearly underlines their importance in general combat. In Halo 3 you can carry a maximum of two of each grenade type; these are automatically collected from the battlefield as you walk over them. Grenades are powerful against crowds (Fig. 4), or strong enemies that can weather the storm of an entire Assault Rifle clip without blinking or breaking stride. However, there are many other ways they can be used; there's plenty of room for creativity. You could, for example, cover a hasty retreat by throwing one at the ground to discourage foes from giving chase.

0 4

BASICS

CAMPAIGN

EXTRAS

MULTIPLAYER

HOW TO PLAY

HALO 3 MEDIA

HALO 3 PRIMER

EQUIPMENT

The inclusion of specialist "equipment" is a new feature in Halo 3. The Master Chief can only carry a single piece of equipment at a time, and will automatically collect an item provided he is not currently carrying anything. Whenever you want to swap a gadget with a different type

positioned at his feet, simply follow the onscreen prompt.

To avoid spoiling any surprises, we explain the function and use of all equipment types in the relevant areas of the Campaign chapter.

ALLIES

Not everyone you encounter in Halo 3 carries a gun with a bullet inscribed with the words "Master Chief" sitting impatiently in the chamber: you will also be frequently accompanied by troops who will fight alongside you. On one level these individuals act as a diversion for enemy combatants, drawing fire away from your position and contributing to each affray with their fair share of kills. On another, they're talkative, highly welcome companions – you'll find that you actively go out of your way to ensure

their wellbeing, often just to see what they'll say or do next.

You can actually swap weapons with certain allies: simply stand in front of them and press the button that appears onscreen to make the exchange. However, some troops will not accept certain firearms, and you should note that you cannot take weapons of a type that the Master Chief is already carrying. It is also not possible to trade weapons with a co-op player.

VEHICLES

There are many vehicles (including unique model variants) to drive in Halo 3, each having its own characteristics and capabilities. To climb inside a vehicle, approach the appropriate side and follow the onscreen prompt. While each mode of transport behaves in a different way, it's generally safe to assume that you steer with one thumbstick, then accelerate and reverse (and, in some instances, strafe) with the other thumbstick. Though it may take a little getting used to, this system soon becomes second nature.

With certain vehicles you can also hop on board as a gunner or a passenger – watch out for the onscreen message that appears as you approach them from different directions. When you take

up one of these positions, nearby allies will often climb in as well, driving you on an attack run if there are enemy forces present. If the coast is clear, they'll simply chauffeur you (and any other troops on board) to the next battle.

Finally, it's actually possible to "board" and take control of enemy-controlled vehicles. We'll offer more detailed advice on this in the Campaign chapter, but remember that it can be achieved by holding the usual button while approaching a vehicle from a specific direction – generally from the side. Covenant troops are far from stupid, though, and will attempt to dodge you or, indeed, simply run you over.

CHECKPOINTS

Halo 3 automatically stores and saves your progress when you reach "checkpoints". These can be triggered by arriving at a particular area, or killing specific enemies; they may occur prior to, during, or after battles. When you die, you will be restored to the exact position and state you were in when you last passed a checkpoint. This is a clean, simple and fair process that runs transparently in the background and encourages experimentation.

If the tide of a battle turns against you, and you'd like to turn back time to put things right, you can enter the pause menu and select "Revert to saved" to start again from the last checkpoint. (We usually prefer to commit suicide in the most spectacular, explosive manner possible to achieve the same effect, but perhaps that's just us.)

AUDIO

As magnificently rich as the Halo 3 audio experience is, it would be a mistake to regard everything you hear as mere incidental ear-candy. If you listen closely, you'll notice that there are a wide variety of audio cues that can help you to stay alive. From the hissing and fizzing of a thrown Plasma Grenade, to shouts and warnings from your allies, to the audible plotting and scheming of emboldened Grunts, it pays to have a keen ear. Incidentally, you should note that when you hear the dull, echoing report of distant gunfire on your travels, that battle is actually *really happening* further forwards – it's not just an atmospheric effect. If you want to save your allies, you'll need to move quickly. Finally, if you're lucky enough to have a Dolby 5.1 sound system, you can use the apparent position of a sound to gauge where your enemy is shooting, walking, or even reloading. If he sounds like he's upstairs, or behind you, he probably is.

ONSCREEN TEXT

Last, but not least, keep an eye on the upper left and (especially) right-hand sections of the screen. This is where useful prompts will appear to inform you when you can perform certain actions, such as collecting weapons, boarding vehicles, or interacting with objects.

CAMPAIGN

This chapter is designed both to guide new players through their first experience of the Halo 3 Campaign on its lower difficulty levels, and to offer a comprehensive walkthrough for the hugely challenging Legendary play mode. This dual-speed approach is unique, so we strongly advise that first-time readers consult the User Instructions section overleaf before they continue.

USER INSTRUCTIONS

CHAPTER STRUCTURE

Most Campaign missions in this chapter have the following structure:

- Two opening pages feature a large overview map of the entire playing area (Fig. 1).
- The walkthrough pages offer guidance, analysis and tips for each mission. There is an enhanced map portion on each left-hand page, annotated with useful advice for those playing on Easy, Normal and Heroic, and a corresponding Legendary walkthrough on each right-hand page (Fig. 2).
- The final two pages for every mission act as a "debriefing" session, discussing the new features (such as enemies and weapons) introduced during the level (Fig. 3).

 Overview map

This map offers a clear view of the entire mission area, with place names added as an aid to orientation. The rectangles indicate the locales covered in each part of the walkthrough that follows. To locate the specific area you need guidance on, simply look at the Roman numerals, and then flick forward to the page with the corresponding number.

 Walkthrough: left-hand page

When you play on the Easy or Normal difficulty levels, you should find all the advice you need on the left-hand page. It focuses on general insights and assistance, with its short captions carefully tailored to help you through occasional flashpoints, or to point out interesting features.

3 **Walkthrough: right-hand page**

The right-hand page, by contrast, provides detailed advice and tactics that are designed to help dedicated players beat the "true" incarnation of Halo 3: the ultra-challenging Legendary difficulty setting. However, the strategies and suggestions made on this page can be just as useful on Heroic, or even Normal and Easy. If you find a particular battle difficult to beat, feel free to refer to this text at any time.

4 **Headline**

The main headline for each left-hand page features a Roman numeral. This links to the corresponding section of the main overview map.

 Map section

Each left-hand page features an enhanced, magnified portion of the overview map. This is annotated with location names, important collectable items, and icons that reveal approximate enemy numbers. The letter icons link to the corresponding paragraphs of the Legendary walkthrough on the right-hand page.

 Captions

Map portions are annotated with captions; some with screenshots, others without. These point to specific locations and usually suggest tactics that will help you to survive the toughest battles. If you are playing on Easy or Normal, these captions will generally tell you everything you need to know.

 Lettered paragraphs

The core of the Legendary walkthrough, these paragraphs offer step-by-step guidance through each key battle. If you encounter difficulties in a particular place, just locate the nearest letter on the area map, then refer to the corresponding paragraph on the right-hand page.

8 **Margin notes**

You can find "margin notes" at the bottom right-hand corner of each Legendary walkthrough page. These offer a wide variety of useful tips and observations, from co-op tactics to enemy weaknesses.

9 **Tab system**

The tab system on the right-hand side of each double-page spread is designed to aid rapid navigation through the different sections of the guide. If you are looking for information on a specific mission, just flip the pages until its entry is highlighted. Note that in order to avoid potential spoilers, missions are referred to by their numbers rather than their actual names.

10 **Debriefing**

Every mission walkthrough ends with a "debriefing" section that analyzes the new enemies, equipment, vehicles and weapons that appeared during the level. Again, this has been designed to keep spoilers to a bare minimum.

QUICK START

This simple diagram shows where you should look for guidance, based on your chosen difficulty setting. This is only a suggestion, of course. If you want to use the Legendary walkthrough while you play on Normal, that's entirely your choice — just bear in mind that it will often reference enemies and events that don't occur on lower difficulty levels.

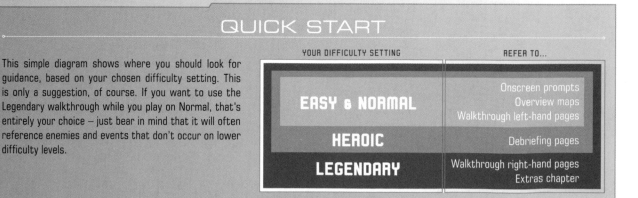

YOUR DIFFICULTY SETTING	REFER TO...
EASY & NORMAL	Onscreen prompts Overview maps Walkthrough left-hand pages
HEROIC	Debriefing pages
LEGENDARY	Walkthrough right-hand pages Extras chapter

BASICS

CAMPAIGN

EXTRAS

MULTIPLAYER

**USER
INSTRUCTIONS**

PREFACE

MISSION 1

MISSION 2

MISSION 3

MISSION 4

MISSION 5

MISSION 6

MISSION 7

MISSION 8

MISSION 9

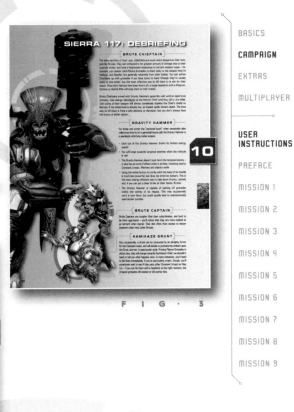

SIERRA 117: DEBRIEFING

BRUTE CHIEFTAIN

GRAVITY HAMMER

BRUTE CAPTAIN

KAMIKAZE GRUNT

10

F I G · 3

1

F I G · 1

2

3

4

[SIERRA 117]

CHIEF CRATER

JUNGLE WALK

GRUNT CAMP

SNIPER ALLEY

5

6

7

8

9

HALO 3

First things first: your Assault Rifle is of relatively little use against this Brute or, indeed, his entire species, on Legendary. You may as well be pelting him with spitballs, or harsh language. You'll need to expend at least an entire clip at close range to destroy his power armor, while simultaneously dodging incoming fire. It's much better, then, to leave habits acquired on Normal (or even Heroic) behind and learn to love one of the tools that will keep you alive on Legendary: the humble yet deceptively powerful Plasma Pistol.

Meanwhile, two Phantoms will deploy Brutes and Grunts further along the riverside, so take cover until they depart. At this point, you should begin to notice enemy behaviors that were perhaps less apparent on other difficulty settings, particularly their tendency to pull back to more defensible positions once the side of battle begins to turn against them. Over the first waterfall, pop the single Brute's power armor with a charged Plasma Pistol shot, then – carefully – dispatch him with a headshot. (This

Grab a Carbine from the dispenser and make your way up to the ledge overlooking the Grunt Camp. There are Jackals with Carbines here (which can sometimes include one to the very far right – you can only see him before dropping down if you stand beside the Arbiter), so deal with those first. Then sit about killing every Grunt you can find. The Covenant troops will take cover or even withdraw, but don't be tempted to sacrifice your excellent vantage point just yet. Lastly, kill the shield-wielding Jackals. It may take more shots than usual to dispatch them from this range (remember, you should ideally shoot for the embrasure on their shields to make them stagger, then follow up with an immediate headshot), but you certainly won't be short of ammunition here.

As soon as you vault over the natural barrier, take cover by the fallen tree and use your Assault Rifle to kill a few Grunts as they come into view. Switch to your Magnum, quickly grab one of the Grunt's Plasma Pistols to dual wield with it, then immediately prepare a charged shot to blow the Brute's power armor. You should aim to finish him off with a pistol headshot immediately, but if there are plenty of Grunts around, it may be safer to duck straight back behind cover. Use your Assault Rifle to begin clearing the area. Note that grenades are used by enemies and allies alike from the first encounter on Legendary. Be vigilant, and steer well clear of explosions.

is by far the best way to kill Brutes at this point, so we'll assume that you've got the message now.)

Move forward cautiously: there are numerous Grunts and two more Brutes along the river's edge. You can swap your Assault Rifle for a Brute Shot to deal with the former quickly from range, and there is a ready supply of Plasma Pistols to help you beat the latter.

The remaining members of the Covenant force (particularly the Brutes) will usually retreat to the top of the slope on the far side of the camp, though they will be less inclined to do so if you have kept some Marines alive. Replenish your supply of Carbine ammo, then make your way to the opposite side of the shallow pool. If there is a Jackal marksman on the high ledge to the right and you didn't kill him earlier, you'll probably notice a succession of searing yellow reminders heading your way any time now. The surviving Covenant troops will either have foolishly backed themselves into a corner near the point where the path upwards turns to the spread thinly on the slope if there are Marines accompanying. This is a good opportunity to have fun with a Needler. When you've cleared the area, take a Plasma Pistol to dual wield with your Magnum (with a Carbine in reserve) before you continue.

You'll have the Arbiter fighting alongside you for the forthcoming jungle battles. Armed with a Carbine, he's a highly useful companion – even when his shots don't hit their mark, he tends to draw fire away from the Master Chief.

Weapons are made available on purple "dispensers" throughout most levels. Feel free to help yourself whenever you encounter one.

There's a Brute standing guard on a tree trunk here, and a sizable group of Grunts will attack shortly after you arrive. As a rule, it's always smart to break enemy forces up into manageable units. On lower difficulty settings, you can also rely on your allies to help you out when things get tough.

Once the first enemies have been dispatched, two Phantoms will drop off reinforcements. The Phantom's cannons can be devastating, even on Normal, so it's prudent to take cover until they fly off. Fight your way along the riverbank until you reach a natural rock passageway marked by red flares.

There are a handful of sleeping Grunts in this area. If you're sufficiently quiet, you can silently kill these with melee attacks without raising the alarm.

The main Covenant force is located on the opposite side of the pool, with further troops set off to the right. These include Jackals for the first time, so make sure you fire at the embrasure on their shields to send them reeling, then follow up with shots to the body or, better still, head. You can also disable a Jackal's shield with a charged Plasma Pistol shot.

F I G · 2

PREFACE

"Know your enemy" is a maxim that rings true throughout Halo 3; it also pays to know how best to kill your Covenant foes. With that in mind, this short preface introduces the main opponents and weapons you will encounter during the first Campaign mission (all of which, you'll notice, are recognizable from Halo or Halo 2). To avoid spoiling any surprises, we'll be gradually providing advice on new adversaries and firearms at the end of each relevant mission walkthrough.

COMMON ENEMIES

[GRUNTS]

Lowly Grunts may be individually weak and occupy the lowest ranks of the Covenant military hierarchy, but their sheer weight of numbers makes them dangerous foes.

- Grunts generally use Plasma Pistols and Needlers — two weapons that are consistently effective against the more powerful Brutes.

- Grunts throw Plasma Grenades, so it pays to keep moving when you fight large groups of them. (Note that killing Grunts is also your primary source of Plasma Grenades.)

- Grunts may seem cowardly, fleeing from battle when they encounter a determined show of force, or when a Brute commander is slain, but they'll still turn and fight ferociously when cornered.

- The quickest way to kill a Grunt is with a headshot. However, they are surprisingly resistant to plasma-based weaponry, especially on higher difficulty settings.

- If you hear a Grunt cry "He was my nipple mate!" as you shoot one of his comrades, there's no need to feel unduly alarmed or perplexed — Grunts eat at devices known as "food nipples".

[JACKALS]

Jackals come in two varieties — those that carry large, sturdy energy shields, and marksmen armed with Carbines or Beam Rifles.

- Shield Jackals are tough to kill when they adopt a defensive position. Their shields can withstand an extended barrage of non-explosive projectiles, so either aim for the firing embrasure on the right-hand side to make them reel backwards (thus revealing more body to shoot), or use a grenade. Melee attacks also work well, but are not always practical in large battles.

- You can temporarily disable a Jackal's shield with a charged Plasma Pistol shot; this generally causes them to turn and flee for cover.

  Shield Jackals carry Plasma Pistols, and are unique (among Covenant troops) in that they use the charged shot feature. Be ready to duck behind cover if you see one of these powering up.

  Jackals armed with Carbines or Beam Rifles are vulnerable to precision headshots. Look out for the distinctive sheen and glow of their headgear during sniper duels, and aim accordingly.

[BRUTES]

More intelligent and cunning than overheard snatches of their gruff conversation may suggest, Brutes are viciously expert hunters.

- Brutes employ a wide variety of weapon and equipment types, and come in many forms. They also perform crushing melee attacks at close quarters.

- Brutes wear protective power armor, which must (generally) be destroyed before they can be killed. The armor emits steam and smoke when it is critically damaged.

- Once its power armor is destroyed, the quickest way to kill a Brute is with a headshot.

- Brutes are known to go berserk if injured, or when their allies are killed. If you have friendly forces nearby, aim to kill berserk Brutes immediately — they can toss fragile Marines aside like ninepins.

- Killing a Brute often causes nearby Grunts and even Jackals to mount a disorganized retreat.

COMMON WEAPONS

BASICS

CAMPAIGN

EXTRAS

MULTIPLAYER

USER INSTRUCTIONS

PREFACE

MISSION 1
MISSION 2
MISSION 3
MISSION 4
MISSION 5
MISSION 6
MISSION 7
MISSION 8
MISSION 9

NAME	GENERAL USAGE ADVICE
Assault Rifle	The Assault Rifle is a solid, dependable close-range weapon on the Easy and Normal difficulty levels, and you generally won't need to look far to find ammunition for it. Its accuracy decreases during sustained fire, so it's sensible to use frequent short, controlled bursts unless fighting at close range.
Magnum	The Magnum is a small sidearm for players who prefer precision over firepower, especially on higher difficulty levels. A charged Plasma Pistol shot followed by a single Magnum headshot will bring down most Brutes.
Plasma Pistol	While its stopping power as a weapon is less than impressive, a charged Plasma Pistol shot can disable energy shields and power armor in a single blast. In a new feature, holding a charged shot will continually drain its limited battery until released. Additionally, charged Plasma Pistol shots have an EMP-style effect that can disable vehicle engines (but not, you should note, weapon systems) for a short but tactically valuable period of time.
Brute Shot	The Brute Shot is used to bludgeon opponents into submission with explosive projectiles. The blast radius of each detonation makes it highly effective when targeting enemies hidden behind light cover, and its wickedly cruel blade attachment makes it a devastating melee weapon. However, it's perhaps less powerful than it feels – you'll need more than one shot to take down a Brute.
Needler	The Needler fires small explosive projectiles that automatically home in on targeted enemies over short distances. Angled correctly, Needler shards will bounce off hard surfaces in a predictable and useable fashion. Note that its effectiveness decreases with range – your opponents will dodge or even dive to avoid the deadly incoming shower. Halo 2 players may be surprised to discover that it is no longer possible to dual wield the Needler, but don't be misled – it is a hugely powerful weapon, especially against Brutes.
Carbine	The Carbine's zoom, range and rate of fire make it perfect for taking down opponents from safe distances. While its precision decreases with range, a single shot to an unprotected head is always deadly.
Battle Rifle	The Battle Rifle is slower than the Carbine but fires in bursts of three bullets, which actually increases its potential accuracy. Like the Carbine, it has a zoom function for mid-range firefights. Skilled players will acquire the knack of deftly flicking the thumbstick to "rake" a small area to increase the likelihood of a headshot, or to take down multiple Grunts.
Sniper Rifle & Beam Rifle	The Sniper Rifle and Beam Rifle are outstanding long-range weapons thanks to their powerful two-level zoom. As you need to take scarce ammunition and limited battery power into account, they should be saved for dispatching priority targets. The Sniper Rifle has a slower fire rate than the Beam Rifle, but the latter will overheat if fired rapidly in quick succession.
Shotgun	It may be extremely satisfying to use, and brutally effective at close quarters, but the limited range of the Shotgun means that it's practically a melee weapon. Its close-quarters stopping power makes it a good choice of backup weapon.
Frag Grenade & Plasma Grenade	The power and distance of grenade throws is determined by elevation – the further away the target, the higher you should aim. The more powerful Frag Grenade is perfect for crowd control, or for covering a retreat. The Plasma Grenade is a more specialized weapon that sticks to living creatures and moving vehicles, but not to inanimate scenery or objects. If you can tag an enemy with one, it's often a guaranteed kill.

I

CHIEF CRATER

JUNGLE WALK

GRUNT CAMP

SNIPER ALLEY

III

DAM

BRUTE AMBUSH

II

SUB-STATION

BASICS

CAMPAIGN

EXTRAS

MULTIPLAYER

USER
INSTRUCTIONS

PREFACE

MISSION 1

MISSION 2

MISSION 3

MISSION 4

MISSION 5

MISSION 6

MISSION 7

MISSION 8

MISSION 9

SIERRA 117

[MISSION 1]

You'll have the Arbiter fighting alongside you for the forthcoming jungle battles. Armed with a Carbine, he's a highly useful companion — even when his shots don't hit their mark, he tends to draw fire away from the Master Chief.

Weapons are made available on purple "dispensers" throughout most levels. Feel free to help yourself whenever you encounter one.

CHIEF CRATER

A

JUNGLE WALK

B

GRUNT CAMP

SNIPER ALLEY

There's a Brute standing guard on a tree trunk here, and a sizable group of Grunts will attack shortly after you arrive. As a rule, it's always smart to break enemy forces up into manageable units. On lower difficulty settings, you can also rely heavily on your allies to help you out when things get tough.

Once the first enemies have been dispatched, two Phantoms will drop off reinforcements. The Phantom's cannons can be devastating, even on Normal, so it's prudent to take cover until they fly off. Fight your way along the riverbank until you reach a natural rock passageway marked by red flares.

There are a handful of sleeping Grunts in this area. If you're sufficiently quiet, you can silently kill these with melee attacks without raising the alarm.

The main Covenant force is located on the opposite side of the pool, with further troops just off to the right. These include Jackals for the first time, so make sure you fire at the embrasure on their shields to send them reeling, then follow up with shots to the body or, better still, head. You can also disable a Jackal's shield with a charged Plasma Pistol shot.

BASICS

CAMPAIGN

EXTRAS

MULTIPLAYER

USER
INSTRUCTIONS

PREFACE

MISSION 1

MISSION 2

MISSION 3

MISSION 4

MISSION 5

MISSION 6

MISSION 7

MISSION 8

MISSION 9

A First things first: your Assault Rifle is of relatively little use against this Brute or, indeed, his entire species, on Legendary. You may as well be pelting him with spitballs, or harsh language. You'll need to expend at least an entire clip at close range to destroy his power armor, while simultaneously dodging incoming fire. It's much better, then, to leave habits acquired on Normal (or even Heroic) behind and learn to love one of the tools that will keep you alive on Legendary: the humble yet deceptively powerful Plasma Pistol.

As soon as you vault over the natural barrier, take cover by the fallen tree and use your Assault Rifle to kill a few Grunts as they come into view. Switch to your Magnum, quickly grab one of the Grunt's Plasma Pistols to dual wield with it, then immediately prepare a charged shot to blow the Brute's power armor. You should aim to finish him off with a Magnum headshot immediately, but if there are plenty of Grunts around, it may be safer to duck straight back behind cover. Use your Assault Rifle to begin clearing the area. Note that grenades are used by enemies and allies alike from the first encounter on Legendary. Be vigilant, and steer well clear of explosions.

B Meanwhile, two Phantoms will deploy Brutes and Grunts further along the riverside, so take cover until they depart. At this point, you should begin to notice enemy behaviors that were perhaps less apparent on other difficulty settings, particularly their tendency to pull back to more defensible positions once the tide of battle begins to turn against them. Over the first waterfall, pop the single Brute's power armor with a charged Plasma Pistol shot, then – carefully – dispatch him with a headshot. (This

is by far the best way to kill Brutes at this point, so we're going to assume that you've got the message now.)

Move forward cautiously: there are numerous Grunts and two more Brutes along the river's edge. You can swap your Assault Rifle for a Brute Shot to deal with the former quickly from range, and there is a ready supply of Plasma Pistols to help you beat the latter.

C Grab a Carbine from the dispenser and make your way up to the ledge overlooking the Grunt Camp. There are Jackals with Carbines here (which can sometimes include one to the very far right – you can only see him before dropping down if you stand beside the Arbiter), so deal with those first, then set about killing every Grunt you can find. The Covenant troops will take cover or even withdraw, but don't be tempted to sacrifice your excellent vantage point just yet. Lastly, kill the shield-wielding Jackals. It may take more shots than usual to dispatch them from this range (remember, you should ideally shoot for the embrasure on their shields to make them stagger, then follow up with an immediate headshot), but you certainly won't be short of ammunition here.

The remaining members of the Covenant force (particularly the Brutes) will usually retreat to the top of the slope on the far side of the camp, though they will be less inclined to do so if you have kept some Marines alive. Replenish your supply of Carbine ammo, then make your way to the opposite side of the shallow pool. If there is a Jackal marksman on the high ledge to the right and you didn't kill him earlier, you'll probably notice a succession of searing yellow reminders heading your way any time *now*. The surviving Covenant troops will either have foolishly backed themselves into a corner near the point where the path upwards turns to the right, or be spread thinly on the slope if there are Marines accompanying you. This is a good opportunity to have fun with a Needler. Once you've cleared the area, take a Plasma Pistol to dual wield with your Magnum (with a Carbine in reserve) before you continue.

- A harsh reality of life on Legendary is that the Marines accompanying you are so very fragile. While it's fun and rewarding to try to keep them alive, their support is not something you should count on.

- If the Brute Shot dropped by the first Brute you encounter has five or more shots, you may be able to use it to detach the Plasma Turret from its mounting on the starboard side of the nearest Phantom dropship when it arrives shortly afterwards. You can then collect it to make light work of the Grunts and Brutes ahead.

Emerging from the jungle, you will immediately encounter Covenant forces on the river bank, with a much larger attack group (including several Brutes) deployed by dropship to the concrete platform a short way along the river. You can use the Battle Rifle you collected earlier to pick off Grunts (perhaps even a couple of Brutes) from distance before you engage your opponents at close range. While you could run directly up the short slope to make a frontal assault, it's safer to take the small pathway to the left.

You can actually save the Marine being interrogated by the Brute if you're quick – a Needler is the fastest way to do so if you're not yet confident enough to use Plasma Pistols.

[SIERRA 117 II]

As you make your way to the sub-station, you can find two Battle Rifles and some Frag Grenades. From this point forward, you'll find that Grunts may also drop Plasma Grenades when killed. The bad news, however, is that they'll now use them with malice aforethought whenever they can...

During the sub-station battle, feel free to jump in the river – it's perfectly safe (unless you unwisely choose to dive over the waterfall), and presents a quick escape route if you need one.

SNIPER ALLEY

SUB-STATION

It's important to avoid being backed into a corner that offers scant protection from explosions while fighting the Covenant here – the blast radius of Brute Shot projectiles and Plasma Grenades means that your enemy doesn't necessarily have to hit you to hurt you. Ideally, keep a reasonable distance, use the crates for cover, and dispatch all foes with a combination of the Battle Rifle, grenades and – as soon as you can acquire one – a Brute Shot.

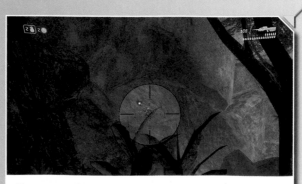

There are several Jackal marksmen armed with Carbines hiding in the trees and on ledges in this area. You can use a weapon scope or the Master Chief's built-in visor zoom feature to find them. Make your way through the gloomy undergrowth carefully, dispatching each one from a safe distance.

BASICS

CAMPAIGN

EXTRAS

MULTIPLAYER

USER
INSTRUCTIONS

PREFACE

MISSION 1

MISSION 2

MISSION 3

MISSION 4

MISSION 5

MISSION 6

MISSION 7

MISSION 8

MISSION 9

D As a point of interest, note that you can save the Marine from the Brute – just hit the latter with a charged Plasma Pistol shot, then follow that up with a quick headshot with a Carbine. If you use a Needler instead, don't forget that the explosion will also hurt the Marine. There is a Jackal marksman here, so you'll need to be quick.

Σ Over the tree bridge, you'll encounter a force of Grunts and Jackals (including at least one marksman), with a Brute loitering with intent further on. In the cave to the left (watch out for the trio of Grunts that emerge) you'll find a Battle Rifle and Magnum ammo next to the fallen Marines. Again, take a Plasma Pistol to accompany your Magnum, then look to collect more Battle Rifle ammunition and Frag Grenades from beside the Marines' corpses as you follow the path.

F The sub-station area is the stage for one of those large, free-form battles that the Halo series is famous for – there's plenty going on, and you can approach it in a number of different ways. The most practical solution, though, is to attend to targets in the order of the danger they pose to you.

Priority 1: Run to the right and kill the Brute there. Deal with all Grunts in the immediate vicinity, and the Jackals with Carbines on top of the low buildings.

Priority 2: Look for (and kill) the Jackal snipers on the far side of the river. However, note that the Battle Rifle isn't very accurate or effective at this range. Sometimes, one shot each will suffice; on another day, you may need to expend the best part of an entire clip to kill them.

Priority 3: While avoiding fire from incoming Phantoms, use the Battle Rifle to pick off any Grunts you can see at the far end of the area; you should also be able to spot another couple of Jackal snipers armed with Carbines. Brutes (possibly accompanied by Grunts) may or may not move forward to attack you here; either way, it pays to have grenades or a Plasma Pistol at the ready just in case. You can find Battle Rifle ammunition and a Machine Gun Turret (which isn't available on Normal) beside the river, though the latter is unsuited to this battle – it's difficult to dodge grenades and Brute Shot blasts when carrying it.

G Once the lower portion of the sub-station area is clear, cautiously move around to the path that leads to the back of the concrete platform. There are two Jackals with shields to deal with and, as you round the corner, up to three snipers armed with Carbines (unless you espied and shot them earlier). While using your Battle Rifle to pick off nearby Grunts, have a Plasma Pistol at hand to quickly deal with any Brutes that approach.

The remaining Brutes and Grunts tend to pull back to a more defensible position on top of, and around the base of, a large rock next to the waterfall, unless you kill them quickly. They are potentially covered by a sniper with a Beam Rifle once they move there, so it can be beneficial to attack aggressively before they commit to an organized retreat. Stock up on ammunition (there's a Battle Rifle near one of the concrete pipes) before continuing.

H Everybody loves sniper duels (bar, perhaps, those wheezing through newly acquired puncture wounds in their chests), and this is a good one on Legendary. The majority of the Jackals here have Carbines, but there are also a few armed with Beam Rifles. You need to move slowly and carefully, identifying and neutralizing each target in turn as you scan the branches and gaps in the trees for the tell-tale purple glow that identifies each enemy. The Arbiter is a great help here, as you'll find that he tends to draw their fire. Pick up a Beam Rifle as soon as you can find one, and watch out for the Jackal on top of the high cliff as you round the corner to the right – he's difficult to spot in the glare of the sunlight. Collect a Carbine (and as much ammo as you can find) before you press forward.

- On Legendary, Brute Captains clad in gold armor are stronger than their peers, and can sometimes survive a grenade explosion at point-blank range. Always be prepared to make an immediate headshot to finish them off.

- Jackal snipers can be surprisingly tough unless you score a headshot. When they stagger backwards, don't relent – if you stop firing, they'll be able to shoot back at you. (Halo 2 multiplayer experts will recognize this principle as a Campaign equivalent of "descoping", a technique for suppressing snipers.)

Use a Carbine or Battle Rifle to kill snipers and targets of opportunity from on top of the ledge, then drop down and fight your way to the bridge. Kill the small attack force that arrives via the cave beyond the bridge, then head back down to the crashed Pelican to collect a Sniper Rifle and a Battle Rifle.

BRUTE AMBUSH

DAM

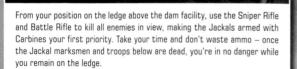

From your position on the ledge above the dam facility, use the Sniper Rifle and Battle Rifle to kill all enemies in view, making the Jackals armed with Carbines your first priority. Take your time and don't waste ammo — once the Jackal marksmen and troops below are dead, you're in no danger while you remain on the ledge.

There is a Brute Chieftain armed with a Gravity Hammer on top of the dam. Unless you'd actively like to meet him at close quarters, you should use the Sniper Rifle to kill him from a safe distance. Additionally, Carbines and Needlers are readily available here if you need them.

As you approach the dam, a Phantom will arrive to deploy troops on the far side of the river. Locate and neutralize the Jackal marksmen first, then cautiously make your way across the dam.

When you deactivate the shield generator to free the Marines, two Phantoms will arrive to drop off a final wave of troops. Stand fast until the Pelican arrives and simply jump inside by following the onscreen prompt to end the level.

BASICS

CAMPAIGN

EXTRAS

MULTIPLAYER

USER
INSTRUCTIONS

PREFACE

MISSION 1

MISSION 2

MISSION 3

MISSION 4

MISSION 5

MISSION 6

MISSION 7

MISSION 8

MISSION 9

1 From the top of the slope on the right, use a Beam Rifle to pick off the Jackal snipers (there is usually one to the left and a few straight ahead; if you move over to the far left of the lower ledge, you should be able to see more to the right), and then switch to your Carbine to dispense with as many Grunts as you can find. Don't drop down until you're absolutely sure that you've killed all potential targets, including the small group waiting below (it will make the next part of the battle much easier). If necessary, retrace your steps to find more Carbine ammunition before continuing.

While watching for snipers – if you didn't deal with them before, there may be one (perhaps two) in a tree, and definitely a third on the far ledge to the right – tentatively move forward to check for Covenant troops sheltering in cover. The rocky alcove to your left and the cave directly ahead are both regular hiding spots for Grunts and at least one Brute. You're vulnerable to shots from above should there be anyone left alive up there, so watch for enemies on top of the cliff. Don't press forward until the nearby Phantom departs – its turrets would tear you to shreds.

There should be one more Brute, and assorted Grunts, as you make your way around to the bridge, but don't venture down to the crashed Pelican just yet. Collect grenades and suitably powerful weapons (such as a Needler), then head onto the bridge to trigger the arrival of Covenant reinforcements from the cave just beyond it. Having just passed a checkpoint, you shouldn't find this battle too much of a challenge (there's plenty of ammo in the vicinity). When the last enemy falls, head back to the Pelican to collect a Sniper Rifle and a Battle Rifle.

2 When the cutscene ends, immediately take a few steps back to avoid being seen by the ever-inquisitive eyes of Jackal snipers. If you're patient and focus on accuracy and ammo conservation, saving the Sniper Rifle for Jackal marksmen and Brutes only, you can turn this potentially complicated battle into a simple mopping-up exercise. From your lofty vantage point, you should concentrate on the following tasks.

Priority 1: Taking care to avoid fire from the Covenant force below the cliff, kill every sniper you can find. Look on the roof just beneath you, on top of the building where Johnson is imprisoned, on the ledge on the large structure behind it, and on the low roof on the far right-hand side of the dam.

Priority 2: Use your Sniper Rifle to kill any Brutes firing from below, and your Battle Rifle to dispatch Grunts and Jackals with shields.

Priority 3: If you can get a clear shot, you can save yourself needless perspiration and swear box contributions by killing the Brute Chieftain on the bridge with your Sniper Rifle before you go any further. It shouldn't take any more than three bullets aimed at his head to drop his shield and remove his helmet; you can even switch to your Battle Rifle for the killing shot. This will usually draw other Covenant troops from their hiding places – a very useful fringe benefit.

- There's plenty of scope for exploration and experimentation in the dam area – for example, you can get up onto the ledge of the long building with the striking glass roof (where you may find a Beam Rifle dropped by a Jackal), or climb a ladder into the upper room of the low building on the side of the dam that you start on.

- The Arbiter is not invincible – he can (and will) be knocked unconscious for a variable period of time if he sustains too much damage. This is a fairly rare occurrence on lower difficulty levels, but it can happen quite frequently on Legendary. He usually takes out his Energy Sword to attack foes at close range when injured or enraged, and will drop it if he is knocked out, but the bad news is that its remaining battery supply is always ridiculously low – barely enough for a single strike.

3 Once you've killed all Covenant forces in view, or exhausted your supply of ammo, drop down to the ground below (though you can backtrack to the crashed Pelican to pick up more Battle Rifle ammo if you wish). You'll trigger a checkpoint as you approach the dam and, with it, the arrival of a Phantom delivering additional troops to the opposite side of the river. Quickly check the pump station door for enemies (they sometimes use the service walkway underneath the top of the dam), then find cover to avoid the Phantom's turrets.

The Covenant reinforcements will be dropped off at the far side of the broken bridge. If you have plenty of Battle Rifle ammunition, you can take down most of the Grunts and both Jackal snipers in this party straight away. There are a few ladders and ledges that are great to snipe from but, given the sheer amount of ammunition at your disposal, clearing up the few remaining Grunts, Jackals and Brutes really doesn't take a great deal of effort.

Last, but not least, grab a Carbine and a Needler from the top of the dam, then free Johnson and the other Marines. This is the cue for two Phantoms to drop troops on top of the dam, and on the opposite side of the river. Sprint up onto the dam and aim to slow the advance of the attack party until the cavalry arrives, then sit back and enjoy the fireworks.

SIERRA 117: DEBRIEFING

BRUTE CHIEFTAIN

The elite warriors of their race, Chieftains are much more dangerous than rank-and-file Brutes. They can withstand a far greater amount of damage due to their superior armor, and have a heightened resistance to certain weapon types – for example, you cannot stick Plasma Grenades to them (only to the weapon they're holding), and Needler fire generally rebounds from their bodies. You can soften Chieftains up with grenades if you have some to hand (though they're usually quick to dive aside), but the most effective way to kill them is to aim for their heads. Once their helmets have been blown off, a single headshot with a Magnum, Carbine or Battle Rifle will stop them in their tracks.

Brute Chieftains armed with Gravity Hammers generally wait until an opportune moment, then charge relentlessly at the Master Chief until they kill or are killed. One swing of their weapon will almost completely deplete the Chief's shield on Normal; if the shield level is already low, an impact spells instant death. The best way to kill them is from a safe distance or elevation, but you don't always have the luxury of either option...

GRAVITY HAMMER

For those who prefer the "personal touch" when xenophobic alien collectives drop by for a genocidal house-call, the Gravity Hammer is a peerlessly satisfying melee weapon.

- Each use of the Gravity Hammer drains its limited energy supply
- You will lunge towards targeted enemies when the reticule is red
- The Gravity Hammer doesn't just harm the targeted enemy – it also has an area of effect when it strikes, knocking nearby Covenant troops, Marines and objects aside
- Using the melee button to strike with the base of its handle is much less powerful, but does not drain its battery. This is the most energy-efficient way to take down Grunts, Jackals and, if you can get a clear strike at their backs, Brutes
- The Gravity Hammer is capable of setting off grenades within the vicinity of its impact. This may occasionally work in your favor, but could equally lead to unintentionally spectacular suicides

BRUTE CAPTAIN

Brute Captains are tougher than their subordinates, and tend to be more aggressive – you'll notice that they are more inclined to go berserk when injured. They also often have access to better weaponry than most other Brutes.

KAMIKAZE GRUNT

Very occasionally, a Grunt can be consumed by an almighty fervor for the Covenant cause, and will decide to prematurely embark upon the Great Journey in spectacular style. Priming Plasma Grenades in either claw, they will charge towards the Master Chief; we shouldn't have to tell you what happens next. In many instances, you'll need to kill them immediately. If you're particularly smart, though, you'll sometimes wait to see if they pass other Covenant troops as they run – if you can hit them with a headshot at the right moment, the dropped grenades will weaken or kill nearby foes.

BASICS

CAMPAIGN

EXTRAS

MULTIPLAYER

USER INSTRUCTIONS

PREFACE

MISSION 1

MISSION 2

MISSION 3

MISSION 4

MISSION 5

MISSION 6

MISSION 7

MISSION 8

MISSION 9

SPIKER

Proof positive that Brutes hold their quarry in contempt, the Spiker is a rapaciously barbarous firearm – but only at close range.

- Can be dual wielded, and is especially powerful when you do so
- Stuns most enemies with its withering rate of fire
- Has a fairly large clip size – one is sufficient to kill a Brute on Normal, with spikes to spare
- Very effective at short range, but its accuracy plummets as the distance increases, and its projectiles have a decaying trajectory – they'll actually fall to the ground before reaching the target at medium range
- The spikes are rather slow, so it's not a good weapon to use against fast-moving or distant targets. Even though you can adjust your aim to hit enemies over longer ranges, the spikes take an absolute epoch to arrive in comparison with other weapons; you'll swear that continental drift shifts your target a few inches to one side as the projectiles float lazily through the air
- You can bounce the spikes off surfaces (even the ground) if you fire from certain angles

BUBBLE SHIELD

A Bubble Shield is the Halo 3 equivalent of a "Get Out of Jail Free" card – and for "jail", read: "death". Once activated, it generates a selectively impervious energy wall, allowing troops and vehicles to move in and out freely, but shielding occupants (or, to a lesser extent, those hiding behind it) from harmful projectiles or explosions outside. Equally, though, shots and explosions emanating from inside the sphere can't harm anyone on the outside. The device can be deployed in a second and, as long as your opponents don't run in to join you, will provide temporary respite from a variety of threats – such as an incoming Phantom or a sniper. It can also offer vital moments of calm to enable your shields to recharge, or even be used as cover for an attack, so long as you wield your weapons outside the protective boundaries. You'll find that Brutes regularly use Bubble Shields, activating them when they feel suitably injured or in danger.

Bubble Shields last up to 20 seconds, but can be destroyed before that point if the central generator is damaged. If you need to remove one quickly, a single melee attack to the base unit will suffice.

BARRACKS

III

IV

LANDING PAD BRAVO

II

SEWERS

OPS CENTER

I

MOTOR POOL

SOUTH HANGAR

BASICS

CAMPAIGN

EXTRAS

MULTIPLAYER

USER
INSTRUCTIONS

PREFACE

MISSION 1

MISSION 2

MISSION 3

MISSION 4

MISSION 5

MISSION 6

MISSION 7

MISSION 8

MISSION 9

CROW'S NEST

[MISSION 2]

Return Journey: It's generally sensible to fight the swarm of Drones from behind the best cover you can find, but there is a partially concealed Machine Gun Turret on the rock outside, to the left of the enclosure you start in, which you can use to make light work of your airborne enemies. Be aware, though, that you may need to retreat occasionally to give your shield time to recharge. Take the turret with you when you leave.

OPS CENTER

(Return journey only) **Rally Point Alpha**

(Return journey only)

(Return journey only)

SOUTH HANGAR

Sharp-eyed marksmen should seek out Fusion Cores and shoot them to engulf nearby Covenant troops in a powerful explosion. This works both ways, though — it's really not sensible to take cover near to or, heaven forbid, behind them.

Fixed turrets have infinite ammunition; your supply is only limited once you detach them from their stand. While choosing to use fixed turrets for more than a few seconds on Heroic or Legendary could be most accurately described as Covenant-assisted suicide, it's okay to do so when you play on Normal.

Although the enemy presence is fairly light as you make your way to the South Hangar, don't underestimate the danger of Grunts — they'll try to stick you with a Plasma Grenade if the opportunity arises. After killing the Brute and heading through the door, watch out for the Jackals at the end of the corridor. They're armed with Carbines, so either move into cover as you approach them, or try to dispatch them from afar with a Battle Rifle.

After you've killed the initial group of Grunts and Jackals, reinforcements (including numerous Brutes) will be dropped off in waves by Phantoms. If you need more ammunition (or a reasonable Battle Rifle sniping spot) you can head upstairs, though it's better to fight this battle from behind cover on the lower level. We advise that you concentrate on dispatching the Grunts first — they can overwhelm you if you let them reach your position.

A Grab a Battle Rifle and a Magnum on your way out of the Ops Center. The Battle Rifle is practically indispensable, and the Magnum/Plasma Pistol (or, in some instances, Plasma Rifle) combo is still often the best way to deal with Brutes.

When you spot the large group of Grunts and Jackals in the road tunnel, keep your distance and pick them off with your Battle Rifle and Frag Grenades. You can also wait until they draw near and take most of them out by shooting the nearby Fusion Cores as they run past. After dispatching the Brute hanging back at the rear, be very careful as you approach the door leading to the South Hangar – Grunts backed up by Jackals armed with Carbines will charge around the corner at the end of the corridor. If you're running low on Battle Rifle ammo (and shame on you if you are – aim for the head, soldier), you can dart into cover on the left or right to get close enough to throw a grenade, or use the SMG found in the water on the right-hand side.

B The battle to repel the invading Covenant forces in the South Hangar can be long and stressful unless you take a systematic approach to eliminating your opponents, and prevent them from gaining a foothold on the upper area. Use your Battle Rifle to kill all Grunts and Jackals, including those that move upstairs. Unless you're quick, they may kill the Marines that are

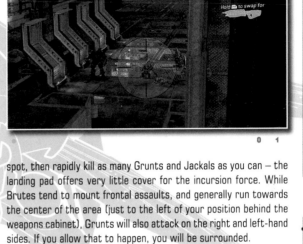

0   1

supporting you, which will make the next part of the battle more difficult. Ensure that you have a full supply of grenades, then sprint to the room upstairs as the Phantoms arrive, to collect more ammunition and, perhaps more importantly, grab a Plasma Pistol on your way. Smash a window in the control room and jump through to make a rapid return journey. You could grab a Machine Gun Turret from the next level down, but this is risky – mobility is more important than raw firepower for the first few Covenant attack waves.

The first two Phantoms will deploy large numbers of Grunts, Brutes and, to a lesser extent, Jackals. Though there are some good places to take cover, the best of all is probably behind the closed weapons cabinet (Fig. 1), which provides excellent protection against all weapons bar Brute Shots and grenades – not to mention a clear view of incoming enemies. Drop your Plasma Pistol in a safe spot, then rapidly kill as many Grunts and Jackals as you can – the landing pad offers very little cover for the incursion force. While Brutes tend to mount frontal assaults, and generally run towards the center of the area (just to the left of your position behind the weapons cabinet), Grunts will also attack on the right and left-hand sides. If you allow that to happen, you will be surrounded.

Dealing with the Brutes is, as you'd expect, somewhat challenging. You have a Plasma Pistol, but you'll need to be unerringly accurate with your follow-up headshots – you really do not want a berserk Brute running rampage right now. If your Marine allies are still alive, you'll find that they will contribute vital kills, and may have weakened some Brutes. They will also draw enemy attention away from you – and it's this attribute, more than anything else, that makes them helpful to have around.

Before the final wave of Covenant troops arrive, there's usually a brief moment of calm when you can run upstairs to pick up supplies, and this is also an opportune moment to grab a Machine Gun Turret. Again, don't forget to kill the Grunts from distance first with the Battle Rifle, then use the Machine Gun Turret to clear up any remaining adversaries.

Pick up a fresh Machine Gun Turret before you return to the Ops Center. It may extend your journey time on the long walk back, but you'll thank us for the tip shortly…

C Though Drones are disturbingly efficient at killing the Chief on Legendary, this battle is only difficult if you insist on leaving the small enclosure. Armed with the Machine Gun Turret collected in the South Hangar, move over to the small corner wall to the right as you enter. Hug it closely to avoid incoming fire (Fig. 2), and concentrate on killing the small number of Drones that attack from the right; if you move further along, you can also get a clear shot at the main swarm at the center of the cave. Move regularly in and out of cover, pressing tightly against the middle of the wall to shelter when your shield is disabled, and this should be an easy battle.

There is another Machine Gun Turret on top of a rock on the left-hand side of the room. Collect it before you continue.

0   2

BASICS

CAMPAIGN

EXTRAS

MULTIPLAYER

USER INSTRUCTIONS

PREFACE

MISSION 1

MISSION 2

MISSION 3

MISSION 4

MISSION 5

MISSION 6

MISSION 7

MISSION 8

MISSION 9

- When you attack from behind cover, take your weapons into account. If you are using a single firearm, such as a Battle Rifle or large turret, it's better to move out to attack from the right-hand side – that way, you will present a slightly smaller target to your opponents. When you dual wield and your "lead" weapon is in your left hand – a Plasma Pistol or Plasma Rifle, for instance – the opposite applies.

- In co-op games, the battle in the South Hangar is one of many instances where you can actually form a more effective partnership by splitting up. One of you could go to the room above, for example, and concentrate on sniping Grunts and Jackals – there is, after all, a plentiful supply of Battle Rifle ammunition up there – while the other player concentrates on Brutes.

If you brought a turret with you, the battle in the Motor Pool is less difficult than it might otherwise be. There is a large force of Brutes here, so it's sensible to take cover behind a wall, or the trailer in the middle of the room, then wait for them to come to you. If you require further assistance with this potentially awkward fight, you can consult the Legendary walkthrough on the right – the enemies may not be as savage or numerous here as they are on Legendary, but the general guidance is equally applicable.

The Motor Pool battle marks the introduction of several new equipment types, including the Regenerator (a green energy field, which replenishes all shields within its boundaries), the Power Drain (a blue field, which has the opposite effect), and the Grav Lift, which enables you to reach high platforms (but also has a few other interesting applications). Oh, and watch out for Spike Grenades – Brutes will use these deadly devices regularly from this point onward.

[CROW'S NEST **II**]

SEWERS

MOTOR POOL

Try to save some of your Machine Gun Turret ammunition for the Brute Chieftain. He charges when you have killed most of his subordinates, and can be difficult to avoid. If necessary, use one of the Grav Lifts to gain access to the upper level, where you can shoot him from above.

Shotguns are available in the cabinets in the Ops Center, and in the right-hand parking bay in the Motor Pool. If you lie in wait until the Brutes are practically within touching distance, you can use one to mount a briskly devastating ambush.

More for fun than an efficient strategy, you can use a Grav Lift during the battle with the Brute Chieftain. Backpedaling as he approaches, drop one in his path and watch with glee as he is catapulted over your head.

Before you leave the Motor Pool, pick up a fresh Machine Gun Turret from the upper platform. This will come in useful in the next corridor, where you'll encounter Drones flying through the ducts; it's also handy in the ensuing battle to retake the Barracks.

Even though this is a zero-checkpoint confrontation against approximately a dozen Brutes and a Chieftain, it isn't actually as difficult as you may initially fear. The key to beating it is to play a cat-and-mouse game with your foes, hiding from view until they move towards your position to investigate, then striking when they draw near.

As you enter the room, immediately take up position behind the back wheels of the trailer in the left-hand parking bay. This will be your base of operations for most of the battle — not only is it a suitably solid piece of cover, it also provides several avenues of escape if required. However, there are a few things you'll need to be aware of. Firstly, the Brutes will use plenty of Spike Grenades. You should be ready to back down the slope behind you to avoid these. Be careful though — Brutes moving towards your position may be able to shoot at you through the gap beneath the trailer. Secondly, explosions can dislodge the containers on top of it, leaving you a little more exposed — if that happens you'll need to stand closer to the wheels to avoid incoming fire, and possibly even abandon the trailer in favor of the wall further along. Finally, you're vulnerable to Brute Shot blasts here — even if they don't hit you, the explosions may leave their mark.

The Brutes will initially run down the center slope in groups of two or three. Generally — but not always — they will retreat once you open fire. The best strategy is to wait until they move into range, then inch out and use controlled Machine Gun Turret bursts to take down at least one Brute at a time, retreating back into cover as required. This is pretty much the procedure for the entire first part of the battle: wait until the Brutes launch an attack, strike fast and hard to break their resolve, then hide out of sight until they move forward again.

When your turret's ammo drops to around 50 bullets, leave it somewhere safe and grab a Plasma Pistol (there's actually one right behind your position by the trailer) to dual wield with your Magnum. As well as dealing with Brutes as they arrive, you should focus on killing any that are armed with Brute Shots, especially those firing from range — these are the biggest danger to you at this stage. Towards the end of the battle, when Brutes tend to attack in smaller numbers (in pairs, sometimes even alone) and your ammo supplies are running low, you can instead use grenade sticks to kill them. However, be very wary of chain-reaction explosions — the lower garage area may be littered with Spike Grenades by now.

At a variable point in this battle's endgame, usually when there are only two or three Brutes remaining, the Chieftain will charge. This is the most dangerous moment in this confrontation, as there's precious little room for maneuver in your location. Grab the turret you dropped earlier, and open fire when the Chieftain marauds into range. You should have sufficient ammo to put him on his back, or at the very least remove his helmet; if not, immediately drop the turret and use grenades (if you have any left) and headshots to finish the fight before he can get close enough to bring his hammer to bear. If things go desperately wrong and you need an urgent escape route, there is a small pile of Grav Lifts in the center of the room that you can use to jump to the upper level. This may also be your only recourse if the Chieftain activates an Invincibility power-up, as he is sometimes inclined to do.

Beware of overconfidence when you deal with the last few Brutes. They're still very dangerous, and may be hiding behind Deployable Cover devices. Again, we strongly advise that you wait for them to come to you. Once you're absolutely sure that none remain, collect necessary supplies (particularly Battle Rifle and Magnum ammunition) before you leave.

BASICS

CAMPAIGN

EXTRAS

MULTIPLAYER

USER INSTRUCTIONS

PREFACE

MISSION 1

MISSION 2

MISSION 3

MISSION 4

MISSION 5

MISSION 6

MISSION 7

MISSION 8

MISSION 9

◆ **Brute Chieftains are most dangerous when they activate Invincibility. Every time you see the telltale sheen of an augmented shield, just run — there's really no point in fighting them while it lasts.**

Σ The battle with the Drones flying through the sewers is a minor one, but you can save ammunition (and avoid unnecessary unpleasantness) by using the following strategy. Approach the first pipe, wait for a Drone to appear, then shoot and kill it

before it flies out of view. Two more will usually emerge from either side; deal with them as you see fit. Repeat the process for the next two pipes, then pick up a Plasma Pistol to dual wield with your Magnum before you drop down at the end of the corridor to meet up with the Arbiter.

◆ **If you dual wield two plasma weapons of the same type, the Master Chief will keep the gun with the highest battery power when you drop one.**

CROW'S NEST III

Bar a handful of Jackals on the upper walkways, the battle to save the Marines in the Barracks is fought entirely against a large party of Brutes, broadly separated into three groups encountered in three corridors. Advance slowly, taking out each Brute in turn, and be sure to check that you've killed all adversaries in an area before you tackle the next lot – they can sometimes be found hiding in the shower rooms.

The Brute Chieftain here is armed with a powerful Plasma Turret, so frontal assaults are extremely risky. You should take this weapon with you when you leave.

Once opened, the door on the right-hand side enables you to ambush the Brute Chieftain and his allies while the Arbiter and Marines draw their fire from another direction.

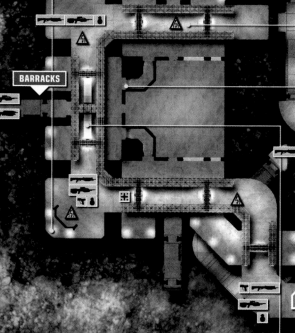

BARRACKS

LANDING PAD BRAVO

Ladders on the upper walkways lead to a ventilation shaft that runs almost the entire length of the Barracks. Use it to launch ambushes on enemies below, particularly those taking cover in the two corner rooms.

If you're sufficiently confident in your abilities, and have plenty of Plasma Turret ammo, you might want to try dashing over to the door to the control room just before the final group of Brutes equipped with jump packs storms the landing pad. It's possible to slaughter all of them before they leave the corridor with a suitably unrelenting hail of plasma fire. (On higher difficulty levels this is much more risky, but it's a real time-saver if you're on a speed run.)

F. We're not going to sugar the pill: this can be a savagely tricky battle, marked by a paucity of checkpoints and an almost malicious number of Brutes. There are no Needlers here, and even Plasma Pistols are in extremely short supply. What really complicates matters is the presence of Jackals and Brutes on the upper walkways.

While there are countless ways to tackle this battle we suggest that, as a rule, you stick to the ground floor; it's too easy to be caught out by unseen Brutes if you don't. The Arbiter and any Marines that you rescue will help draw attention away from you, and they may even contribute a few kills; the Arbiter's dual Plasma Rifles are excellent at destroying power armor. Equally, your supply of grenades is precious: you'll need to make every throw count, and actively search for Spike Grenades as you move forward.

So: from the start, employ Plasma Pistol charged shots followed by well-aimed bullets to the head to dispatch the Brutes nearest to you, then use your Battle Rifle to kill the two Jackals on the upper walkway. This gives you access to a pair of additional Plasma Pistols. Climb up there and "fix" them in position (see the margin tip) so that you can come back for them later. This increases your tactical options no end. You can then use long-range Battle Rifle blasts as you fight your way to the corner rooms, or fight at relatively close range with a Plasma Pistol and Magnum. When you reach the corner, be careful — there may still be one (or even two) Brutes hiding in the showers. Check to your right before heading up to investigate.

The second long corridor is lightly populated by comparison — and there are, thankfully, no Jackals on the walkway above — but the stakes are higher here. Though you may sometimes get a checkpoint in the previous corridor, the most likely place to hit one is after clearing *this* corridor. The biggest danger here is the Brute wielding a Brute Shot, who generally positions himself outside the second shower area. Use a charged Plasma Pistol shot to take down his power armor as quickly as you can to make the situation much more manageable.

Around the final corner you'll encounter the remaining group of Brutes, accompanied by a Brute Chieftain wielding a deadly Plasma Turret. The moment the first volley of plasma hits you, you'll need to dive behind cover immediately — there's really no time to squeeze in a final shot before you move. The door on the right just before the corner is the key to winning this closing encounter. You can use the short corridor behind it to periodically ambush the Brutes while your allies distract them; a Plasma Pistol or some Spike Grenades will enable you to wreak havoc in small, carefully delivered portions.

Grab Battle Rifle ammunition and a Carbine to replace your Magnum, then collect the Brute Chieftain's turret before you leave. Having escaped the frying pan, so to speak, it's now time to attend to a pressing appointment with a fire…

BASICS

CAMPAIGN

EXTRAS

MULTIPLAYER

USER INSTRUCTIONS

PREFACE

MISSION 1

MISSION 2

MISSION 3

MISSION 4

MISSION 5

MISSION 6

MISSION 7

MISSION 8

MISSION 9

G. Let's start with the basics: unless you are a particularly gifted player, venturing onto the landing pad is suicide. There's very little cover down there, and the Jump Packs used by the Brutes make them highly mobile and — most importantly — much more unpredictable than usual. They also tend to use equipment frequently, particularly Radar Jammers and Trip Mines.

Once you start fighting the first group of Brutes, reinforcements will drop down from the control room above the landing pad. Later in the battle, approximately half a dozen more will enter the fray via the door which leads to the control room. If you have plenty of grenades, you can greet the new arrivals with a rain of explosives as they run out. You're highly unlikely to hit a checkpoint before the final Brute draws its last lungful of breath, so this is one of those fights where patience and prudence really are important.

Though you can head for the lower level beneath the landing pad and make your stand from a variety of locations — and please, feel free to try — the simple fact is, taking up position by the large metal crate just outside the elevator door is probably the safest thing to do. If you brought the Plasma Turret dropped by the Brute Chieftain in the Barracks, you can wait for Brutes to jump into range, then batter them with short, controlled bursts until their power armor fails. You can then either continue firing to put them down for good or switch to a Battle Rifle to make an immediate killing headshot. (If you didn't bring the turret along, this confrontation is much more difficult, but you'll find a supply of Battle Rifles on the wall dispensers to the right of the elevator.)

The metal crate isn't perfect cover, but it does offer a "sweet spot" where Brutes located to the left and right can't hit you. Better still, some of the Brutes have a tendency to jump to a position at the bottom of the nearby steps, where you can easily pummel them into submission with the Plasma Turret. Though you may be unlucky enough to have a Brute jump on top of the crate, or even land next to you, this actually happens less than you might expect.

When you finally reach a checkpoint, stock up on Battle Rifle ammo and, if possible, grab a Carbine before you move on.

• By now, you should have noticed that Halo 3's code periodically "cleans up" areas that you have passed through, by removing corpses and, more importantly, dropped weapons. However, you can use a classic Legendary-grade trick from previous Halo games to make potentially useful firearms exempt from these bouts of housecleaning — just pick them up and then (here's the science bit) drop them again to "fix" them in place. If you need one at a later date, you can backtrack to collect it.

[CROW'S NEST IV]

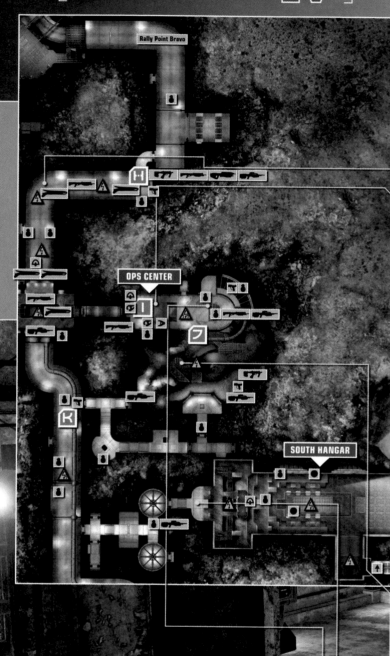

Rally Point Bravo

OPS CENTER

SOUTH HANGAR

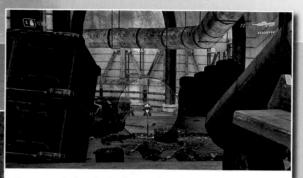

On your way back to the Ops Center, a large force of Grunts and Jackals bar your way. They wouldn't usually be a great threat, but there are also numerous Plasma Turret emplacements. From cover, you can inch out and dispatch the Grunt operators in two shots with a Battle Rifle or Carbine. Be careful as you approach the Motor Pool – there are Jackals armed with Carbines on the upper walkway.

Retaking the Ops Center is complicated by the presence of a Brute Chieftain armed with a Fuel Rod Gun. Stay in cover behind the metal barrier, and make long-range shots to his head to take him down. We strongly advise that you dispatch his minions (two Brute Bodyguards, plus Grunts) before you engage him.

The door leading to the Motor Pool will be locked when you activate the bomb in the Ops Center, so go back there before you press the button if you need to pick up supplies.

Though it may appear that the Master Chief is in danger of being engulfed by an enormous explosion at any moment as you make your way to the South Hangar, feel free to make the journey as leisurely as you see fit – there's no fixed time limit to worry about.

There are no more Brutes to fight as you make your way to the South Hangar, and the initial force of Grunts in the large cave is too panicked to put up much resistance (though you should be wary of the two Jackals with Carbines on the slope to your right as you enter). The Grunts in the road tunnel are more spirited, but are nevertheless easily killed. When you reach the hangar, you can simply sprint for the elevator to end the level.

BASICS

CAMPAIGN

EXTRAS

MULTIPLAYER

USER INSTRUCTIONS

PREFACE

MISSION 1

MISSION 2

MISSION 3

MISSION 4

MISSION 5

MISSION 6

MISSION 7

MISSION 8

MISSION 9

H The two indoor roadways that lead to the Motor Pool are infested with dozens of Grunts backed up by Jackals with shields. There are also several Plasma Turret emplacements manned by Grunts, though these are less dangerous than you may at first presume — you can usually kill the operator in a couple of quick shots. Just dart from cover to cover, methodically picking off all targets within view as you make your way forward.

However, once you turn the corner and fight your way to the Motor Pool entrance, proceed with extreme caution — there are two Jackals armed with Beam Rifles on the upper platform inside. Due to their elevation, they can see your legs and body before you even cast eyes on them, which is problematic. It's advisable to kill all Grunts in the vicinity (including the turret operators) before you try to approach them.

Collect grenades if your supplies are low, stock up on Battle Rifle ammunition (there's plenty in the upper level in the Motor Pool), pick up a Beam Rifle, then grab a Plasma Turret before you head into the Ops Center.

I Inside the Ops Center, drop the Plasma Turret somewhere it can be easily retrieved. You'll find that the Covenant troops you come across have their backs turned to you. The temptation to slap the nearest Grunt on the back of the head is hard to resist, granted, but you'll be better served by taking the opportunity to stick a grenade to one of the Brutes further ahead. If you're swift, you can even dispatch both of them this way. Use your Battle Rifle to kill Grunts as you shelter from Fuel Rod Gun missiles behind the metal partition; with a little luck, the Chieftain's indiscriminate firing may cause collateral damage that works in your favor.

Dealing with the Chieftain in such confined quarters is tough, and much depends on his behavior. If he holds position at the back of the room, you can inch out and wear him down with Beam Rifle fire. If he opts to engage you up close, you're in trouble. One option should this happen is to pick up the Plasma Turret, press yourself tightly against the metal partition, then move over and open fire at point-blank range as he reaches the steps — the volley of plasma might stagger him and prevent him from returning fire. The second is to attempt to stall his advance (and, ideally, kill him) with grenades. When he finally falls, don't forget to deal with the Brute manning the Plasma Turret on the balcony before you rearm the bomb.

⊐ Entering the cave again en route to the hangar, you'll find that it is populated by a disorganized, panic-stricken rabble of Grunts, but also by two Jackals with Carbines on the slope to your right. This would usually be an extremely simple fight, but the periodic rumbling and blackouts caused by explosions throughout the base can make it hard to aim. You may find that activating your Flashlight makes the temporary loss of the lights marginally less disorientating when it occurs.

- While enemies are firing their weapons, they are much less likely to dive to dodge charged Plasma Pistol shots, grenades and, to a lesser extent, Needler fire. They are especially vulnerable to all of the above when throwing a grenade, but you should be careful to keep moving to avoid being "stuck".

- Even though certain weapons are occasionally carried forward to subsequent missions, there's no need to be frugal once you're sure that the end of a level is in sight — you'll always find adequate replacements or additional ammunition when you arrive.

K You will encounter a large group of fleeing Grunts in the road tunnels. Try to kill these quickly — they annoyingly regain their composure and fight when you least expect it, so it's best to deal with them immediately. The small swarm of Drones that flies past may cause a brief moment of alarm, but you'll soon notice that they don't actually stop to exchange plasma-based pleasantries. You can either let them pass, or try to stick a Plasma Grenade to one to see how many you can take out with a single explosion.

Finally, your return trip to the South Hangar is much less fraught with danger than your first visit. The remaining Covenant presence here consists of disorganized Grunts and Jackals, easy meat for even mediocre marksmen with a Battle Rifle. There's additional ammunition at your disposal in the upper level room, but you can simply (and, with a few choice shots and grenade throws, pretty much safely) sprint straight for the elevator if you're in a hurry.

CROW'S NEST: DEBRIEFING

PLASMA & MACHINE GUN TURRET

Though they differ in terms of the ballistic ammo used, the Plasma Turret and Machine Gun Turret are broadly analogous – not to mention devastating.

- You can wrench either type of fixed turret from its mounting by following the onscreen prompt that appears when you use one.

- If you are dual wielding, the weapon in your left hand will be dropped when you pick up a turret.

- When you carry a turret, the view switches to a third-person perspective. Although this shouldn't have a massive influence on the way you play, note that it can enable you to study enemy movements from behind cover.

- Both turrets stun targets (even Brute Chieftains) with their ferocious rate of fire.

- Carrying a turret slows the Master Chief down, making him vulnerable to grenades, turret emplacements (including fixed cannons on the Phantom dropship), and the Brute Shot. If you find yourself dangerously exposed and under fire while carrying one, just drop it and run – you can always retrieve it later.

RADAR JAMMER

For those panicked "there's movement all over the place!" moments, the Radar Jammer is a recipe for Motion Tracker madness.

- When deployed by Brutes and the Master Chief alike, the Radar Jammer causes the Chief's Motion Tracker to be filled with phantom contacts for as long as the device is active.

- The Radar Jammer will automatically self-destruct after a relatively short period of time, but it can also be destroyed by gunfire or explosions.

- When you use it against Covenant enemies, it can cause Grunts to panic, and Brutes to enter their berserk state. That may not necessarily be a good thing...

SMG

If the Magnum or Battle Rifle could be said to possess the precision and accuracy of a surgeon's scalpel in the right hands, the SMG is more akin to a rusty chainsaw.

- The "bullet hose", as those in the know affectionately call it, can be dual wielded, and has an extraordinary high rate of fire

- It suffers from bone-jarring recoil – especially when you use two at once – and its accuracy drops

alarmingly when fired continuously. As with the Assault Rifle, you'll find that frequent controlled bursts are more effective

- While it's very powerful on the Easy and Normal difficulty levels, the SMG is less potent on Heroic and Legendary.

PLASMA RIFLE

A mainstay of previous games in the series, the Plasma Rifle is actually relatively rare in Halo 3.

- The Plasma Rifle overheats if fired continuously. Use medium-length bursts to take advantage of the accelerating fire rate, but be sure to ease off the trigger before it cuts out.

- Can be dual wielded – ideally with a weapon such as the Magnum (for finishing headshots), an SMG or a Spiker.

- The Plasma Rifle tends to be marginally more effective at destroying shields and power armor than ballistic weaponry such as the SMG or Spiker, but is slightly less efficient against flesh and bone.

- On Heroic and Legendary, the Plasma Rifle is a solid substitute if there are no Plasma Pistols available

SPIKE GRENADE

With a design brief worthy of Torquemada's most feverishly evil dreams, and an end result that connoisseurs of artist Jackson Pollock would find eerily familiar, this is a pitilessly cruel type of grenade.

- The Spike Grenade will stick to practically any surface – even Bubble Shields and the shields used by Jackals.

- When it detonates, the Spike Grenade fires a payload of viciously sharp metal. However, the blast radius is smaller than that of Frag Grenades and Plasma Grenades.

- "Sticking" an enemy with a Spike Grenade is often a guaranteed kill.

- As with other grenade types, be careful when the floor is littered with Spike Grenades – a single explosion could set off a lethal chain reaction.

BASICS

CAMPAIGN

EXTRAS

MULTIPLAYER

USER
INSTRUCTIONS

PREFACE

MISSION 1

MISSION 2

MISSION 3

MISSION 4

MISSION 5

MISSION 6

MISSION 7

MISSION 8

MISSION 9

GRAV LIFT

Don't underestimate the Grav Lift, as it's more than a simple means of conveyance. Players with imagination and a degree of cunning will soon realize that it can be deployed to send charging Brutes and even onrushing light vehicles flying overhead — but don't forget to duck. As a fringe benefit, you should bear in mind that it also has an influence on the trajectory of thrown grenades, which may have some interesting applications...

DEPLOYABLE COVER

First encountered in its deployed form in the jungle battles of the Sierra 117 mission, the Deployable Cover equipment is simple to use — just face the required direction, press the magic button, and that's it. If you need to destroy one in a hurry, aim for the base unit. The degree of punishment that the energy shield can withstand is linked to the difficulty level you are playing on. With Legendary battles, it offers little more than very temporary respite from incoming fire.

POWER DRAIN

There are a few parallels that may lead you to erroneously assume that the Power Drain is simply a yin to the Regenerator's yang — after all, the similar visual appearance (though blue in color) and deleterious effect on energy shields certainly suggests that. However, there is more to this powerful piece of equipment than meets the eye. Not only does it quickly strip all shields in range, it also explodes once its power source expires, potentially killing any weakened Brutes (or, for that matter, Spartan or Arbiter) within range. Most interestingly, though, it also has an EMP-style effect on all vehicles that pass through it, stalling their engines for as long as it lasts. In all game modes (especially multiplayer matches), it's a device you'll learn to love and loathe in equal measure.

JUMP PACK BRUTE

Equipped with special "jump packs" that enable them to leap to higher ground and over large distances, this class of Brute can attack without warning, and from any direction — and that makes them extremely dangerous. Their weakness is that it's often possible to track their trajectory as they take off or land, and there's little (bar returning fire) that they can do to avoid your shots. Additionally, they tend to pause in place for a moment as they activate the jump packs, and when they land.

REGENERATOR

When deployed, the Regenerator creates a green spherical energy field that rapidly replenishes all personal shield devices in range. However, don't make the mistake of believing that this is equivalent to a form of temporary immunity from death or pain for either the Master Chief or Brutes. Incoming fire or nearby explosions will cause just as much damage as usual, and a suitably accurate hail of bullets will still kill a target within its boundaries. What it offers, though, is an astonishingly fast shield recharge time. Duck into cover for a second while inside the green field, and the Master Chief's shield will be completely restored. This enables you to launch rapid, aggressive attacks.

DRONE

Individually weak but collectively lethal. Drones can be hard to hit as they flit from one point to another. You should find cover straight away when they first spill into the air, as their sheer weight of numbers often makes them overwhelming. Ideally, you'll have access to a turret when you face them, but Battle Rifles or Carbines are reasonably reliable if you pick your shots carefully. If you have a Needler to hand when a swarm arrives, though, use it instead — it can be amazingly effective.

TSAVO HIGHWAY

[MISSION 3]

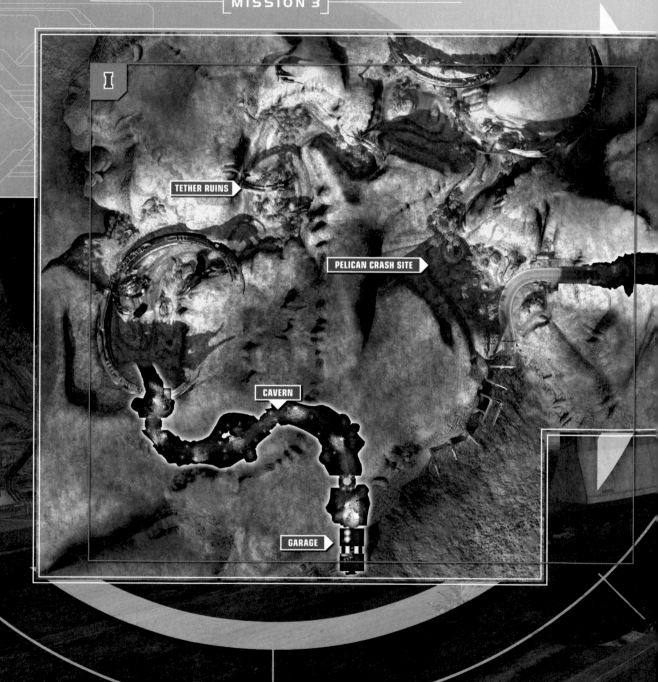

I

TETHER RUINS

PELICAN CRASH SITE

CAVERN

GARAGE

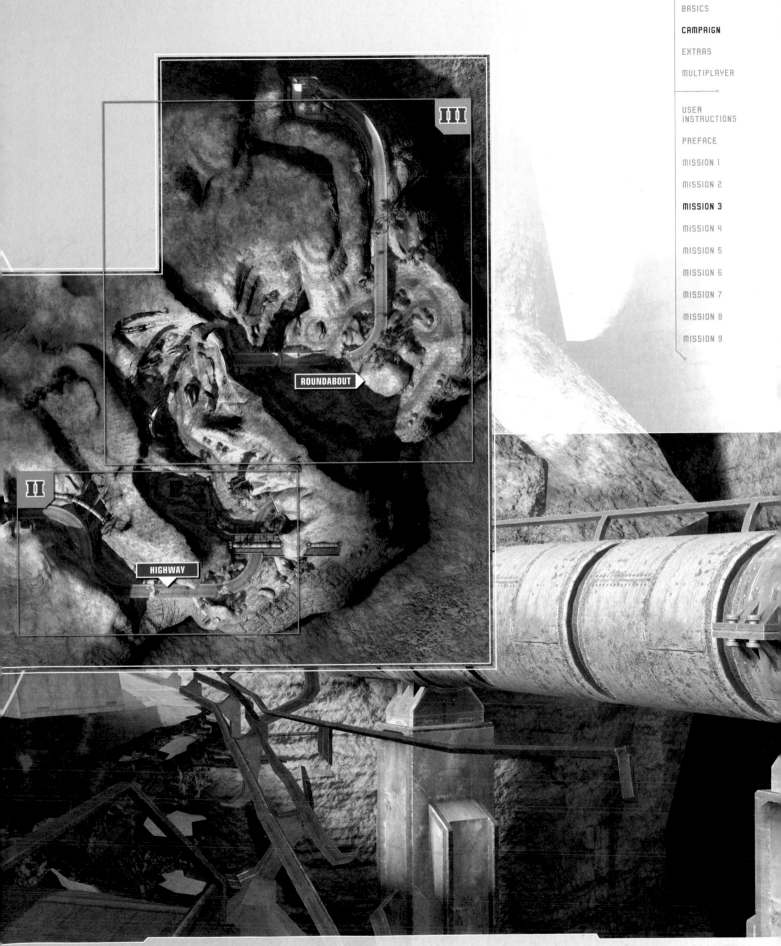

BASICS

CAMPAIGN

EXTRAS

MULTIPLAYER

USER
INSTRUCTIONS

PREFACE

MISSION 1

MISSION 2

MISSION 3

MISSION 4

MISSION 5

MISSION 6

MISSION 7

MISSION 8

MISSION 9

III

II

ROUNDABOUT

HIGHWAY

In this area, the Covenant has established an ad-hoc blockade. The main danger is the Shade turret; the position of this can vary, and you'll encounter more than one on Heroic. Note that it isn't actually mandatory that you kill all enemies in this area before you depart. Bar denying yourself the satisfaction of a job well done and an additional checkpoint (plus points, of course, if Campaign Scoring is activated), there's no penalty for just driving through.

The two Choppers patrolling this area should not be underestimated – not only can they ram both vehicles and infantry with predictably unpleasant results, they are also armed with powerful forward-firing cannons. The trick when fighting these deadly vehicles is to stay behind them, preventing their pilots from cutting you to shreds with their weapons. Capturing one of the Choppers is a definite bonus here.

Jump into a Warthog, and wait for the Marines to join you before you drive out through the caves. Outside, the enemy forces are light in both number and resolve, and can easily be run down as they retreat. At the top of the hill, past the Jackal snipers, be cautious as you approach the Covenant forces that are surrounding a crashed Phantom – they have fixed Plasma Turrets, though you can ram these to disable them.

[TSAVO HIGHWAY I]

TETHER RUINS

PELICAN CRASH SITE

CAVERN

GARAGE

As you approach the tunnel, a number of Drones will fly out to attack. Pull back immediately and aim to kill these before they move within firing range. If you are driving a vehicle, don't let them get too close – they will land on the hood and pummel you with melee attacks.

The tunnel entrance is covered by an energy shield that permits the Master Chief, Marines and Covenant troops to move through, but blocks the passage of weapon fire, explosions and vehicles. Destroy the generator behind this screen to disable it.

You may be playing on Legendary, but there's still no reason why the underside of your Warthog shouldn't be looking like a tie-dyed T-shirt after you encounter the small attack force outside the base exit. Over the brow of the next slope, plough into the two Jackal snipers, then collect a Beam Rifle. (If you chose to ride the troop-carrying Warthog at the beginning of the mission, you should give the other one to a Marine – see the margin tip at the bottom-right of the page.)

 Taking the route to the right, you will encounter a Jackal with a Beam Rifle on top of a floating observation post as you round the corner. Don't take any risks – jump out and carefully snipe him before you drive into his field of vision. At the top of the slope, there is a Covenant party that has set up a defensive perimeter of Plasma Turrets around a crashed Phantom.

There is a Brute with a Fuel Rod Gun here, so park your Warthog out of harm's way at the bottom of the slope, snipe him, and then kill a couple of turret operators. You can run the remaining Grunts over. If by any chance your Warthog is destroyed, revert to the previous checkpoint – you will really need it in the next area. Equip the Marine riding shotgun with the Fuel Rod Gun before you press forward.

The Covenant has established a blockade featuring Shade turrets and several snipers in this area. Usually, you'd lack the appropriate equipment to deal with this threat, but the Marine armed with a Fuel Rod Gun is your secret weapon. Staying on the entrance path (which offers cover from most enemies), move back and forth to dodge incoming fire as your ally pummels all targets in range with deadly green missiles. Once the Shade turrets and most of the infantry have been neutralized, carefully make your way around the area and mop up any stragglers. Some Covenant troops might retreat to the path on the far side of the small dam, but it should be safe to just run these over.

If you have difficulties with the above strategy, or simply forgot to collect the Fuel Rod Gun, the best tactic is to barge your way through in the Warthog. As you enter the area, turn left (watch out for the Brute – he may have a Brute Shot) and swing around in a semi-circle. Without easing off the accelerator, carefully line up the jump over the small slope (a crash at this point is always fatal), then slalom past the two barriers, and aim to be out of sight before anyone can get a clear shot at you.

BASICS
CAMPAIGN
EXTRAS
MULTIPLAYER

USER INSTRUCTIONS
PREFACE
MISSION 1
MISSION 2
MISSION 3
MISSION 4
MISSION 5
MISSION 6
MISSION 7
MISSION 8
MISSION 9

 The Chieftain on the rooftop to your left as you enter this area is your utmost priority – he'll absolutely slaughter you and the handful of Marines here unless you kill him immediately. You can get behind cover and try to snipe him straight away, but we've found that skidding the Warthog against the building he stands on, jumping out, then sneaking around the back to melee him from behind works well. Speed is everything here – there are Brutes armed with Beam Rifles in this area, so there's no time for mistakes.

This vital first task completed, move yourself (and the Warthog, if necessary) out of the line of fire – the right-hand side of the building the Chieftain was on top of is perfect. Switch to your Beam Rifle and, with ammo conservation in mind, eliminate any visible snipers first, then pick off other Grunts and Brutes; the latter targets may hide behind the crashed truck, so be patient. There is also a Shade turret on the far side of the road. You can use the Fuel Rod Gun dropped by the Chieftain to destroy this if you wish.

The two Choppers are your next target. Though you should be perfectly safe in your current position, know this: a Chopper's cannons can kill the Master Chief in the time it takes you to blink in astonishment. At this point, both Choppers should be driving in a patrol pattern on the broken highway. No matter how tempting it may be to use the Fuel Rod Gun, don't do it – you actually need at least one of the two vehicles intact. Sniping the drivers from this range is difficult, but eminently achievable if you carefully trace their movements and wait until they slow down to turn.

Once the two Brutes have been forcibly separated from both their vehicles and this plane of existence, run behind the crashed trailer and kill the Brute sniper on the floating platform to the left. Another Shade turret beside the tunnel entrance will open fire as you move into its field of vision. Grab a Chopper to destroy it, then collect a fresh Beam Rifle and replenish your supply of Battle Rifle ammunition.

A small swarm of Drones will emerge from the force field covering the tunnel entrance as you approach it; you may also find that a few Brutes and Grunts have retreated here. Use the Chopper to make light work of these troops (it's sensible to reverse as the Drones fly forward), then destroy the shield generator. Grab a fresh Beam Rifle and some Battle Rifle ammunition, then jump on your Chopper to travel to your next destination.

- Arming Marines with powerful weapons is always a good idea – it makes them more efficient killers. If you have a spare Beam Rifle, for example, approach a Marine wielding a less effective firearm, make the trade, then go collect the gun that you actually want to use. Note that Marines cannot carry certain weapon types.

- Whenever you have a valuable weapon with one shot left (especially the Beam Rifle or Sniper Rifle), give it to a Marine – in their hands, it has infinite ammunition.

[TSAVO HIGHWAY **II**]

A second, more dangerous Covenant attack group will be dropped off by a Phantom once you have wiped out the initial force. This includes a Chieftain (armed with a Fuel Rod Gun) and several Brutes. If you're feeling creative, you can deploy the Trip Mines found inside the buildings to form a lethal perimeter defense. Use the Sniper Rifle found here to pick off opponents from behind cover.

If possible, try to leave this area with a Fuel Rod Gun, as it can prove useful in the next battle.

A Wraith will appear on the path running through the middle of the area during the battle. You can save it until last and then board and hijack it, but there's no shame in simply choosing to destroy it.

If you have a penchant for marksmanship, there is a Sniper Rifle on top of the bridge above the highway. (You can find another in one of the buildings that the Marines are fighting to defend.)

HIGHWAY

Rally Point Alpha

When you reach the broken bridge section, it may appear that you need to proceed on foot, but you can actually drive a Chopper across the gap. This is particularly useful on Heroic and Legendary, and it's a definite bonus on Normal, too. Align the Chopper as demonstrated in this screenshot, whisper a silent prayer for luck, then boost forward. You'll need to make a few hasty thumbstick adjustments to help it gain sufficient purchase on the opposite side. If you fall through the gap, simply revert to the last saved checkpoint, and try again.

The coming battle is much easier if you have the firepower of a Chopper at your disposal, though it's not essential. The initial wave of Covenant troops will be attacking a beleaguered group of Marines trapped inside the buildings on the left of the area. The most important task is to neutralize the Brute armed with a Fuel Rod Gun.

We strongly recommend that you take a Chopper over the broken bridge to use in this (frankly enormous) battle. When you first arrive, Brutes and Grunts can be found battling with Marines trapped inside the buildings to the left; a handful of Jump Pack Brutes will enter the fray shortly afterwards. Once this initial force has been defeated, two separate Phantoms will each deploy a group of Brute reinforcements, both including a Chieftain. The icing on the cake is the presence of a Wraith, which will move into position (and, if you're really unlucky, begin a bombardment) at a variable point between the arrival of the first and second Phantoms. There's no doubt about it: this is one of Legendary's most demanding fights.

It's hard to offer a single definitive strategy for this battle, as there are so many variables to consider. It truly never plays out the same way twice. There is a trio of main positions that we recommend you operate from, which we have marked on Diagram 1. In all likelihood, you'll probably use all three.

AREA A: The bridge above the highway offers an unrivalled view of the battlefield; you can also find a Sniper Rifle there.

- **PROS:** If you have a Beam Rifle from earlier, you can make many "safe" sniper kills from up here.
- **CONS:** You're exposed to attacks from Jump Pack Brutes (though there are Plasma Pistols here that you can use against them), and the arrival of the Wraith complicates matters even more — usually unleashing a relentless bombardment that precludes further sniping from this location.

AREA B: The crashed trucks further ahead provide a degree of cover, which makes this a good place to fire from if you have a Chopper.

- **PROS:** You can kill Brutes very quickly with the Chopper's cannons, and pull back through the gate if you need to make a rapid escape.
- **CONS:** Enemies armed with Fuel Rod Guns are a problem when you're in a Chopper, as it's hard to avoid the homing missiles. There's also a danger that you will be overwhelmed by Jump Pack Brutes, or struggle to deal with the Wraith.

AREA C: The buildings offer the best cover of all, and also contain useful weapons and equipment.

- **PROS:** This area features not only plenty of places to hide, but also a Sniper Rifle, loads of Battle Rifle ammunition, and a collection of Trip Mines that you can position to disrupt or deter frontal assaults.
- **CONS:** Once reinforcements arrive (especially the Wraith), it's very difficult to escape from this locale. Jump Pack Brutes operate on the ridge to your left, and Brutes equipped with Flares and Power Drains may rush your position unless you practice careful crowd control. Given the sheer number of enemies you face, running low on ammunition can also be a problem.

While there's plenty of room for experimentation here, we suggest the following strategy:

- **Step 1:** When you first arrive, kill any Brutes and Grunts within range at position B, then move onto the top of the bridge at position A (there's a slope that leads up there next to the closed highway tunnel). Snipe all enemies you can see (but use the Battle Rifle for Grunts), with the Brute carrying a Fuel Rod Gun and Jump Pack Brutes being your most immediate concerns.

- **Step 2:** It can be difficult to kill every single enemy and trigger the arrival of the first Phantom from on top of the bridge, so you'll probably need to venture down to the buildings to pick off any stragglers. If you have a Chopper, park it somewhere safe (by the tunnel entrance, for example) before you set off.

- **Step 3:** As the Phantom flies in, either make a stand in the buildings at position C (noting that it's hard to escape if you commit to this plan), or run back to your Chopper with a view to wearing enemies down from a distance. There's a chance that not everyone will have a Chopper, so we're going to assume that you'll take the first option.

- **Step 4:** There are numerous Brutes in the first wave of reinforcements. You have plenty of Sniper Rifle and Battle Rifle ammo, but you'll need to ensure that you make every shot count as the next fight is even more taxing. The most economical strategy is to use the Sniper Rifle to destroy each Brute's power armor with headshots, then quickly switch to the Battle Rifle to finish them off. Try to kill the Chieftain immediately, and use a varied range of firing positions (from behind cover, naturally) to confuse your opponents.

- **Step 5:** The final attack wave features plenty of Jump Pack Brutes, who operate on the ridge to the left, and — among other Brutes — another Chieftain. If you have sufficient time, pick up and deploy the Trip Mines in front of the buildings before they arrive. The Wraith should definitely have moved into position by now. Try to avoid engaging the attention of its driver by staying out of sight and not firing at it — a mortar bombardment would make your life pretty miserable at this juncture.

- **Step 6:** When the last Brute falls, and you're absolutely sure that there are no more, you can either destroy or hijack the Wraith. Snipe the secondary gunner first, then sneak forward and board it to kill the driver. If you want to be extra careful, use a charged Plasma Pistol shot to disable it beforehand. If you don't have a Chopper waiting nearby, we strongly recommend that you take the Wraith into the next battle.

Pick up a Fuel Rod Gun, collect Battle Rifle ammo, and jump into the Wraith or a Chopper. The next battle is only moments away.

DIAGRAM 1

BASICS

CAMPAIGN

EXTRAS

MULTIPLAYER

USER
INSTRUCTIONS

PREFACE

MISSION 1

MISSION 2

MISSION 3

MISSION 4

MISSION 5

MISSION 6

MISSION 7

MISSION 8

MISSION 9

- If you play this battle in co-op mode, divide your attack so that one player snipes from the bridge, while the other defends the base. This is much more successful, we've found, than simply sticking together. As an added bonus, the player taking the risky option of engaging the Covenant up close will respawn on the bridge if killed.

- An alternative strategy for the battles that follow this lengthy confrontation is to take the Warthog troop carrier and equip everyone aboard with Fuel Rod Guns. Though you might at first dismiss this vehicle due to its lack of turret, it's actually an extremely powerful platform if you can fill it with heavily-armed allies — and for sheer maneuverability, it's hard to beat.

The first roadblock is guarded by several Brutes (including the Jump Pack variety), but these are easily dealt with in a Chopper – just pummel away with its dual cannons until the last one falls. Your priority in the final fight is to destroy the Shade turret; thereafter, you can blast away with the Chopper or snipe from a safe distance until the last Brute falls.

The final group of Brutes have a Chieftain armed with a Plasma Turret to support them, so don't move too close before you've dealt with him. The easiest way to do that is to use a Sniper Rifle.

The weapons scattered here include a Sniper Rifle, which is enormously useful (and especially so if you don't have a vehicle). As both fights on the final roadway feature Jump Pack Brutes, watch out for those that leap to or behind your position.

Aim to destroy the two floating sniper platforms straight away (either with the mounted gun on a Warthog, or with a Chopper if you still have one), then press forward to engage the Choppers. As before, try to stay behind them at all times to avoid their cannons.

You can actually shoot one or even both Wraiths from a position on top of the broken roadway. You'll need to be quick to dodge incoming mortar blasts, though.

ROUNDABOUT

The "roundabout" area is guarded by Wraiths and several waves of Choppers, and you'll also encounter at least one Shade turret. Take one of the Choppers at the start of the broken highway, and aim to deal with the enemy Choppers on the near side of the central hill first. Use extreme caution when you engage the Wraiths – try to tackle them one at a time, from a distance, moving by a couple of vehicle lengths to avoid incoming mortar fire.

BASICS

CAMPAIGN

EXTRAS

MULTIPLAYER

USER
INSTRUCTIONS

PREFACE

MISSION 1

MISSION 2

MISSION 3

MISSION 4

MISSION 5

MISSION 6

MISSION 7

MISSION 8

MISSION 9

F. This can be a very intense and frustrating confrontation unless you have a Wraith or Chopper to use. You face several Choppers, two floating platforms manned by Brute snipers, and at least one Shade turret. Your first priority is to kill the nearest snipers. The second is to get into a position that enables you to avoid the initial enemy charge. This is difficult, but not unreasonably so – the presence of Marines in Warthogs means that you have a small window of opportunity while they distract the Brutes. The enemy Choppers tend to drive between the two rocks for their first attack, so the best place to position yourself is just to the left of this opening (in approximately the same position as the "F" icon on the map).

The secret to winning this fight is to constantly adjust your position to avoid cannon fire, using what little cover is available, then blast the Choppers as they drive by. Though you can kill any remaining snipers (there are usually two) and destroy the Shade turrets if you get the opportunity to do so, we suggest that you leave these until later, and focus exclusively on the enemy vehicles. If you experience difficulties you can pull back into the previous area, and aim to shoot the Choppers from a greater distance – Brutes tend not to use their cannons until they move within a set range. It's harder to evade their attention if you're piloting a Wraith (you obviously present a much bigger target), but the power of its main cannon more than compensates for the reduced mobility.

G. We don't recommend fighting in a Wraith in this area, as the tank's lack of speed makes it extremely vulnerable over open ground – pick one of the two free Choppers instead. You'll usually pass a reasonable number of checkpoints during this battle, but it's still extremely tricky – enemy Choppers attack from the left and right paths, often in pairs, and it's far too easy to get caught up in a deadly crossfire. If you choose to dive straight into the fray, you should stay on the near side of the central hill, only venturing briefly to the other side to lure additional Choppers around if required. Once the Choppers have been destroyed, you can move on to attack the Wraiths – though it's important that you separate these and fight them individually. It may be hard to manoeuvre a Chopper over short distances (especially in reverse), but you should try to get into a rhythm of firing a few blasts before moving to avoid the inevitable searing plasma-based retort. Use distance to your advantage (the further away you are, the better) and don't even think about attacking from close range – the Wraith's secondary cannon would make confetti out of you.

Given the steep odds you face, you should be pleased to hear that there's a decidedly cheap and dirty tactic you can use to make this fight much easier. After arriving in this area, hang back at the start and fire at the Wraiths from long range. If you operate from the part of the highway just in front of the sloped section of broken road, you'll find that there's sufficient room to avoid incoming mortar fire, and that you're also largely covered from

the Choppers milling around below. Once the Wraiths have been destroyed, you can stay on this platform to deal with the Choppers. If you're careful, the only real dangers are passing Phantoms, and the possibility that the Covenant may deploy an additional Wraith. We definitely found that making a stand from this position leads to far fewer deaths, and potentially none if you're very careful – a definite plus for those playing with Campaign Scoring activated.

H. With a Chopper at your disposal, beating the penultimate battle at the small roadblock is simple. The Brutes may be numerous, but they're no match for a pragmatic (though some purists would argue "craven") barrage of cannon fire from a safe distance. The only possible threat is that Jump Pack Brutes may attempt to close the gap, but these are easily dispatched if you pay attention. Collect the Sniper Rifle from the right-hand side of the road before you continue – it's useful in the next fight.

I. Again, having a Chopper makes this final battle much easier to complete than it would be on foot, but you should bear in mind that the Brutes have more potential hiding spots. Destroy the Shade turret immediately, then set about showering Brutes with ranged cannon blasts. We advise against moving too far down the slope in the Chopper, even if it appears safe to do so – the Brutes may use a Power Drain to disable your vehicle. Once you've thinned their numbers to a manageable level, jump out and use the Sniper Rifle to pick off the rest. Ensure that you have killed the Chieftain before you move closer (he tends to be better at taking cover than the other Brutes), and study certain positions carefully through your scope to be sure that his subordinates are all dead before you move down to end the mission.

- As Tsavo Highway is the first Halo 3 mission that features vehicles, this seems as good a place as any to remind you that the Plasma Pistol is an invaluable tool whenever you face vehicles on foot. One charged shot will incapacitate a vehicle's engine for a short (but significant) period of time, though you should remember that the EMP effect does not disable their weapons systems.

- On a similar note, be careful if there are Brutes in close proximity when you drive vehicles. If they deploy and hit you with a Power Drain unit, your vehicle will stall immediately, and you'll also lose all shield energy.

TSAVO HIGHWAY: DEBRIEFING

[WARTHOG]

An iconic part of the Halo games since the second level of the first episode, the Warthog is as fun to drive now as it ever was.

- The Warthog comes in three flavors: the M12 LRV (armed with a chain gun), the M12 LAAV (or "Gauss Hog", equipped with an anti-vehicular Gauss cannon), and the M831 TT (a troop carrier with room for up to five, including the driver).
- The Warthog's hood is an offensive weapon in its own right at high speed, but you can also use the e-brake to slide and increase the surface area you present as you collide with Covenant infantry.
- With the M12 LRV and LAAV, the gunner is partially protected from incoming fire in the direction that he or she is facing, but is vulnerable from all other compass directions. Good driving is not simply a question of helping your gunner to get a clear shot — you also need to take their wellbeing into account.

[CHOPPER]

As whimsical as an autopsy, as amiable as a grave, there's really no poetry to a Chopper in motion — it's an ugly, inhumane instrument of death.

- The Chopper is the "alpha" of light ground vehicles in Halo 3: its strength, durability (especially its armored front), speed and firepower make it deadly in the right hands. Its principle weaknesses are its lack of maneuverability, and the scant protection offered to its driver from the rear.
- The hood of the Chopper is specifically designed to gouge its way through metal; we shouldn't need to tell you what it can do to flesh and bone. It also shields the driver from small arms fire.
- The Chopper is equipped with lethal dual cannons. Their direction of fire can be adjusted up and down and, to a much lesser extent, left and right. Even if a Chopper isn't directly facing you, it doesn't mean the Brute pilot can't hit you.
- The Chopper's limited boost function can be used offensively to increase the force of a deliberate impact, but also defensively to accelerate away from danger.

[WRAITH]

Equipped with two weapons systems and impervious to small arms fire, a Wraith's only true weakness is its lack of speed.

- The Wraith's mortar cannon is enormously powerful. It's especially effective against vehicles — the sheer force of the blast radius can cause light vehicles to roll, rendering them vulnerable to a follow-up shot.
- The secondary plasma turret is also a weapon to be feared. Its unremittingly fast fire rate enables it to shred vehicle armor, and send infantry fleeing for cover. Fortunately, a Brute manning this turret will generally only use it when you move within medium-to-close range.
- The Wraith's speed boost function, though brief, can be used to accelerate away from danger, clear awkward obstacles, and splatter infantry unfortunate enough to be hit by its imposing front end.
- If you board an enemy Wraith from the side or front, you can bludgeon its driver and hijack it, or throw grenades inside to destroy it. Jumping to reach the hood can also work, but be careful — a last-minute use of its speed boost can be fatal.
- You can also board the Wraith from behind if you simply wish to wreck it. This technique is especially useful if you lack the appropriate weapons to deal with its turret operator.

BASICS

CAMPAIGN

EXTRAS

MULTIPLAYER

USER
INSTRUCTIONS

PREFACE

MISSION 1

MISSION 2

MISSION 3

MISSION 4

MISSION 5

MISSION 6

MISSION 7

MISSION 8

MISSION 9

SHADE

The latest evolution of the Shade fixed turret is the most powerful to date, as it provides far greater protection for its Grunt operator than previous models.

- The Shade fires slow-moving yet powerful bolts of plasma. Jump and dodge to avoid these at range, but be warned – not all Grunts are stupid, and the operator may anticipate your movements if your evasive maneuvers are all zig and no zag.

- The Shade's front armor is impervious to small arms fire, though you may be able to hit the operator and cause him to jump out and flee if you have a precision weapon (such as a Sniper Rifle) that enables you to fire through the tiny gaps.

- If you can get a clear shot from the side or behind, a single headshot is sufficient to disable the Grunt inside.

- The Shade is especially vulnerable to "sticky" grenades – one tag equals instant death for the unfortunate Grunt manning it.

FUEL ROD GUN

One of the most powerful weapons you can lay your hands on, the Fuel Rod Gun turns a common infantryman into a walking tank.

- As with other "power weapons", the Fuel Rod Gun has limited ammo while in the care of the Master Chief, so it's often more useful in the hands of allies. If a Brute has one, they're also free to fire for as long as they please – which is why such enemies should always be top of your hit list.

- The "splash damage" that occurs when a Fuel Rod Gun shot hits home can tip light vehicles over, and cause anything combustible within range to explode.

- The Fuel Rod Gun is best used against vehicles and concentrated groups of infantry. With the obvious exception of Chieftains, using it on individual Brutes is wasteful.

- If you find that a long-range shot appears to be tracking your movements, that's because it *is* – the Fuel Rod Gun's projectiles have a limited homing function when correctly aimed. This effect is far more pronounced on higher difficulty levels.

TRIP MINE

Tread on one of these, and the Marines that find the Master Chief's remains will need to requisition a specially made Spartan-sized body bag… and a spade to fill it.

- There is an audio cue that helps you to detect the presence of an activated Trip Mine, even if you can't actually see it.

- A Trip Mine will detonate shortly after its proximity trigger is activated by a nearby vehicle or pedestrian.

- Trip Mines can also be activated by gunfire or explosions, and have a wide blast radius.

- Don't make the mistake of thinking that Trip Mines are only appropriate for use against vehicles – they're actually perfect for many close-quarters infantry battles, especially if you want to lay a trap for attacking enemies.

- If a Brute deploys a Trip Mine and it poses no immediate danger to you, don't be too quick to destroy it. Instead, wait to see if enemies move into range at a later point, then fire at will if they do.

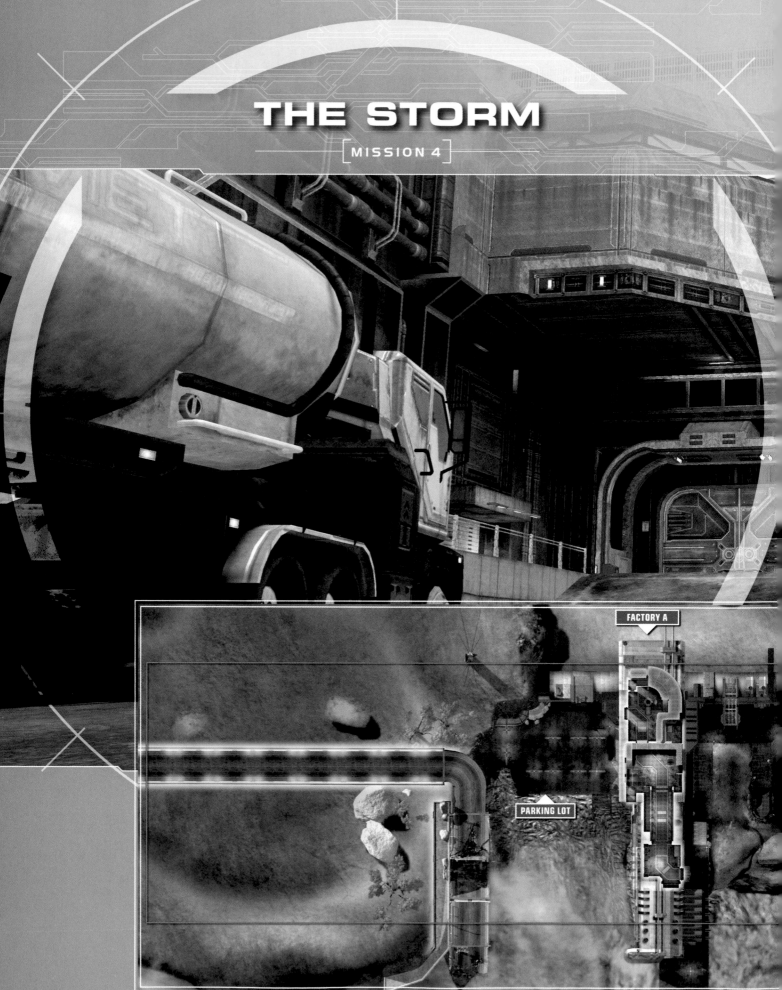

THE STORM

[MISSION 4]

FACTORY A

PARKING LOT

BASICS

CAMPAIGN

EXTRAS

MULTIPLAYER

USER
INSTRUCTIONS

PREFACE

MISSION 1

MISSION 2

MISSION 3

MISSION 4

MISSION 5

MISSION 6

MISSION 7

MISSION 8

MISSION 9

III

STORAGE AREA

WAREHOUSE

FACTORY B

LAKE BED B

LAKE BED A

I

II

Run upstairs and attack the Covenant watching the Prophet of Truth's sermon. Try to hit them with a Frag Grenade before they notice your arrival. You might be tempted to press the button above the gate to allow your Warthog through straight away, but be warned – it only takes a single unseen Grunt to wipe out the vehicle and its entire crew with a grenade stick.

[**THE STORM** I]

Collect the Battle Rifle in this small room before you continue – it's more useful in the coming battles than the Assault Rifle that you start with.

FACTORY A

PARKING LOT

LAKE BED A

During the battle inside Factory A, there's a danger that Grunts (or even Brutes) will jump aboard the Ghosts parked just out of view. You can take cover on the walkway to the right (note that a Bubble Shield and a Battle Rifle are located at the end of it) while the Warthog deals with these.

Your first objective when you arrive outside is to kill all Covenant infantry. There is a group to your left as you pass through the gate, and another force deployed by a Phantom on the roof of the nearby building. You'll need to dispatch these first to secure some powerful weapons. Don't go down onto the dry lake bed yet – the patrolling Ghosts will annihilate you on the open ground.

You can find a Missile Pod and a Sniper Rifle on top of the small building at the end of the wooden boardwalk. Collect the turret and use it to neutralize the Ghosts (including the two delivered by Phantom later). Eliminate the gunners on both Wraiths with the Sniper Rifle, as this makes it easier to board and smash them to pieces once you've dealt with the Ghosts. Be careful when you approach the exit – a small Covenant force will run out to bar your advance after the Anti-Air Wraith has been destroyed.

BASICS

CAMPAIGN

EXTRAS

MULTIPLAYER

USER
INSTRUCTIONS

PREFACE

MISSION 1

MISSION 2

MISSION 3

MISSION 4

MISSION 5

MISSION 6

MISSION 7

MISSION 8

MISSION 9

A Grab a Battle Rifle from the room upstairs (to your left when you enter Factory A) before you ambush the Covenant in the next room. Though it's tempting to press the door release button and let the Warthog roll through to provide assistance, you'll almost certainly lose it to a Plasma Grenade if you do.

Clear out the initial force from a safe position on the metal walkway (watch out for Grunts or Jackals attacking from the stairs to your left), and a succession of further Grunts will arrive via an opening in the far right-hand corner of the room, which is partially obscured by crates and barrels. Deal with these before you allow the Warthog to roll through. You can collect more Battle Rifle ammunition from beside a fallen Marine to the left of the closed gate.

B There's not a great deal of cover if you simply open the gate and follow the Warthog along, so it's generally better to press the button, then immediately run through and jump onto the walkway to your right. From this position you can catch the Covenant in crossfire, with enemy troops often too distracted by the turret to worry about you. Two Ghosts are parked at the very end of the corridor, which surviving enemy infantry may (or may not) use against you. If you hear the distinctive sound of one accelerating or firing, get out of the way immediately. Use Plasma Grenades against these if your ally on the turret is slow to deal with the threat; note that a charged Plasma Pistol shot followed by a hijack can work just as well.

As the Warthog will rarely survive this short yet furious encounter, you might prefer to head through the side passageway to launch an initial solo attack with a Battle Rifle. Bring a Plasma Pistol along with your Magnum (it's handy if you need to deal with an aggressive Brute), then aim to thin enemy numbers by killing Grunts, Jackals and the two more adventurous Brutes. When the final few enemies hang back at the end of the corridor, let the Warthog roll through to finish them off.

C After you open the gate, jump into the Warthog's driving seat and try to catch up with the roadkill-to-be running along the side of the dry lakebed. Skid through the crates to reach the start of the boardwalk leading to the low building, and jump out as your gunner lays waste to the Covenant on its roof. You need to clear this area of enemy combatants quickly; a Phantom will deploy a Wraith outside the far exit at this point, and the Ghosts milling around below will already be moving towards your position.

Get on top of the small building, and collect the Sniper Rifle and the Missile Pod. Use the former to shoot the gunner in the distant Wraith (not the Anti-Air variant – leave that alone for now). The Missile Pod enables you to destroy some (though probably not all) of the Ghosts that are milling around below as you make your way over to the Wraith. Drop the turret when you draw near to the tank, then sprint over and board it. If you hijack it successfully, it makes the rest of the battle much easier.

(Incidentally, the Missile Pod can occasionally be knocked over the edge and down onto the dry lake bed by a grenade explosion or suchlike. If this happens, going down to collect it is a risky business. You'll need to take cover below and destroy any nearby Ghosts before you even consider running to the slope that leads back up to the dockside path.)

The final part of this skirmish is a cat and mouse game against the remaining Ghosts. If your Warthog crew is still alive, they'll engage any that come within range, creating a welcome diversion. You may either attempt to snipe the Grunt drivers from afar, or bombard them from range with the Wraith's main cannon.

With the Ghosts out of commission, kill the gunner in the Anti-Air Wraith from a safe distance, grab yourself a Ghost, then drive over to the target. Leap out and board it to kill the driver (shooting it with plasma cannons takes an absolute eternity), then jump off and back into the Ghost. Two Banshees will fly in to attack you. There's usually a friendly Hornet that will engage and destroy them on your behalf, but it's wise to boost to cover with the Ghost before one (or both) can open fire.

The door to the next area will now be open, with a small force of Grunts and one Brute outside. Kill these in any way you see fit (watch out for the turret, though), then steel yourself for the next encounter...

If you capture the Wraith deployed in the far corner during the Lake Bed A battle, it's actually possible to take it through to Lake Bed B, using it to utterly annihilate the Covenant encountered on the way. If you smash one of the two "wings" on either side of its hood with melee attacks – be warned though, this may destroy the vehicle if it's seriously damaged – you can squeeze it through the entrance and exit to the next building with a little creative maneuvering. It's not actually very practical in the Lake Bed B fight (the light vehicles, especially the Choppers, will make light work of you), but it's fun to try.

[THE STORM II]

Take the Plasma Turret from outside, then deal with the Covenant just inside the door. There are Brutes (including a Chieftain) upstairs. If you're feeling creative, you can flank them by taking the set of stairs through the small door to the left of the entrance; the Marine on the Machine Gun Turret should distract them from the other side.

A swarm of Drones will attack from above after you enter this room. They're much easier to deal with if you have a Plasma Turret. If you experience difficulties, you can collect the one dropped by the Chieftain earlier.

FACTORY B

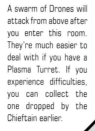

Rally Point Alpha

LAKE BED B

There is a Sniper Rifle on top of the crane nearest the far wall. You can use this to shoot troops on the Scarab's deck before you jump on board.

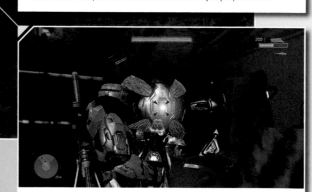

The Scarab will move under one of the two cranes after it arrives, so take an elevator up and jump onto its deck from above. Grab one of the fixed Plasma Turrets, then head around to the back of the machine. When you reach the opening pictured here, you've found the engine core — and it's this that you need to shoot to destroy the Scarab. Retreat a safe distance before it explodes.

Jump on a Mongoose with a Marine riding pillion and head out onto the dry lake bed. The Wraiths are actually the least important targets when you arrive (though you should drive quickly to avoid their cannons). Instead, concentrate on destroying other enemy vehicles first. Watch out for reinforcements, and keep moving to avoid incoming fire from the Phantoms that deliver them.

If you need to escape a chasing Chopper or Ghost in a hurry during the fight to destroy the Anti-Air Wraiths, use the ramps in the center of the area to jump from one side to another.

BASICS

CAMPAIGN

EXTRAS

MULTIPLAYER

USER
INSTRUCTIONS

PREFACE

MISSION 1

MISSION 2

MISSION 3

MISSION 4

MISSION 5

MISSION 6

MISSION 7

MISSION 8

MISSION 9

Quickly kill the Grunts and Jackals in the room beyond the gate with your Ghost, then jump out and grab the Plasma Turret from outside; the Brutes upstairs have Power Drains, so it's unwise to engage them in a vehicle.

The Chieftain won't come downstairs to attack you, but you can lure his Bodyguards to your location. Pick these targets off with the Plasma Turret, being careful to dodge similar ripostes from the Chieftain. Once the Brutes are dead, you can switch to your Battle Rifle and patiently wear your main opponent down with headshots. If you still have a few Sniper Rifle bullets from earlier, this is a good time to use them. Collect the Chieftain's Plasma Turret, then make your way through the open gate.

As soon as you enter the next room, Drones will smash through the skylights above — be warned that a number of them carry Needlers. Open fire with the Plasma Turret while they descend, then run back through the gate and take cover once they begin to return fire. This is the best place to operate from — the Drones will rarely (if ever) follow you through, and you can make darting forays into the open to dispatch them in twos or threes before hiding to give your shield time to fully replenish.

Grab a Rocket Launcher and stock up on Battle Rifle ammo at the weapons cabinet prior to departing. The Rocket Launcher is actually needed for a battle that occurs much later in the mission, so you should endeavor to save it until then. Trust us: you'll be thankful for the tip later.

Though it's possible to destroy all vehicles and the Anti-Air Wraiths while driving a Mongoose, as you did on Normal, the odds are resolutely stacked against you on Legendary. The Choppers and Ghosts alone are intimidating enough; add the Wraith turret operators and passing Phantoms to the mix, and surviving this fight requires 70% perspiration, 30% skill, and approximately 434% luck.

There is, fortunately, a different way to play it — and one that those making a speed run or Campaign Scoring high score attempt will appreciate for its brevity and simplicity. As soon as you hit the dry lake bed at the bottom of the ramp, drive directly to the more distant of the two fixed Missile Pod emplacements on the far dockside. There is a small group of Grunts and a Brute at this position; quickly run them down, or angle the Mongoose to give your driver a clear shot. That important opening task achieved, drive up the ramp and park the Mongoose safely. As a fringe benefit, your passenger will help protect you from incoming vehicles.

Take control of the Missile Pod (leave it on its mounting, of course, for infinite ammunition), and aim to smash absolutely everything within sight. You may need to take cover when enemy vehicles threaten you, or alternatively run and use the other turret temporarily. The Ghosts, Choppers and Banshees are your priority — the sooner you wipe these out, or at least thin their numbers, the better the chance your allies on

Mongooses have of destroying the Anti-Air Wraiths and surviving this opening part of the battle. If you have the other vehicles under control, incoming fire from the Phantoms is the only danger to you here, so you should also aim to blow these from the skies. The only reason you might have to leave this location is if your allies have difficulties taking down one of the Anti-Air Wraiths. We hardly need to remind you what happens next, so return to the Missile Pod promptly.

As soon as the enormous Scarab passes overhead open fire on its deck, turrets and leg joints, with the intention of sufficiently weakening both vehicle and crew before it can turn to attack you. If a number of Mongooses survived the earlier confrontation, you may find that the Scarab won't open fire on your position for a while, which is a blessing. Should you arouse its ire, retreat immediately — remember, there's another working turret to your right.

When the Scarab moves underneath one of the two cranes, use the appropriate elevator to travel up, then run over and jump onto its deck; from there, it's a short journey to the engine core at the back. You can grab one of the Plasma Turrets to dispatch any surviving infantry, and then finish off the walking tank with ease. If your opening rocket salvo didn't go entirely as planned, and there are still an alarming number of enemies on board, use the Sniper Rifle at the top of the crane nearest the exit to eliminate the most dangerous targets from afar before you launch a direct assault.

With a little good fortune, it's actually possible to annihilate the Scarab without leaving your original position behind the Missile Pod. If you aim exclusively at the armor on its back from the moment it arrives, you can expose the engine core and then maybe even hit it before the Scarab's gunners realize where you are firing from. This is more likely if there are still Mongooses around to distract it, but it's definitely something you should try on a speed run.

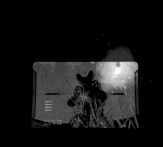

Your principle objective in this closing battle is to kill the Chieftain carrying a Fuel Rod Gun as soon as you can. Getting close enough to kill him is tough, but fortunately there's another Sniper Rifle beside the missile launcher just in front of the slope. Try to dispatch all nearby Grunts and Jackals from a safe position (that is, one that doesn't put you in the direct line of fire of the Chieftain) before you pick him off from range.

[**THE STORM** **III**]

STORAGE AREA

Shoot the white panel that appears when the cannon vents gas to destroy it. If you're running low on ammunition, you can find a Fuel Rod Gun on a nearby Covenant weapons dispenser.

WAREHOUSE

If you have trouble surviving a direct attack on the Chieftain and his entourage outside, there is another option. Head up the steps next to the warehouse exit and go through the door at the top. In the second office along, you'll find a Sniper Rifle. Smash the window with a melee attack, then snipe the Brutes (especially the Chieftain) from this position.

Welcome the pair of Hunters with grenades as they burst explosively into the warehouse. Strafe to avoid their cannons, and don't linger close enough to be hit by a melee attack. The exposed orange flesh on their backs is their weak spot.

Collect a Machine Gun Turret as you pass through the rooms controlled by Marines. You face three separate groups of Brutes in the warehouse. The first isn't too hard to beat, but the second is larger — try cutting through the open shipping container on the left to flank them, or holding back to fight them from a distance. After defeating the third attack party, ensure that you have a full stock of Spike Grenades before moving on.

HALO 3

BASICS

CAMPAIGN

EXTRAS

MULTIPLAYER

USER
INSTRUCTIONS

PREFACE

MISSION 1

MISSION 2

MISSION 3

MISSION 4

MISSION 5

MISSION 6

MISSION 7

MISSION 8

MISSION 9

G As you pass through the rooms filled with Marines, grab a Machine Gun Turret and ensure you have a full supply of Battle Rifle ammunition before you head into the warehouse area. The first battle against a small group of Brutes isn't particularly tough. However, if you save the Marine on the upper walkway, you'll make the next fight (which features a larger group of Brutes) relatively easy, as he will man the nearby fixed turret; the Arbiter and Marines should hold the others at bay while you do this.

Once you have dealt with the advance party, run over to, and head through, the empty shipping container on the far left, then shoot the Brute on the other side. This will enable you to flank the larger Brute pack from the left. If you saved the Marine earlier, the turret crossfire can wipe the Brutes out in mere seconds. If not, or should they deploy Bubble Shields, you'll need to be a little more patient. Watch out for Spike Grenades (you can retreat inside the container to take cover), and try not to waste unnecessary Battle Rifle ammunition – you'll need it later. If your Machine Gun Turret is almost dry, go back and grab the one on the walkway before continuing.

H As you round the corner, you will usually encounter two workers battling against another group of Brutes. Run around to the right to flank them. If you operate from behind the crate, you can pick each Brute off in turn while they are distracted by your allies.

I If you've been patiently saving the Rocket Launcher since acquiring it earlier, your diligence pays dividends against the Hunters. Sprint over to the exit (watch out for the explosion), and hit them with rockets as soon as they enter the warehouse. It should take no more than three or four shots to kill them both.

The Chieftain outside is flanked by two Brute Bodyguards armed with Carbines, and a number of Grunts. From the warehouse exit, switch to your Battle Rifle (your main weapon in this fight) and kill the Grunts first, being careful to avoid incoming Carbine fire. At this point, the Chieftain and his guards will usually withdraw. Aim to take at least one Bodyguard out while his back is turned towards you as you cautiously move outside. Take out the second Bodyguard straight away, then turn your attention to killing the next wave of Jackals and Grunts before additional Brutes arrive. We strongly recommend that you make the most of every opportunity to shoot at the Chieftain – if you're lucky, you can even kill him before he charges (with the added bonus of being able to collect his Invincibility equipment), or at least weaken him in advance. Note that there is a Battle Rifle just outside the warehouse if you're running low on ammunition.

You might think that halting the charge of the Chieftain would be easy with a Rocket Launcher, but that isn't always the case. If he's still at full strength, he can survive the first shot; more often than not, he'll then activate his Invincibility unit, necessitating approximately ten seconds of panicked running, dodging and jumping. If you simply run away, he'll usually take the easier option of attacking the workers and Marines that accompany you... but bear in mind that this shameful act of cowardice will deny you additional support in the following battle.

As the battlefield is positively littered with useful weapons (particularly Carbines, Needlers and Plasma Pistols), the final Brutes aren't too difficult to finish off. Before you press forward, collect a Carbine and as much ammo as possible, then pick up the Sniper Rifle from the office (see area map for location).

J Take cover behind the Marine missile launcher and have your Sniper Rifle at the ready. A Chieftain armed with a Fuel Rod Gun will briefly move into the line of fire before retreating, usually after sending a few green blasts in your direction. If you can at least weaken him and remove his helmet with a barrage of four shots – you won't get to make any more than that – then you'll give yourself a massive starting advantage.

Kill the Jackals and Grunts that run down the slope with your Carbine; watch out for the Grunts carrying Plasma Turrets in particular. Collect some Sniper Rifle ammo from in front of the missile launcher, replace your Carbine with a Battle Rifle if necessary, and make your way up the slope. When you reach a large rock on your right, stop and dispatch any Jackals and Grunts in the vicinity. With that achieved, inch forward until you can see the Chieftain (if you didn't manage to kill him earlier) and other Brutes in the distance. Dispatching the Chieftain is your foremost priority; well, that and dodging the Fuel Rod Gun missiles that he fires your way, of course. Marines and workers should be protecting you from Grunts and Jackals, but watch out for grenades – it's infuriating to have your plans foiled by a lucky Plasma Grenade stick from an unseen Grunt.

Once the Brutes are dealt with, the final task is to mop up any stray infantry before you complete the last objective. As a word of caution, we should remind you that overconfidence is deadly on Legendary, so explore the area slowly and methodically. It's usually a long way back to the previous checkpoint...

- In the final battle, you'll notice Banshees circling overhead. Don't be alarmed – these attack sporadically, if at all, and can be safely ignored if you operate from cover. If you're aiming to get maximum kills with Campaign Scoring activated, it is possible to bring a Missile Pod along with a little preparation and forward planning – but you might be losing potential points on the time multiplier by doing so.

- If you are using a Sniper Rifle to dispatch a Chieftain, you'll find it much easier (and economical in terms of ammunition) to switch to a Battle Rifle or Carbine to make the final headshot once his helmet is removed.

THE STORM: DEBRIEFING

[HUNTER]

HUNTER

These giant "living tanks" are extremely difficult to beat unless you know how to exploit their weaknesses. Hunters perform lethal melee attacks at close range, and use their arm-mounted cannons to fire deadly green energy bolts from afar. The latter can be dodged by running at full speed. Unless you have a powerful weapon or a vehicle, you should always aim at the exposed flesh on a Hunter's back to kill it. To get a Hunter to present its vulnerable hind quarters, though, you'll need to get close enough to encourage it to lunge at you, then sidestep at the last moment and fire away until it turns. Be careful to move out of range of the inevitable follow-up melee attack.

MONGOOSE

It doesn't have any weapons, both driver and passenger are exposed to the elements, and it can be difficult to drive — and yet, riding a Mongoose is never less than exhilarating.

- Unlike Weebles, the Mongoose wobbles and frequently falls down. It takes a deft touch to keep one on all four wheels over uneven terrain. Keep practicing and you'll soon find there's a knack to moderating your acceleration that makes the Mongoose easier to control.

- As with the Warthog, the Mongoose has an e-brake that you can use to slide around obstructions.

- Remember that the Mongoose is much lighter than the Warthog. If you want to run over and kill a Brute, you'll need to hit him directly at top speed.

SCARAB

Arachnophobes have got it all wrong: as it transpires, absolute mind-numbing terror has only *four* legs.

- The Scarab has two primary weapons systems: the bolts fired by its rotating "eye", and the devastating green energy beam fired from its front-mounted cannon. Avoid both at all costs.

- There are a few fixed Plasma Turrets on its main deck. If these are manned, try to destroy them straight away. When you jump on board, aim to grab one and turn it against its Covenant owners.

- To destroy a Scarab, you need to shoot the "engine core" situated at the back of the vehicle.

- The Scarab has two secondary weaknesses. The first is that if one of its leg joints sustains too much damage, it will move into an emergency "crouching" position while its auto-repair systems deal with the fault. This gives you the opportunity to jump on board from the ground. The second is the protective armor on its back. If this is destroyed, you can get a clear shot at the exposed engine core from afar.

- To avoid the Scarab's weapons, one of the safest places to be is actually underneath it. Just steer well clear of its legs…

BASICS

CAMPAIGN

EXTRAS

MULTIPLAYER

USER
INSTRUCTIONS

PREFACE

MISSION 1

MISSION 2

MISSION 3

MISSION 4

MISSION 5

MISSION 6

MISSION 7

MISSION 8

MISSION 9

MISSILE POD

You don't get to use them very often in Campaign mode, but finding a Missile Pod is always a blessed relief during fights against Covenant vehicles.

- The Missile Pod will automatically acquire a lock-on when you face an enemy vehicle. With larger craft, you can even target individual sub-systems, such as the turrets on a Phantom dropship.
- Its missiles have a homing function, but you'll need to take the intervening landscape into consideration – they won't fly over or around obstructions.
- The Missile Pod has infinite ammunition while attached to its mounting, but holds a mere eight rockets once ripped from its fixed position.

ROCKET LAUNCHER

It may lack the homing function that made it the ultimate anti-vehicular weapon in Halo 2, but the Rocket Launcher is still an intensely satisfying tool when you have some serious smiting and waxing of wroth to attend to.

- The rockets are extremely powerful, and will destroy almost anything other than dropships and Scarabs within two shots on Normal difficulty.
- Take the blast radius into consideration when you aim. Ideally, you should be attempting to obliterate entire attack parties with one shot.

INVINCIBILITY

Though carefully rationed, Invincibility devices enable the Master Chief to sustain outrageous levels of damage with almost absolute impunity. The same, alas, is true of the Chieftains that carry them.

- Invincibility units are carried by the Brute Chieftains that wield Gravity Hammers. The only way to acquire one is to kill a Chieftain before he activates it.
- This device renders the user invulnerable to weapons damage and explosions for ten seconds. Falling from a great height is still lethal, though.
- Two words: rocket jumps. With this device, you can make one and survive. What you do with this knowledge is entirely at your discretion...

GHOST

Piloted by Grunts and (less commonly) Brutes, the supremely maneuverable Ghost excels against infantry or small vehicles.

- If you're on foot, take cover when Ghosts arrive – their dual cannons are deadly, and the drivers will use the hood as a battering ram.
- The hood protects the driver from small-arms fire. To hit the Grunt or Brute behind it, you'll need to get a clear shot from the back or side. At close range, grenades are very effective.
- The Ghost has a speed boost function (default **LT**), but using it deactivates the weapons systems. There is also an air-brake (default **Ⓐ**) that can be used to steady the vehicle while it is airborne.

ANTI-AIR WRAITH

You can't actually drive this Wraith variant, sadly, but it should be treated with the same degree of caution as its close cousin. The secondary gunner is your principle concern at close proximity, but be wary of its main flak cannon – the driver may decide to employ it against you if you make a nuisance of yourself.

FLOODGATE

[MISSION 5]

FLOOD SHIP

LAKE BED A

STORAGE AREA

WAREHOUSE

FACTORY B

LAKE BED B

I

II

BASICS

CAMPAIGN

EXTRAS

MULTIPLAYER

USER
INSTRUCTIONS

PREFACE

MISSION 1

MISSION 2

MISSION 3

MISSION 4

MISSION 5

MISSION 6

MISSION 7

MISSION 8

MISSION 9

Collect weapons and grenades as you make your way back to the warehouse. The Gravity Hammer and Shotgun are the best choices, though some may prefer to have a Battle Rifle or a pair of Spikers (instead of the melee weapon) to knock Combat Forms down over longer distances. The most important thing in the opening fight is to avoid getting surrounded. If necessary, retreat along the path, backpedaling as you fire at the chasing hordes.

STORAGE AREA

WAREHOUSE

When you encounter Infection Forms, try to smash all Combat Form corpses in the vicinity with melee attacks to prevent the skittering menace from reanimating them. If Infection Forms move past you, they're probably making a beeline for a dead body. Destroy them before they reach their target. Note that you cannot destroy corpses that are untainted by the Flood.

Stay in the small office and fire at the Flood to attract their attention. If you brought a ranged weapon along, try to knock a number of them down from afar; aim for the Infection Forms situated in their chests to fell them quickly. Be ready with the Shotgun when they attack at close quarters, and take every opportunity to reload. If you're caught short at any moment, you can usually dispatch Combat Forms with a melee attack.

After the first couple of encounters, Combat Forms will regularly carry weapons. Use cover whenever possible, switching to the Shotgun when they draw near. Remember that the Shotgun is a close-range weapon only. It will atomize Combat Forms within melee attack distance, but its potency diminishes rapidly as you fire at targets further away.

Collect grenades, a Gravity Hammer and a Shotgun en route to the first encounter with the Flood. When the Combat Forms drop down to attack outside the warehouse, hang back at the destroyed trailer and wait for them to approach you. It may be tempting to jump in and try to save the Marines, but given that a single Infection Form can kill them, they won't last for long whatever you do. Be restrained in your use of the Gravity Hammer, taking full advantage of its wide area of effect. When you encounter several targets moving in close proximity to each other, you can usually wipe them all out with a single blow.

Pick up more Shotgun ammo before continuing. This is your primary weapon in this mission, so refer to the map sections to find cartridge supplies when needed.

BASICS

CAMPAIGN

EXTRAS

MULTIPLAYER

USER INSTRUCTIONS

PREFACE

MISSION 1

MISSION 2

MISSION 3

MISSION 4

MISSION 5

MISSION 6

MISSION 7

MISSION 8

MISSION 9

Inside the warehouse, engaging the Flood over open ground is suicidal. Though only a few of them carry weapons, their sheer numbers (and the presence of scattered Infection Forms sequestering additional corpses for the undead army) will soon overwhelm all but the very best players. Better, then, to perfect the strategy that makes fighting against the Flood bearable: tackle them on your own terms. Pick a defensible position, and encourage them to come to you.

The best place to make a stand in this battle is the doorway beside the metal stairs. Generally, you'll find the Flood attack individually or in small groups, leaping or running up the steps, which makes them easy to deal with. Larger packs of Combat Forms are more dangerous, but you have an obvious escape route: just backpedal as they draw close, firing point-blank Shotgun blasts into their vulnerable chests. If it's a *really* big group, that's your cue to break out the Gravity Hammer.

There are a variety of interesting devices in this area, including a Trip Mine, a Bubble Shield, and a Regenerator. You'll find that such items are common (even unusually so) throughout the mission. The Regenerator is probably the most useful of these, especially when fighting Combat Forms that carry weapons. We've marked the location of all necessary equipment on the area maps.

The next wave of Flood is smaller. If they charge in a large group, shoot the Fusion Cores on the trailer to engulf several of them in an explosion as they pass. As long as you avoid being surrounded, this fight should pose you no problems.

As you probably recall from previous visits, there is a Flame Thrower on the metal walkway that leads to the next room. While it's enjoyable to use, you really need to destroy Combat Forms with greater speed on Legendary. Feel free to take the Flame Thrower along to torch prone Flood bodies (burning them is quicker than making melee attacks), but you don't actually *need* it per se.

When you reach the twisting metal corridor, have your Gravity Hammer at the ready as you approach the first corner. There is a big group of Combat Forms waiting to ambush you. If you run forward quickly, you can wipe them all out with just two well-aimed strikes.

- Let the Arbiter take the strain if you struggle during your encounters with the Flood in this mission — he'll draw his Energy Sword when surrounded, and cut through hordes of Combat Forms with ease.

- Don't forget that standard melee attacks are highly effective against smaller Combat Forms. One strike is usually sufficient to knock them down, or even destroy them entirely. It's a little more risky against the bigger or shielded varieties, though.

The two Carrier Forms that waddle down the slope here will explode if damaged, or if they are in close proximity to a viable target (such as the Master Chief or Arbiter). Be ready to eradicate the Infection Forms that emerge before they can find corpses to occupy.

Employ the fixed Machine Gun Turret here to destroy Combat Forms and Pure Forms from afar. It takes a little time, but you can even reach Flood situated close to the burning vessel, including Stalker Forms and Ranged Forms positioned on walls.

Work your way along the dockside path, methodically pausing to destroy Flood as you encounter them. There is no one weapon configuration that truly excels against all Flood forms, but a good choice would be dual Plasma Pistols to deal with Combat Forms, Infection Forms, Stalker Forms and Ranged Forms, with an Energy Sword in reserve for use against Tank Forms (or, for that matter, anything that moves within range).

[FLOODGATE II]

Rally Point Alpha

FACTORY B

LAKE BED A

LAKE BED B

FLOOD SHIP

Follow the waypoint indicator to locate the entrance to the Flood ship. Once inside, avoid shooting the large, fleshy sacs — these contain Infection Forms.

Your approach to the crashed Flood vessel is barred by a new threat. The Pure Form can morph into three physical shapes: the Stalker Form (the least dangerous; performs melee attacks), the Tank Form (the strongest, with a high resistance to many weapon types; uses melee attacks), and the Ranged Form (which fires Carbine-like projectiles over long distances). Refer to the Debriefing section overleaf if you need tips on how to fell them.

There are three separate battles against Flood in this building. You can safely sit back and let the Elites fight on your behalf, though your allies may announce their displeasure with sarcastic comments if you don't contribute your fair share of kills. Pick up and deploy the Regenerator found in the room at the end of the corridor to help the Elites survive the two waves of Combat Forms that attack.

BASICS

CAMPAIGN

EXTRAS

MULTIPLAYER

USER
INSTRUCTIONS

PREFACE

MISSION 1

MISSION 2

MISSION 3

MISSION 4

MISSION 5

MISSION 6

MISSION 7

MISSION 8

MISSION 9

D Most of the Elites don't tend to survive very long after landing on Legendary. In some ways, this is a blessing in disguise. Though you lose the opportunity to sit behind a suitably solid rock while they fight Combat Forms ("practical cowardice" is, after all, a valid strategy), the bustling, aggressive Elites can be more trouble than they're worth. If you're playing with Campaign Scoring active, they steal valuable kills; they also have an alarming tendency to throw Plasma Grenades with furious abandon, or leap into the line of fire when you least expect it.

Still: the Elite landing party will reduce the number of Combat Forms you need to kill as you make your way down from the metal walkway. Destroy any intact bodies you encounter (this prevents Infection Forms from occupying them later), then hunt around for a pair of Plasma Rifles to dual wield. Approach the ramp slowly, then pull back into cover the moment the Combat Forms leap up from behind the cliff to your left. As some of these are carrying powerful weapons (including a Brute Shot and a Shotgun), it's better to pick them off from range — and the Plasma Rifles are a very effective way to do so.

Further Combat Forms will make their way down the ramp, so try to knock these over before they open fire. The arrival of two Carrier Forms waddling down the slope indicates that the battle is nearing its end. The way that you handle these dictates how quickly you can move on. We suggest that you toss two Frag Grenades or Plasma Grenades in rapid succession. The first will knock the Carrier Forms over; the second should pop the majority of Infection Forms that emerge. Quickly dispatch those that survive the blast before they reanimate nearby corpses, and you should be all set to move on.

While you may lament the loss of the Gravity Hammer, the Plasma Rifles are probably the best weapons you can have for the next few encounters.

Σ As you enter Factory B, don't try to fight the Combat Forms in the open. Instead, stay by the burnt-out truck after firing to gain their attention, then shoot each one in turn as they draw closer.

Further Combat Forms will drop down from the ceiling when you leave the low corridor. As most of these land in close proximity to one another, plant a grenade in their midst, then retrieve your second Plasma Rifle and blast any that remain. Quickly run underneath the walkway to avoid the weapons of the second wave that arrives through the door above, then wait at the bottom of the stairway to dispatch any that run down it; the Arbiter will eliminate the rest. It helps if you deploy a Regenerator at the bottom of the stairs to give yourself a slight but sure advantage.

You can find a Flamethrower on the upper level of this building (see map for location). Though not entirely efficient against Combat Forms, it's definitely one of the best weapons for eradicating the Pure Forms you'll encounter outside, especially the Tank Form.

- If you're trying for a high score with Campaign Scoring active, you can potentially benefit by leaving Combat Form bodies intact, allowing Infection Forms to revive them. However, linger for too long on any given battle, and you're almost certain to miss the full time multiplier…

- You can destroy Infection Forms as they begin to burrow their way into the chest cavities of living creatures or corpses. However, you should refrain from shooting cadavers during the Flood transformation sequence — until they begin to clamber to their feet, you're simply wasting ammunition.

F A further force of Elites is usually (but not always) dropped off as you head outside, so take advantage of their aid as you fight the initial wave of Combat Forms and the handful of Pure Forms that approach. However, if you choose to move ahead of your allies (especially during a speed run), be warned that they show little restraint or consideration when fighting the Flood — as previously, it's not uncommon to be caught up in the crossfire as they shoot at targets near to you, or be unceremoniously killed by one of their Plasma Grenades.

When the immediate area is clear, pick up an Energy Sword (if you don't find one straight away, collect one later) and grab the Machine Gun Turret, then walk carefully along the concrete path. Employ short bursts of turret fire to temporarily disable Ranged Forms that attack from distance as you push forward. There's a definite danger that you might be surrounded by Flood, so don't rush — deal with any Combat Forms that draw near, and choose cover that protects you from incoming projectiles.

From the far end of the concrete path, you can usually switch to an Energy Sword and wipe out the Pure Forms, weakening large groups with grenades beforehand. If you move into the corner area, you should be able to entice any remaining Flood over in manageable numbers.

FLOODGATE: DEBRIEFING

INFECTION FORM

The base unit of the Flood scourge. Underestimate them at your peril.

- A single Infection Form can reanimate a Combat Form body that is still in a functional state, and turn Brute, Elite or Marine corpses into fresh Combat Forms.

- The amount of damage that individual Infection Forms inflict is small, but the cumulative effect when several attack at once is lethal — especially on Heroic and Legendary.

- Infection Forms can be popped with a single shot. Other Infection Forms within proximity will also explode if hit by this small blast.

- Automatic weapons such as the SMG and Assault Rifle are the best firearms against Infection Forms — and yet, as these are less efficient against Combat Forms and Pure Forms, you rarely have the luxury of having one to hand.

CARRIER FORM

This foul Flood piñata is guaranteed to enliven *any* party with its surprise contents. It helps if you have something more substantial than a stick to break it with, though…

- Carrier Forms waddle slowly towards their target, then collapse and explode when they draw near. This detonation is hugely destructive — it alone can kill the Master Chief or his allies, and will also set off nearby explosives.

- After a Carrier Form detonates, it will shower the immediate area with Infection Forms. You can avoid this by tagging them with a Spike Grenade or Plasma Grenade — the blast will also destroy its payload.

- Carrier Forms are more resistant to firearms than they were in previous Halo games. If you want to blow them up from a safe distance, use grenades.

COMBAT FORM

The Combat Form is the most common (and, in large numbers, most deadly) part of the inexorable Flood army.

- There are three distinct varieties of Combat Form, with their physical appearance and attributes governed by their former species, be it human, Brute or Elite.

- A Combat Form will fall immediately if you hit the Infection Form embedded in its chest. More powerful attacks (particularly melee strikes, Shotgun blasts and explosions) will cause their bodies to fall apart.

- In the presence of Infection Forms, you should use melee attacks or a Flamethrower to destroy prone Combat Forms.

- "Human" variants are the weakest, and can often be dispatched with a single melee attack or close-range Shotgun blast.

- "Brute" versions are larger, stronger, and more resilient.

- "Elite" types can be the most difficult to kill, as they are sometimes still protected by shield systems and armor. Aim specifically for their flesh, and be particularly wary of those that carry Energy Swords.

ENERGY SWORD

Though some will prefer the Gravity Hammer's massive impact radius, the swift and deadly Energy Sword is still the purist's choice for close-quarters battles.

- The Energy Sword has two functions: a basic close-range swipe when you press the melee attack button (default **Ⓑ**), and a lunging strike triggered by **RT** when the targeting cursor is red.

- Each use of the Energy Sword drains its battery by a small amount.

- The Energy Sword truly excels when employed against the Flood. A solitary strike is enough to eviscerate most forms, with only occasional exceptions when you face Combat Forms that are derived from Brutes or shielded Elites.

BASICS

CAMPAIGN

EXTRAS

MULTIPLAYER

USER
INSTRUCTIONS

PREFACE

MISSION 1

MISSION 2

MISSION 3

MISSION 4

MISSION 5

MISSION 6

MISSION 7

MISSION 8

MISSION 9

PURE FORMS

This new form of Flood can mutate into one of three distinct body types, each conferring tactical advantages in specific situations.

Stalker

- The Stalker Form is the least dangerous Pure Form body type. You will generally encounter it when the creature wishes to travel from one place to another, or has yet to notice you. Note that they can climb walls, and jump rapidly to avoid weapons fire and grenades.

- Stalkers use melee attacks at close range, but are only sporadically aggressive – they are more likely to transform into a Tank when their prey is near, or a Ranged Form when further away.

- Stalkers can be disposed of quickly with fire, grenades and melee attacks.

Tank

- The Tank Form is enormously strong, and carries out savage melee attacks at close range.

- Its body is highly resistant to many weapon types. Ballistic or plasma shots need to be aimed specifically at its "mouth" to inflict damage – though be warned that the creature will cover this area with one of its arms when threatened.

- The Tank Form occasionally spits out Infection Forms to reanimate nearby corpses, or to distract its prey.

- The Energy Sword, Gravity Hammer, Flamethrower and grenades are the best weapons for bringing Tank Forms down.

Ranged

- Ranged Forms fire incessant volleys of Carbine-like projectiles over long distances. These are easily dodged by strafing when fired from afar, but are devastatingly accurate up close.

- This is the least mobile Pure Form body type, frequently found clinging to walls. Though they will rotate to face you, they tend to shift into another shape (usually a Stalker) to move.

- If you damage a Ranged Form, it will fold up on itself temporarily. While it is possible to kill it in this state, it generally withstands a greater number of shots before dying. Tactically, forcing Ranged Forms to perform the Flood equivalent of "duck and cover" is important when you need to close the intervening gap without being fatally perforated as you run.

- Ranged Forms are weakest against grenade sticks, fire and melee attacks. The Brute Shot is also highly effective.

FLAMETHROWER

Despite its salient drawbacks, the Flamethrower is immensely satisfying to use.

- Like all turret weapons, the Flamethrower slows down the Master Chief. When you face large numbers of Combat Forms, this can be a definite disadvantage.

- The Flamethrower has a very limited range, and is suited to close-quarters engagements only.

- It's almost instantaneously lethal against Pure Forms and Infection Forms – a short burst of flame will suffice.

- Combat Forms, by contrast, will continue to run, use weapons and perform melee attacks until the flames consume their bodies. This necessitates a large amount of awkward dodging and jumping.

- Fires started by the Flamethrower on floors, walls and even ceilings will burn for a short period, and damage anything that passes through them – including the Master Chief.

ELITES

Floodgate marks the return of the Elites to the forefront of the battle against the Flood and the Prophet of Truth. These formidable shielded warriors favor Plasma Rifles and Energy Swords, and toss Plasma Grenades with alarming enthusiasm.

THE ARK

III

IV

CARTOGRAPHER BUILDING

SHIELD WALL

DOWNWARD SLOPE

BASICS

CAMPAIGN

EXTRAS

MULTIPLAYER

USER
INSTRUCTIONS

PREFACE

MISSION 1

MISSION 2

MISSION 3

MISSION 4

MISSION 5

MISSION 6

MISSION 7

MISSION 8

MISSION 9

LANDING ZONE

DUNES

II

ROCKY PATHS

I

The second sniper battle is very similar to the first. If you run low on ammunition, you can simply run back to the previous area to collect more from the green weapon pods. The Hunters are easier to defeat if you have a Plasma Turret (found, again, in the previous clearing), which can also help you to make light work of the small group of reinforcements that appears on the far slope.

ROCKY PATHS

This is the first of a number of Terminals that appear in Halo 3's later missions, with each one offering text extracts that reveal tantalizing (and often rather cryptic) information. You can unlock an Achievement worth 40G if you access them all.

Use your Sniper Rifle to eradicate the two Brutes standing guard by the crashed Pelican, then quickly finish off the Grunts. When the two Prowlers attack, killing the Brutes operating their turrets takes precedence. If you're quick, you can run over to the Pelican and pick up a Rocket Launcher to use against them, though take care not to destroy both vehicles — it's good to have a Prowler for the next fight.

Take cover behind the rocks at the top of the sloped path, and concentrate on sniping the Brutes first; you can save ammunition by using the Battle Rifle against Grunts and Jackals. Your Marine and ODST companions will usually protect you from enemies that try to flank your position from the right, but you should still offer assistance when you hear gunfire or shouts of alarm from that direction.

A You shouldn't experience too many problems in this first battle. Get behind cover at the top of the slope, and take the time to survey the positions and numbers of the enemies you're about to face before you make the first shot. Once the firefight is underway, there are only two real dangers. The first is the threat posed by Brute Shot blasts – make killing any Brutes wielding them a priority. Secondly, certain Brutes (particularly those that have gone berserk) and Grunts may attack from the bottom of the path to your right. Listen out for their arrival, and be ready to make a quick kill.

Ensure that no Grunts are operating the Plasma Turrets on the floating platform, then move back down the sloped path to check that no further enemies are hiding behind cover. Two Jackals armed with Carbines usually guard the entrance to the tunnel that leads to the next area. Kill these, then pick up a Plasma Turret and stock up on ammunition before moving on.

B Drop your Plasma Turret somewhere safe, and – once again – study the Covenant force situated in the area ahead before you announce your arrival. Naturally, the Jackal standing on the incomplete anti-air battery should be your opening kill. As with the previous battle, Brute Shot blasts are the only true danger that should concern you. If you break the resolve of your opponents by killing the most dangerous Brutes quickly, you shouldn't need to worry about anyone moving over to attack your position.

Towards the end of the fight, a Phantom will fly in to deploy a pair of Hunters and two Jackals armed with Carbines. Try to kill any members of the initial Covenant force before this happens – having a hidden Grunt or shield-bearing Jackal to worry about while you fight against the Hunters can be hugely irritating. Stay in cover behind the rocks once the reinforcements land, and try to locate and kill the two Jackal marksmen first. With that task accomplished, pick up the Plasma Turret that you brought along, and wait for the Hunters to separate as they search for you. Pick the nearest of the two; quietly make your way over to it, then open fire and don't stop until it falls. It helps to pull back and sidestep as you do this – the Hunter will be stunned by the volley of plasma fire, but not paralyzed, and may well strike out with a melee attack or short cannon blast. When the second Hunter begins to charge in search of retribution, get behind cover, wait for it to move within range, and repeat the previous tactic.

After the second Hunter falls, a Brute and a small force of Grunts will run down the slope from the cave entrance above; a couple of choice Sniper Rifle shots to the head of the former will break the resolve of the latter.

We advise that you backtrack to the previous area to restock your supply of Battle Rifle and Sniper Rifle ammunition before you make your way into the cave. You should also collect a fresh Plasma Turret to be as well prepared as possible. It isn't strictly necessary, but you will appreciate the extra firepower later.

BASICS

CAMPAIGN

EXTRAS

MULTIPLAYER

USER INSTRUCTIONS

PREFACE

MISSION 1

MISSION 2

MISSION 3

MISSION 4

MISSION 5

MISSION 6

MISSION 7

MISSION 8

MISSION 9

C When you reach the group of Marines hiding in the cave above the crashed Pelican, switch to your Sniper Rifle, move behind cover, and kill the two Brutes in the basin below. The panicked Grunts should be easy to dispatch, but watch out for incoming Plasma Grenades – the sneaky little devils will frequently regain their composure just long enough to stick you unless you're careful.

How you conduct the fight against the two Prowlers actually determines how difficult subsequent battles will be. We strongly advise that you keep at least two (and ideally three) of the Marines alive; if you don't, you're really going to struggle afterwards. Should things go awry, simply "Revert to Last Save" and try again.

Drop your Plasma Turret in a safe position, then immediately run back behind cover close to the Marines. Try to greet the arrival of the first group of Brutes with a couple of choice grenade throws. Usually, one of the two Prowlers will drive around the area with a gunner manning its turret, while the second remains in place (with a Brute manning its gun). Dart quickly from behind cover and use your Battle Rifle and Sniper Rifle to pick off the Brutes, with the turret operators a priority. If your Sniper Rifle ammunition is reduced to one bullet, save it – you'll need it later. You also have the Plasma Turret to fall back on if needs be (and, indeed, some may prefer to use it exclusively rather than sniping).

Once the battle is over, requisition a Prowler and arm the surviving Marines with the best weapons you have. This takes a little patient preparation – they tend to want to drive off in the second Prowler, or ride on a Mongoose, so you'll need to treat them like a group of unruly children. Ideally, you should have one Marine operating the turret, and two more on either side – one equipped with the Rocket Launcher found beneath the crashed Pelican, the other with your Sniper Rifle. Though it may be a little awkward to set up, this leaves you exceedingly well equipped for the confrontations ahead.

- Throughout this mission, keeping your allies alive is a definite bonus on Legendary. The more vehicles there are to accompany you, the fewer enemy shots will be fired in your direction.

- If you would like to arm Marines riding as passengers on a Prowler or Scorpion with superior weapons, you can force them from their seats by tipping the vehicle over. Strangely, this is always more difficult when you try to do it deliberately…

Clearing out the entrenched Covenant to secure a landing area isn't difficult in a Chopper, but you'll need to destroy the Wraith and Ghosts immediately. As the enemy numbers and behavior are similar on all difficulty levels (though the weapons do vary), we suggest that you follow step **G** of the Legendary walkthrough if you experience difficulties.

When you fight the group of Covenant guarding the cave entrance, try to lure the Ghosts over the edge of the slope and destroy them before attacking the infantry.

LANDING ZONE

DUNES

Once you jump over the top of the slope, you will face a group of Choppers and Ghosts. If you're feeling suitably adventurous, you can speed forward to the next hill and kill the drivers before they reach their vehicles. Be wary of the Grunts, though – they may attempt to stick you with Plasma Grenades.

You can find a free Chopper positioned here that you may prefer to use during the forthcoming battles. There are small groups of Covenant posted at either end of the bridge that leads to the upper shield wall entrance, and a pair of Choppers that will speed forward to intercept you. These can all be destroyed safely from long range.

When Johnson asks you to follow his Pelican to the potential landing site, you'll see a group of Sentinels set out along the same path. If you hold back, you can watch them destroy the Ghosts in the next area; they will also attack the Covenant force standing guard outside the next cave.

BASICS

CAMPAIGN

EXTRAS

MULTIPLAYER

USER
INSTRUCTIONS

PREFACE

MISSION 1

MISSION 2

MISSION 3

MISSION 4

MISSION 5

MISSION 6

MISSION 7

MISSION 8

MISSION 9

 With your Prowler kitted out with such impressive firepower, this battle is much easier than it would usually be. It's important to preserve this advantage for as long as possible, so you should revert back to the previous checkpoint if any of your Marines are killed.

The number of enemies you face (both in terms of infantry on top of the next slope, and the Choppers and Ghosts that attack) is practically identical to those encountered on Normal or Heroic – they're just that bit more dangerous. Your role as a driver, then, is to use the Prowler's outstanding speed to set up shooting opportunities for your Marines. Try to stay behind Choppers and Ghosts, and angle your approach so that the Marine wielding the Rocket Launcher can get a clear line of fire. When it's time to deal with the infantry on the hill, just move close enough for your sniper to do his work.

You can find a Sniper Rifle by the Warthog behind the crashed Longsword. It may seem like an unusual tip, but we suggest that you pick it up and save it until this mission's final battle. There's also some Battle Rifle ammunition nearby if you need it. A few Grunts have deployed a couple of Plasma Turrets by the wreckage of their downed Phantom further along, but these pose no threat – park just out of range and let your passengers destroy them.

E: A free Chopper is available to your right as you enter this large open area, but we suggest you stick with the Prowler as long as your Marines are alive. Enemy Choppers will move towards your position, so head down and engage them, again choosing an approach vector that provides the Marine carrying the Rocket Launcher with a clear shot, while avoiding incoming cannon blasts. You can also park on one of the upper rock ledges, and wait (largely in safety) for your Marines to deal with them from distance. In the far corner before the bridge, there is a Brute and a group of Grunts – one of which will be using a Fuel Rod Gun. The final group of enemies you need to deal with are fighting Sentinels outside the upper door. Again, if you can remain just out of range of the Shade turrets, your Marines will destroy them for you.

F: Two Ghosts will assail you as you make your way to the landing zone; to be extra careful, you should stay back until the Sentinels attack them.

Further on, you will encounter a small but determined Covenant force guarding the cave entrance, including Ghosts and a Brute wielding a Fuel Rod Gun. Try to make short, focused attacks, moving over the brow of the hill to make a few kills, then retreating to safety before your opponents can put up concerted resistance. Try not to damage the parked Chopper – you'll need it shortly. While it can be fun to attempt the huge fight that follows in the Prowler, it's not really practical to do so – you'll find it much easier if you switch to the Chopper. We're going to assume that you do so from this point forward.

G: As you exit the cave, use the Chopper's cannons to disable the Wraith from a safe distance, then turn your attention to destroying turrets, floating platforms, and the Ghosts that move towards your position. If you're quick, there's very little danger. Move forward along the right-hand slope, and destroy both Anti-Air Wraiths as soon as you can see them – but don't get too close, or they'll open fire.

The tricky part of this fight is killing the Brutes (and the handful of Grunts) located inside the rock formation at the centre of the area. Some of these adversaries have Brute Shots, one has a Fuel Rod Gun, and they are very quick to use Power Drains against your vehicle. You can either inch forward carefully in an attempt to kill each one in turn, or simply boost through to the edge of the cliff, then turn and launch your attack from there.

If you need to pick up weapons and equipment, do so quickly before the Dawn lands – all small items (and even vehicles) will be scattered over the battlefield by the high winds that accompany its arrival. As you will have four Marines riding on your tank, you might find it beneficial to collect and arm them with better weapons, such as a Fuel Rod Gun and a Sniper Rifle, before you roll out in a Scorpion.

• In co-op games, the obvious temptation is to share vehicles, with one player driving while the other operates a turret. While this is undeniably fun, you can maximize your firepower (and tactical options) by driving separately.

• When facing incoming Fuel Rod Gun missiles while driving vehicles, the obvious reaction is to move in reverse. Unless this enables you to move straight behind cover, or over the brow of a hill, it's actually the worst thing you can do. The most efficient way to evade these deadly projectiles is to accelerate at full speed, veering to the left or right (whichever is appropriate) at an angle that their limited homing function can't fully track. The *best* way to dodge Fuel Rod Gun missiles, though, is to kill the user before he can open fire...

On your way back to the shield wall you visited earlier, advance slowly and use the Scorpion's powerful cannon to destroy each target from afar. Avoid engaging Wraiths at close range – their secondary turrets can tear through the tank's armor with alarming efficiency.

There is a Terminal situated behind the panel that you use to activate the Light Bridge. Don't forget to access it before you continue.

You are free to hop inside the Gauss Warthog as driver or gunner. The latter is more fun, but taking the wheel enables you to get down the slope and meet the main Marine force more quickly. You can even jump straight over the cliff edge, if you like.

Use the Scorpion to bombard the ramp that leads to the entrance of the Cartographer building before continuing on foot.

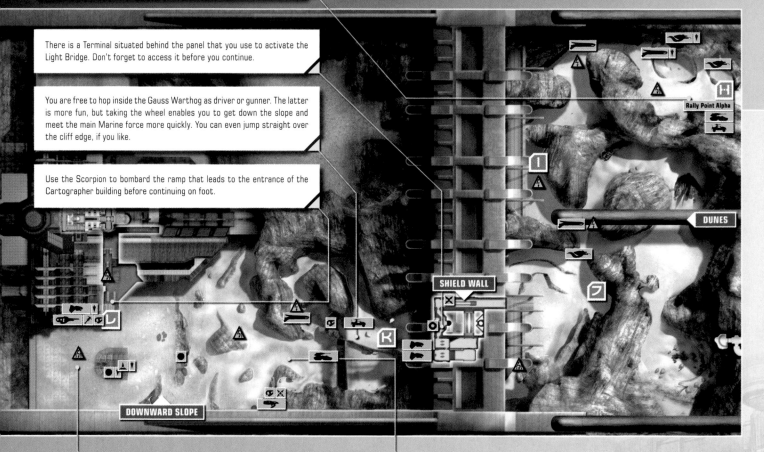

Rally Point Alpha

DUNES

SHIELD WALL

DOWNWARD SLOPE

The best strategy for beating the Scarab is to drive underneath it, where its weapons cannot reach you, and shoot one of its legs until it is disabled. You can then move behind it, destroy the armor on its back end, then blast the exposed engine core to finish it off. If you'd like to topple it in style without using a vehicle, you can find a handy supply of Grav Lifts inside the nearby low building.

Take control of a Scorpion to fight your way down the slope – the Gauss Warthog is well-armed, highly mobile and fun to use, but you'll need armor plating in addition to firepower for this engagement. There's no need to rush as you fight the numerous Wraiths, Choppers and Ghosts; indeed, you should take it steady, and allow your Marine allies to contribute their fair share of kills.

BASICS

CAMPAIGN

EXTRAS

MULTIPLAYER

USER
INSTRUCTIONS

PREFACE

MISSION 1

MISSION 2

MISSION 3

MISSION 4

MISSION 5

MISSION 6

MISSION 7

MISSION 8

MISSION 9

H The key to using the Scorpion is measured, careful progress. If you move forward too quickly you'll be overwhelmed by smaller vehicles, and dodging is rarely an option with this slow-moving tank. Instead, try to draw enemies towards you, use cover, and make your long-range shots count.

The battle that ensues after the Dawn lands isn't particularly taxing – you just need to hit the Ghosts (and the solitary Prowler) before you move within range of their cannons. The Hunters that emerge from the tunnel entrance are laughably easy to dispatch, as is the Phantom on the other side, though you will need to destroy the Shade turrets quickly.

I Be careful as you round the corner – there are several Ghosts in this area, and they're supported by a Wraith. You might not expect it, but the Ghosts are actually the biggest danger here. If you allow them to get close or, even worse, behind your position, this mildly challenging fight can soon become unmanageable.

Blast the floating platform at the top of the next slope, then bombard the Grunts around the barricades (even if you can't see them) with cannon fire before you move any further. At least one of them has a Fuel Rod Gun, and it's very tricky to dodge their projectiles in a Scorpion.

J You need to fight your way to the upper entrance of the Forerunner facility, so it's best to just head straight around the outside of the area – the Marines can deal with any hostiles in the center of the map. Concentrate on destroying the Wraith directly ahead (and the two Ghosts that usually appear from behind it) as you move forward but watch out for the arrival

of a Phantom to your right. This will drop off a third Wraith, then move into position in front of the entrance to deploy troops. You will make life much easier for yourself if you destroy this as quickly as possible – the explosion will usually take out any surrounding infantry – but remember to keep moving to avoid mortar fire from the two remaining Wraiths as you do so.

K Run swiftly to the Gauss Warthog, and immediately man its turret to destroy the chasing Ghosts. You'll need to be accurate and composed during the short journey to the area below – miss two shots at a Ghost or fixed Plasma Turret on the way down, and you won't have the opportunity to make it a hat trick.

As you emerge onto the main slope, hop out of the Warthog and grab yourself a Scorpion. This initial section of the battle is extremely chaotic. Prioritize the vehicles that pose the most danger (usually those closest); don't be in too much of a hurry to press forward, and you'll be fine. You should also aim to take down the hovering Phantom before you move in range of its weapons. However, be careful as you approach the natural stone "arch" – there's a group of Brutes hiding in the rocks just beyond it, and they all have Fuel Rod Guns. The best way to deal with this problem is to drive past a couple of times, firing at the Brutes as you go.

At this point the Scarab should return, which is when things get really interesting. Rush behind cover immediately – its weapons are deadly, and have an extremely long range. To make matters worse, you can also expect a pair of Choppers to strike at this very moment; do your best to destroy these straight away. The most obvious place to seek shelter is behind the low building dead ahead but, typically, it's occupied by Grunts armed with Fuel Rod Guns.

It's possible to dispatch the Scarab in several different ways, but the strategy we recommend is to throw caution to the wind and go straight on the offensive. Head around the left-hand side of the low

building at full speed, firing at the balcony to kill the Grunts stationed there. The Scarab's guns will cut your tank to shreds if you attempt to circle it, so don't. Instead, drive straight under its body – avoiding its legs, of course – then shoot its knee joints out from beneath it. As soon as the klaxon heralds its imminent collapse, drive to the back of it and blast the protective shielding covering the engine core. You may need to disable the Scarab more than once to destroy it. Finally, be aware that additional Choppers may enter the fray at any moment. Dealing with these should always be a priority.

- When you have the advantage of the Scorpion's firepower, it's extremely satisfying to shoot down passing Phantoms. On Legendary, five or six blasts will usually suffice.

- If you'd like to experience a great example of Halo 3 co-op at its finest, try fighting the entire battle leading up to (and including) the struggle to destroy the Scarab in a Gauss Warthog with a friend. It's absolutely superb.

L The slope that leads up to the entrance to the Cartographer building is absolutely teeming with Covenant troops, including several snipers and a new enemy – a Brute Stalker, who is equipped with a Cloaking device and Incendiary Grenades. You're more than welcome to fight your way through on foot (it's a very enjoyable battle), but there's actually a quicker and easier way – simply drive your Scorpion up one of the slopes. The one

on the right seems the easiest of the three routes, as it offers the clearest shot at the group of Brutes lying in wait on the first level. You may not be able to secure a direct line of fire for most enemies, so you'll need to make intelligent use of splash damage – just aim at a wall section or "space crate" that you suspect a hiding enemy is close to, and let the blast radius do the hard work for you.

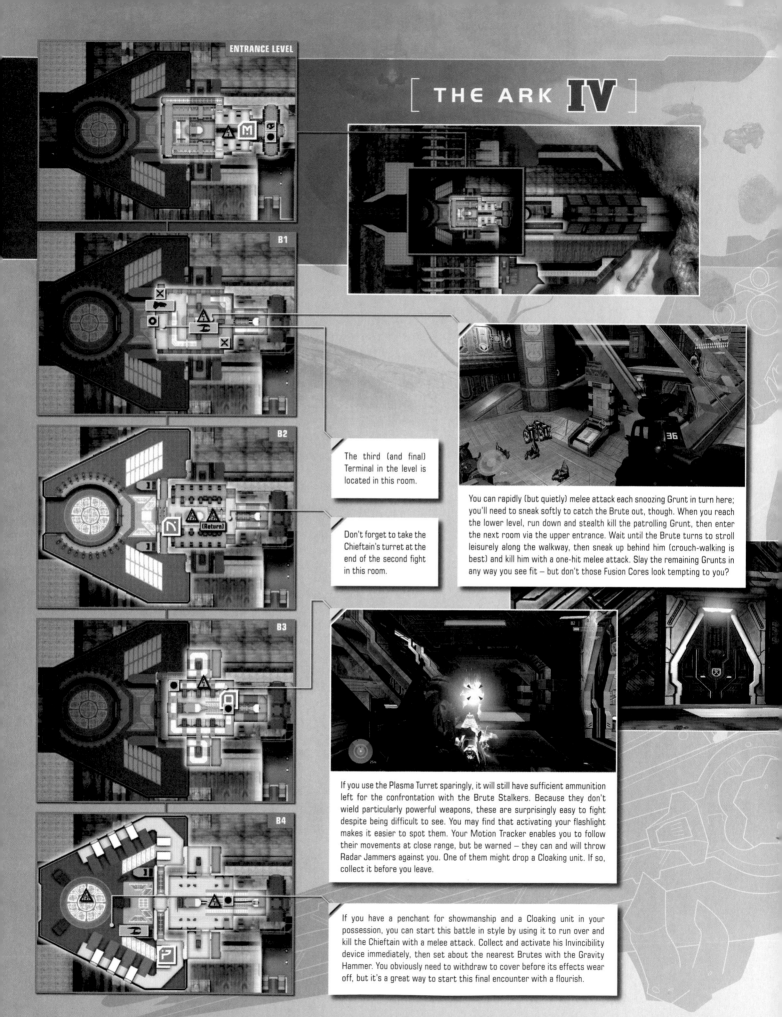

ENTRANCE LEVEL

B1

B2

B3

B4

The third (and final) Terminal in the level is located in this room.

Don't forget to take the Chieftain's turret at the end of the second fight in this room.

You can rapidly (but quietly) melee attack each snoozing Grunt in turn here; you'll need to sneak softly to catch the Brute out, though. When you reach the lower level, run down and stealth kill the patrolling Grunt, then enter the next room via the upper entrance. Wait until the Brute turns to stroll leisurely along the walkway, then sneak up behind him (crouch-walking is best) and kill him with a one-hit melee attack. Slay the remaining Grunts in any way you see fit — but don't those Fusion Cores look tempting to you?

If you use the Plasma Turret sparingly, it will still have sufficient ammunition left for the confrontation with the Brute Stalkers. Because they don't wield particularly powerful weapons, these are surprisingly easy to fight despite being difficult to see. You may find that activating your flashlight makes it easier to spot them. Your Motion Tracker enables you to follow their movements at close range, but be warned — they can and will throw Radar Jammers against you. One of them might drop a Cloaking unit. If so, collect it before you leave.

If you have a penchant for showmanship and a Cloaking unit in your possession, you can start this battle in style by using it to run over and kill the Chieftain with a melee attack. Collect and activate his Invincibility device immediately, then set about the nearest Brutes with the Gravity Hammer. You obviously need to withdraw to cover before its effects wear off, but it's a great way to start this final encounter with a flourish.

BASICS

CAMPAIGN

EXTRAS

MULTIPLAYER

USER
INSTRUCTIONS

PREFACE

MISSION 1

MISSION 2

MISSION 3

MISSION 4

MISSION 5

MISSION 6

MISSION 7

MISSION 8

MISSION 9

M The two rooms where you pummel sleeping Grunts and less than vigilant Brutes are identical on Legendary, bar the graver consequences if everyone wakes up at once. The fight that follows downstairs, however, is potentially much harder. As you make your way down the ramp that leads to the room, a patrolling Brute will approach the entrance. Stick him with a grenade as you run down. If your throwing skills are excellent, you should be able to tag another Brute further inside the room as he clambers to his feet. Dive straight into the separate area that runs along the right-hand side of the room, and kill both Jackals. The first of these is a problem — you'll need to hit the embrasure on his

shield to stagger him as you run, then finish him off with a headshot at point-blank range. Have grenades at the ready, as one or more Brutes will usually move into position at the end of the room — and there's really not enough space to dodge incoming Brute Shot fire here. At this point, finishing off the remaining Covenant is simply a matter of being patient, and not doing anything rash.

Collect a Brute Shot and as much ammunition as you can find before you leave. (If you still have the Sniper Rifle we advised you to carry earlier, congratulations — you're going to feel pretty smug when you reach the final battle.)

N There are Grunts waiting to greet you as you return to the site of the previous battle, but there's actually worse to come: four Brutes and a Chieftain carrying a Plasma Turret. Raw aggression works best in this fight. With your Brute Shot equipped, melee attack the nearest Grunt, then run to the left to kill the two Brutes stationed there; they will often deploy a Bubble Shield, which gives you license to bludgeon them into insensibility with melee attacks.

If you're quick, you should be able to fire at the door (ideally from a position in cover on the left-hand side of the room) before the final Brutes arrive. Throw a couple of grenades as the Chieftain and his escort move inside, then finish off your weakened foes with a relentless barrage of Brute Shot blasts. Stock up on ammunition, then collect the Plasma Turret before continuing downward.

O If you run around the corner to the right, you can usually spot and kill the Brute Stalker at the very end of the walkway before he has a chance to react. Head through the door and down the ramp, then take up position by the lower doorway. Cautiously wait here for your camouflaged foes to come to you, and kill them with the Plasma Turret before they can escape. This strategy has two main benefits: you are well covered from weapons fire in this position (with the option to pull back

to safety at any time), and there's less danger of being hit by an Incendiary Grenade. When the last Brute falls, be careful if you're standing near the downstairs door — two Jackals will run through. It would be really frustrating to be caught out by this pair after laboring to beat the Stalkers.

Should one of the Brutes drop a Cloaking device, be sure to collect it before continuing.

P If you took our advice and kept the Sniper Rifle from earlier in the level, that decision pays dividends here. The Brute Chieftain is likely to charge as soon as he notices your arrival. Take cover behind one of the glass screens and snipe him straight away. Picking the Jump Pack Brutes off from range with a Sniper Rifle is also a relatively simple exercise. The only dangerous moments occur when some (especially the ones carrying Brute Shots) opt to leap over to your position. Provided you stay close to the door, though, you can retreat to safety if needs be.

Without a Sniper Rifle, this battle can be troublesome. Two Carbines are at your disposal on a Covenant weapons dispenser situated a short sprint away to your left. The Chieftain has an Invincibility unit that he will use when he feels suitably threatened, so you might want to force him to trigger it early by throwing grenades in his path as he approaches. Resorting to a Cloaking

device to try to sneak around and kill him with a melee attack from behind is another effective option.

While having a Carbine will enable you to kill a number of Brutes from distance, it lacks the stopping power to trouble them at close range. When they leap towards you — fortunately, they generally attack one at a time — take cover behind the screens during their approach flight, then run over to hit them with a melee attack as they land, and follow up with a headshot. (Alternatively, if the Chieftain's Gravity Hammer is within reach, you can equip and use that instead.)

Two Jackals armed with Carbines are posted on the far side of this platform. These are no trouble while you fight the Brutes from behind cover, but you'll need to kill them both for the Pelican to arrive. It's wise to save a small amount of Carbine ammunition for that very purpose.

- If you take up position outside a doorway, Brutes that run through are easier to hit with sticky grenades, as it's harder for them to dive aside.

- If you have difficulty following the movements of camouflaged Brute Stalkers, try using a Spiker against them — the projectiles will stick in their bodies, making them easier to track as you fire.

THE ARK: DEBRIEFING

BRUTE STALKER

Opaque to all but the most inquisitive eyes, Brute Stalkers utilize Cloaking devices to conceal their approach from oblivious prey. If you look closely, it's possible to spot the distinctive "distorted air" that marks the outline of their bodies. If not, the sudden hail of Spiker shards sticking out of the Master Chief's corpse is, quite literally, a dead giveaway. Stalkers are detected by your Motion Tracker when they move within range, but tend to deploy Radar Jammers before they strike. They also use (and are your primary source of) deadly Incendiary Grenades. Note that the homing function of certain weapons – particularly Plasma Pistols and Needlers – often fails to lock on to Stalkers while their Cloaking is active. Once you destroy their power armor, Stalkers lose this important advantage, remaining fully visible until killed.

PROWLER

This fast-moving support vehicle is used by Brutes to make rapid troop deployments.

- The Prowler's turret has a full 360 degree field of fire, which makes it highly dangerous in close-quarters engagements. On foot, killing the gunner is your priority; in vehicles, try to keep your distance and disable it from range.

- The Prowler has excellent acceleration, speed and stability – you can really throw it around over jumps and bumps in a way that wouldn't be safe or practical in a Warthog, Mongoose or Chopper.

- If you have Marines in tow, equipping prospective passengers with powerful firearms (such as the Rocket Launcher) will enable you to turn the Prowler into a lethal heavy weapons platform.

SCORPION

Arguably the most destructive vehicle you can drive, the Scorpion can make light work of an entire Covenant platoon.

- Unlike in previous Halo games, the Scorpion's secondary turret can only be controlled by a separate gunner.

- Thanks to their raw power and splash damage, the missiles fired by the main cannon are incredibly effective against both infantry and vehicles. They are also extremely fast, though you'll still need to aim at a position slightly ahead of moving vehicles to hit them.

- The Scorpion's main weakness is its lack of speed and mobility. When you drive one, you should make regular use of cover to avoid incoming fire.

AUTO TURRET

It isn't particularly reliable or blessed with notable firepower, but the Auto Turret can still be an efficient device if you know what to expect from it.

- There is a short time delay before an Auto Turret becomes active.

- The Auto Turret will, as its name suggests, fire automatically at any hostiles in range once active. When you deploy it, try to face the direction in which you would like it to fire.

- Though rather weak, this piece of equipment is often a great way to distract opponents, if only for a moment – and sometimes, that's all you need.

- The Auto Turret lasts indefinitely, but can (and often will) be destroyed by weapons fire and explosions.

HALO 3

BASICS
CAMPAIGN
EXTRAS
MULTIPLAYER

USER
INSTRUCTIONS
PREFACE
MISSION 1
MISSION 2
MISSION 3
MISSION 4
MISSION 5
MISSION 6
MISSION 7
MISSION 8
MISSION 9

WARTHOG M12 LAAV

It's the same Warthog that we all know and love when you're behind the wheel, but this variant packs a bigger punch. The "Gauss Warthog" cannon is an excellent anti-vehicular weapon (it can destroy a Ghost in two shots on Legendary), but a steady hand is required to pull off the precision aiming necessary to hit smaller targets.

MAULER

On one hand, the Mauler is a slightly weaker version of the Shotgun... but in two hands, however, it's an absolutely devastating dual wield weapon.

- First things first: at anything other than close range, firing a Mauler at an enemy is akin to insulting their mother – it's just hot air and noise, and it's going to make them angry.
- At very close ranges, the Mauler's rate of fire and ability to stun enemies makes it a worthy rival to the Shotgun when dual wielded.
- Sadly, ammo for the Mauler is actually quite rare. It's a weapon that you simply make the most of when you find it.

SENTINEL BEAM

More damaging than in previous Halo games, the Sentinel Beam is also encountered less frequently.

- The Sentinel Beam overheats when used continuously, so try to unleash short, focused bursts.
- This weapon has a distinct "stun" effect on Brutes – they will rarely be able to return fire while recoiling from the impact of the beam.
- On Normal, this is extremely potent against Brutes, enough to both destroy their armor and kill them very quickly.
- On Heroic and Legendary, the Sentinel Beam is still very effective against power armor, but securing a kill takes longer. You may prefer to use it to weaken Brutes, then switch to a Battle Rifle or Carbine for the final headshot.

INCENDIARY GRENADES

Carried (and dropped) by Brute Stalkers, Incendiary Grenades have a whole range of interesting applications

- Hitting an enemy with an Incendiary Grenade has much the same effect as sticking them with a Plasma or Spike Grenade – it's an instant kill. The same, alas, applies to the Master Chief.
- While the flame from an Incendiary Grenade burns, it will damage anything that it comes into contact with.
- The localized fire that breaks out when an Incendiary Grenade explodes will stick to anything – floors, walls, even ceilings. This means that you can use it in a defensive capacity to block entrances or corridors.

CLOAKING

Used wisely, the Cloaking device can enable you to secure an early advantage in otherwise difficult firefights.

- Cloaking renders the Master Chief effectively invisible for approximately 12 seconds.
- If you fire a weapon, the camouflage effect will cease for a moment; gunfire or explosion damage will also make the Chief visible. If you stop firing, or avoid contact with anything painful, you will fade out of view again.
- Be careful not to bump into Brutes with Cloaking active, or they will try to hit you with an immediate melee attack.
- Chieftains appear to be more receptive to your presence when you use Cloaking than other Brutes, and may turn to track your movements.

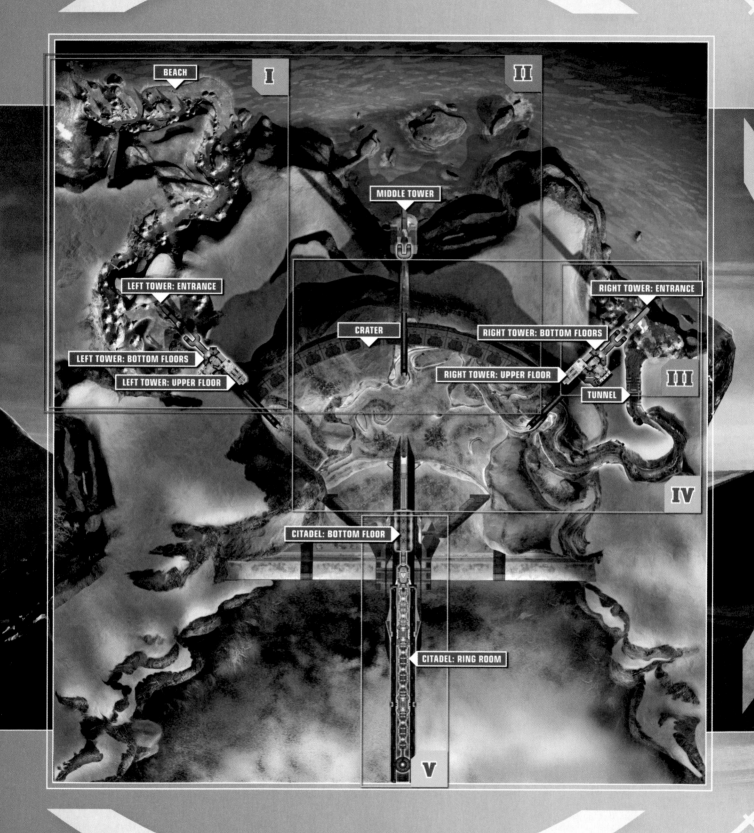

BEACH

I

II

MIDDLE TOWER

LEFT TOWER: ENTRANCE

RIGHT TOWER: ENTRANCE

CRATER

RIGHT TOWER: BOTTOM FLOORS

LEFT TOWER: BOTTOM FLOORS

RIGHT TOWER: UPPER FLOOR

III

LEFT TOWER: UPPER FLOOR

TUNNEL

IV

CITADEL: BOTTOM FLOOR

CITADEL: RING ROOM

V

THE COVENANT

[MISSION 7]

BASICS

CAMPAIGN

EXTRAS

MULTIPLAYER

USER
INSTRUCTIONS

PREFACE

MISSION 1

MISSION 2

MISSION 3

MISSION 4

MISSION 5

MISSION 6

MISSION 7

MISSION 8

MISSION 9

It's tempting to break out the Spartan Laser straight away, but you should save it for the targets that really matter – the two Shade turrets and the Chieftain. Eliminate the Grunts on the right before you attack the infantry directly ahead to avoid being caught in a deadly crossfire, then try to dispatch all visible targets from a safe distance. Blast the Chieftain with the Spartan Laser, but take care to dodge incoming Fuel Rod Gun missiles.

The best way to destroy the Anti-Air Wraith is to sneak around behind it, board the vulnerable rear quarters, then pummel it with melee attacks. Don't risk a frontal charge, or engage the attention of the driver – those green cannon blasts really *are* as painful as they look.

Jump into the Warthog; if you're feeling creative, equip the Marine riding shotgun with the Fuel Rod Gun dropped by the Chieftain. This, along with your vehicle's turret, should give you enough firepower to deal with the Ghosts and the small blockade featuring a Shade turret and assorted infantry that you'll meet en route to your objective. There are further Ghosts to fight as you approach the Forerunner structure. Deal with these before you engage the forces below .

If you hold back when you encounter the Wraith, and dodge any incoming mortars, your turret operator should destroy it rather easily. The two Prowlers that emerge pose a greater threat. Retreat a safe distance, then either try to engage them individually, or hop out of the Warthog and kill their gunners from range. If you need a long-distance weapon for this, you can find Beam Rifles at the top of the path you arrived on.

BEACH

LEFT TOWER: ENTRANCE

A Shade turret and assorted Covenant troops guard the entrance here. If you park the Warthog just out of their firing range, your gunner will deal with them for you.

Don't forget to collect the Cloaking device on your way inside – it will be very handy in a forthcoming battle.

A

While there's always room for a little improvisation in Halo 3, a methodical approach works best as you fight to establish a beachhead at the start of this mission on Legendary – unless, that is, you're actively seeking an opportunity to choke with impotent rage.

- **Priority 1:** Grunts attack from the right, as well as directly ahead of you, and there may also be some to your left. Throw a grenade at the party in front of you, then kill any to your left with your Battle Rifle. The objective here isn't to be thorough; it's just to rapidly thin their numbers so that your allies can deal with the rest while you move on to another task. Spartan Laser ammunition is precious at this point: don't use it unless we offer explicit instructions to do so. There's a method to this restraint madness that you'll genuinely appreciate later.

- **Priority 2:** Edge out to the left end of the natural rock cover until you see the first of two Shade turrets. Destroy it with your Spartan Laser, then walk further to the left to get a clear shot at the second. If you want to keep your allies alive for the later stages of this battle, speed is of the essence here.

- **Priority 3:** Return to the starting position. Your allies should still be fighting a band of Grunts and a sole Brute armed with

a Brute Shot. Though you can get rid of the latter with your Battle Rifle, it's easier – and safer – to collect a Needler or Plasma Pistol for this purpose. You should find some among the corpses to the right.

- **Priority 4:** Run around the rocks to the right, and – once behind cover – clear out any surviving Grunts in the vicinity, then snipe their peers in the distance with the Battle Rifle. A Chieftain armed with a Fuel Rod Gun is positioned on the hill, so be vigilant – if he fires at you, you'll need to hide without delay.

- **Priority 5:** Dispatch the two Brute Bodyguards from range with your Battle Rifle, then head for the cliff wall to the far right. Climb the slope carefully, and pick a spot where you can get a clear shot at the Chieftain with the Spartan Laser. If you're swift and silent, you can make a lethal headshot before he spots you; if not, you'll need to dodge incoming Fuel Rod Gun missiles as you aim. However, it's vital that you save one remaining charge. You should also keep an eye on the Anti-Air Wraith – if it turns to fire at your position, get to safety immediately.

- **Priority 6:** Finally, destroy the Covenant tank. After ascertaining in which direction it's facing, sneak over carefully, board it from behind, and smash it to bits.

BASICS

CAMPAIGN

EXTRAS

MULTIPLAYER

USER INSTRUCTIONS

PREFACE

MISSION 1

MISSION 2

MISSION 3

MISSION 4

MISSION 5

MISSION 6

MISSION 7

MISSION 8

MISSION 9

B

Run over to the passenger side of the Warthog and give the Spartan Laser to the Marine riding shotgun. Once behind the wheel, drive forward to trigger the arrival of Banshees, then immediately retreat back along the beach. Your Marine with the Spartan Laser will deal with the aerial threat with casual aplomb, saving you the trouble of attempting to dodge volleys of plasma fire (not to mention deadly mortar blasts) from above.

As you push forward towards the bottom of the slope leading to the interior of the island, Ghosts will move to attack. Again, reverse and let your ally with the Spartan Laser skewer them. Take the route to the left when the path splits in two, and park so as to give the Marine a clear shot at the Shade emplacement; you can then drive up and let the Marine on the turret mow down the infantry.

C

As you reach the high pass above the entrance to the Forerunner building, you will encounter two Grunts – one in a Ghost, the other on foot. Neutralize both without moving any further along the path. This is the moment when your Marine with the Spartan Laser *really* gets to shine. In the area below, a Wraith will begin bombarding your position as soon as it notices your arrival. If you carefully drive over to the cliff edge, you can give your heavily armed passenger a clear shot at the tank. Although you'll have to perform some precision driving to avoid incoming mortars, it should be destroyed by four or five direct hits.

After the tank is reduced to wreckage, remain parked at the edge of the cliff, and your supremely diligent companion will blast the Shade turret and surrounding infantry on the rock outcrop in the distance, even if you can't actually see it through the trees. When he stops firing, slowly make your way down the slope. A

Shade turret and additional Ghosts await you, so err on the side of caution.

The trickiest part of this battle is luring the two Prowlers into the open, then escaping before they cut your Warthog to shreds. There are a number of ways to do this, but the safest is to drive to the area behind the entrance, head up the ramp that leads to the Beam Rifle dispenser, and then park your vehicle in a way that gives your Marines a clear shot. If necessary, grab a Beam Rifle to take out the turret operators. That feat achieved, you simply need to clear the mixed infantry and Shade turret situated inside the entrance. With a little considered reversing and accelerating at the top of the path that leads inside, your Marines will – once again – complete this task for you.

Pick up Battle Rifle ammunition from one of the pods dropped off by the Pelican and a Beam Rifle from the dispenser, and collect the Cloaking device before heading through the door.

- If you want to give yourself a huge advantage during the battles fought on the way to the first tower, equip the Marine that rides pillion on the Mongoose with the Fuel Rod Gun dropped by the Chieftain.

- A curious side-effect of having a Marine shoot the Wraith with the Spartan Laser is that its driver is almost always killed first. If you use one of the Beam Rifles at the top of the slope to snipe the turret operator, you can keep the tank intact. How useful it is against the Prowlers is debatable, but you could certainly employ it against the troops inside the tunnel leading to the entrance.

If you make a detour and land at the middle tower, you'll discover a Terminal outside the locked entrance.

BEACH

Rally Point Alpha

MIDDLE TOWER

LEFT TOWER: ENTRANCE

During the first part of the aerial battle, don't forget that the Hornet has two weapons systems – a machine gun, and homing rockets. You'll need to use both to take down enemy Banshees quickly and cleanly. Watch out for an Anti-Air Wraith deployed on a small island below – it's advisable to destroy it immediately, especially if you're flying within range of its cannons.

When you reach the elevator, jump across the small gap to the enclosure opposite. You'll find a Terminal there, plus a handy supply of Carbine ammunition and Plasma Grenades.

There's only one Brute inside the first room, accompanied by numerous Grunts and Jackals. Neutralize him, then carefully make your way through the room, dealing with his underlings. Watch out for the Grunts on the level above, and two Jackals with Carbines at the far end. In the second battle on your way to the elevator upstairs, shoot the Fusion Cores to kill several enemies at once.

LEFT TOWER: BOTTOM FLOORS

(Return journey only)

LEFT TOWER: UPPER FLOOR

In the tower control room, you face four Brutes and a Chieftain. If you still have the Cloaking device that you collected earlier, activate it as you run towards the Chieftain. Dispatch him with a melee attack to his vulnerable back (if you time this badly, you may need two strikes), then grab his Gravity Hammer. It's not mandatory that you use it, but stalking the remaining Brutes this way is really quite satisfying. After activating the console, use a vehicle parked outside to return to the beach.

BASICS

CAMPAIGN

EXTRAS

MULTIPLAYER

USER
INSTRUCTIONS

PREFACE

MISSION 1

MISSION 2

MISSION 3

MISSION 4

MISSION 5

MISSION 6

MISSION 7

MISSION 8

MISSION 9

D Grunts and Jackals are abundant inside this room, so be frugal with your limited Battle Rifle ammunition. After taking cover behind the screen, pick off the nearest Grunts, then use the Beam Rifle to kill the solitary Brute before he can retreat behind cover. Try to kill all adversaries in sight, including those on the upper walkway, then take the route to the left, where you will encounter two Jackals armed with Carbines. The remaining infantry will usually be congregated around the doorway, so toss a grenade into their midst and finish off any survivors with the Battle Rifle. You should be running low on bullets for this weapon by now, so replace it with a Carbine.

Σ Watch out for a potential barrage of grenades as you walk up the slope — there are Grunts and Jackals awaiting your arrival, and a further group that attacks from the floor level above. Hang back around the corner, and shoot the easier targets in the immediate vicinity first. Disable the Brute (or, at the very least, his armor) with the Beam Rifle, but don't fire too freely — you need to save this weapon's limited battery supply for the next battle. If the opportunity arises, blow the Fusion Cores on both levels to dispatch multiple enemies at once.

Jump over to the room that contains the Terminal to collect more Carbine ammunition prior to riding the elevator up.

F. Several Brutes and a Chieftain with a Gravity Hammer are guarding the control console, but worry not — you're more than well equipped to deal with the situation. Switch to your Beam Rifle and, using the transparent barrier as cover, snipe the first few that move forward to attack. If you're a less-than-stellar marksman with scoped weapons, weaken your opponent's power armor by aiming for their body, then switch to the Carbine to make finishing headshots.

Before the last few Brutes attack, inch out and snipe the Chieftain. Stubbornly, he often stands in plain view and will not (usually) charge until all of his subordinates have been slain, so it's really easy to assassinate him from range. If you're still carrying the Cloaking device from earlier, activate it to evade him should he run at you, and kill him with a melee strike to the back.

On the way back out of the building, you'll find Marines fighting a small Covenant force by the exit. Shoot these from above (your allies tend to struggle more against the Jackals, if that's any help), then collect the Power Drain from beside the Terminal. You should also pick up a fresh Beam Rifle from the dispenser before you return to the beach.

- If you have kept him alive this far, get the Marine carrying the Spartan Laser to climb on board your Hornet for the aerial battle: he'll be a valuable asset.

- If you can attack them at close range, Brute Chieftains are surprisingly susceptible to melee attacks. Once they are staggered by the initial blow, you can usually bludgeon them into submission with a rapid succession of hits. This is trickier to achieve against those that carry Gravity Hammers, but it's definitely an option for players brave enough to attempt it.

G The dogfights en route to the third tower really aren't difficult as long as you take a patient approach. Accelerate into the fray too enthusiastically, and you'll be easy prey for Banshees, no matter how well you dodge.

From takeoff, ascend to maximum height straight away — it's hard to see, let alone shoot, Banshees operating at a higher altitude if you make a low-level approach. Flying high also has a secondary benefit, as it makes it easier to avoid the Anti-Air Wraith and the small group of Brutes deployed on the little island. You should deal with these once the initial squadron of Banshees has been shot down.

Around the cliff corner, a smaller force of Banshees will engage you. Again, remain out of their attack range, moving just close enough to launch homing rockets, but retreating before your foes choose to make an attack run. Finally, destroy the Phantom before you begin bombarding the land-based force protecting the third tower.

Be careful when shooting at the Brutes guarding the landing zone after destroying the Wraiths: Elites will land to fight on foot shortly afterwards. You need their help in the coming battles, so make sure you don't confuse friend with foe from range.

Collect a Brute Shot and as much ammunition as you can find after landing; it's also advisable to hunt for grenades if your stocks are low. A large group of Brutes will rush out as you approach the entrance. Being careful to avoid harming your allies, throw a grenade through as the door opens. If you then pull back, the ever-enthusiastic Elites will take care of the rest for you.

As with the previous Forerunner tower you visited, there is a Terminal located in a small enclosure a short jump away from the elevator.

RIGHT TOWER: ENTRANCE

RIGHT TOWER: BOTTOM FLOORS

RIGHT TOWER: UPPER FLOOR

A number of camouflaged Brute Stalkers are barring your path to the console, so quickly grab a pair of Maulers from the weapons dispenser, and wait for them to come to you. The Chieftain is more difficult to beat, but the Incendiary Grenades dropped by his erstwhile companions will help.

A veritable cloud of Drones and a pair of Hunters await you in the first room. Focus on blasting the Hunters with the Brute Shot from a safe position while the Elites deal with the troublesome space bugs. Pick up a Needler and plenty of ammo to eliminate the two small groups of Brutes on the upper level. This weapon is also handy when a second (thankfully smaller) swarm of Drones attacks as you approach the elevator.

BASICS

CAMPAIGN

EXTRAS

MULTIPLAYER

USER
INSTRUCTIONS

PREFACE

MISSION 1

MISSION 2

MISSION 3

MISSION 4

MISSION 5

MISSION 6

MISSION 7

MISSION 8

MISSION 9

H Once you've nullified the aerial threat, your next task is to devastate the enemies on the ground. The three Covenant tanks should top your hit list, with the Anti-Air Wraiths the most pressing concern. We advise that you stay as far away as possible, strafing to avoid incoming fire (it's really embarrassing to be taken down by a mortar fired by the standard Wraith if you linger in one fixed position). While this means you can't use the automatic lock-on feature of the Hornet's missile system, it's not something that you actually need – your targets don't have much room to maneuver, so manual aiming will suffice.

With the mobile artillery out of commission, turn your attention to individual Brutes and Shade turrets. Despite the presence of a Chieftain armed with a Fuel Rod Gun amongst the enemy infantry, you can usually afford the risk of moving a little closer at this point.

Make the most of both your weapons to tear your targets asunder while simultaneously blowing them sky-high (after several levels of approaching Brutes cautiously on Legendary, this is truly cathartic), and aim to wipe them all out before they can withdraw to cover.

Towards the end of this massacre, Elites will land to continue the fight on solid ground. It's vital that you don't accidentally shoot them in your haste to finish off the final Brutes, so move in closer still and pay attention to the color of the targeting reticle as you fire. Indeed, once the Elites enter the fray, it's better to avoid firing rockets at all, just to be on the safe side.

After landing, locate the Fuel Rod Gun dropped by the Chieftain, and swap it for your Beam Rifle. Make a mental note of the latter weapon's location – you'll be returning here shortly to reclaim it.

I Given the numbers you faced before landing, a few stragglers are to be expected in the U-shaped corridor that leads to the structure's entrance, so deal with these from a safe distance. The moment you draw near to the door, a large and determined force of Brutes will rush out to bar your passage. If you get there before the Elites charge, you can plant the Power Drain collected earlier through the entrance as it opens, thus depriving the attack party of their power armor. Pull back and finish them off with headshots as they emerge.

J Now here's a winning combination on Legendary: Hunters and Drones. Stay in the open, and you have absolutely zero chance of surviving. Fortunately, there is one quirk that you can exploit – the Drones will not spill out from the middle of the room as long as you don't move too far forward, which enables you to take cover in the areas just to the left and right of the opening.

Switch to the Fuel Rod Gun collected earlier and unleash a barrage of shots at the nearest Hunter as you dash from behind the transparent barrier to take cover behind one of the two walls. You

should definitely have sufficient ammunition to kill one of these, and at least severely weaken its partner. If you can finish the second off with grenades before it reaches your allies, this is very much a positive thing – the Elites will be helpful later, and it would be a blow to lose their support straight away.

Once the final Drones retreat, go back outside to retrieve your Beam Rifle before continuing. If you would like to have a big advantage in the next fight, temporarily trade your other weapon (which should be a Carbine or Battle Rifle, of course) for a Needler with as much ammunition as is available.

K On your way to the elevator, you'll face a fairly large force of Brutes. Three or four will run forward as an advance party; their peers will be lying in wait through the next door. Welcome those that rush to meet you with a grenade, then pepper the surprised Brutes with needles. Any survivors will retreat back up the walkway at this point. Wait at the bottom of the slope until your quarry feels sufficiently bold to press forward again, then remind them pointedly as to why that was a bad idea. Grenades work well – toss

Spike Grenades if you have any, as your victims are likely to leave replacements behind.

Replenish your supply of Needler ammo if required (a couple of full clips will suffice), then continue forward to deal with the anticipated "surprise" Drone attack. If you dive into the alcove to the right of your position, you can simply emerge and pick them off at will, though a little urgency wouldn't go amiss if you still have Elites in support. The Needler isn't a good choice for the next fight, though, so now would be a good time to collect the weapon that you hopefully set aside earlier, prior to riding the elevator to the tower control room.

L This battle plays out in much the same way as the earlier one in the first tower. The moment you step off the elevator, switch to your Beam Rifle and dispatch the Chieftain professionally with three headshots. Take up position behind the transparent barrier, and wait for each Brute Stalker to move into the open. In this light, they're actually quite easy to see and pick off with the Beam Rifle.

You should have a clear recollection of what happens next, so grab two Maulers from the weapons dispenser before you deactivate the shield barrier.

- If you can stick a Drone at the center of a swarm with a Plasma Grenade, you can wipe out several at once.

- With a Beam Rifle in hand, the self-contained battles that take place in the two tower control rooms are perfect for practicing "no-scope" sniper kills – the act of shooting an adversary with a Beam Rifle or Sniper Rifle without using their zoom function. This isn't an important attribute in Campaign, but time spent honing your skills here can pay dividends in multiplayer mode.

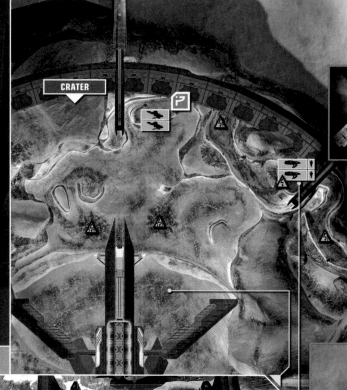

CRATER

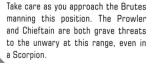

RIGHT TOWER: ENTRANCE

Rally Point Bravo

TUNNEL

Take care as you approach the Brutes manning this position. The Prowler and Chieftain are both grave threats to the unwary at this range, even in a Scorpion.

Before you jump into the Scorpion, take the time to collect weapons, grenades and ammunition. Either a Battle Rifle or Carbine (or indeed both) will be useful in a later showdown.

RIGHT TOWER: BOTTOM FLOORS

RIGHT TOWER: UPPER FLOOR

Hop in one of the two Hornets when they land, destroy the Banshees first to take control of the skies, then attack the Scarab of your choice. Shoot one of its legs repeatedly to disable it (this prevents it from rotating to face you), then move around to its rear to blast the protective armor and, naturally, the engine core behind it. Flying in wide circles can help you avoid incoming shots.

You'll encounter numerous Covenant vehicles and turrets as you drive towards the giant Forerunner structure, but few of these pose any great threat as long as you don't rush. You can blast most of them before they open fire; the same applies to Shade turrets and enemies stationed on floating platforms.

Pick up the turret dropped by the Chieftain to clear the invading Flood, making sure you don't let them surround you. Grab two Maulers from the dispenser near to the elevator on your way out, as these are extremely efficient against the Flood at close range. Fight your way to the exit once you return to the lower level, but be very careful when you approach the door – there are two Carrier Forms outside. Dispatch them with grenades.

BASICS

CAMPAIGN

EXTRAS

MULTIPLAYER

USER
INSTRUCTIONS

PREFACE

MISSION 1

MISSION 2

MISSION 3

MISSION 4

MISSION 5

MISSION 6

MISSION 7

MISSION 8

MISSION 9

M: As soon as the cutscene ends, drop one of the Maulers for now and grab the Plasma Turret discarded by the Chieftain. You should endeavor to meet the charging Combat Forms with a constant barrage of plasma, especially if you see the shielded "Elite type" bearing down on you. It's hard to manage the swarm of Infection Forms while you deal with ostensibly more threatening targets, so expect them to occupy the bodies of the Brutes you dispatched earlier. When the battle ends, retrieve your second Mauler and make your way over to the elevator – but be vigilant, as there may be further Combat Forms hidden out of sight.

N: As the elevator touches down, you will see the Arbiter (and any surviving Elites) fighting Combat Forms. Immediately run down to offer your assistance. The number you face can vary, but it's generally not too intense. Ensure that the Flood bodies are smashed before you continue.

Be on your guard as you approach the door: the two Carrier Forms outside can sometimes be found lurking directly behind it. The fight that ensues is, once again, not too complicated, but it pays to focus on shooting the Infection Forms immediately to prevent them from reviving nearby corpses. This isn't really possible if you're fighting on your own. However with the Elites and the Arbiter in attendance, it's the first task you should attend to. (Naturally, the opposite applies if Campaign Scoring is activated, in which case the Infection Forms aren't worth the time it takes to even look at them.)

Though weapons aren't important for the next section of this mission, forward planning can save you a lot of later suffering. Ranged weapons are key – so keep your Beam Rifle if you still have it, and back it up with a Carbine or Battle Rifle. The Combat Forms will usually have dropped at least one of the latter.

O: The journey to the Control Room in the Scorpion is fun, and only carelessness will get you killed. If you move forward at a measured pace, stopping regularly to survey the terrain ahead for potential dangers, there's nothing that poses so much as a minor threat, let alone an insurmountable one.

Oddly enough, it's the first battle that you fight in the Scorpion that is potentially the most dangerous. After you pass through the gate you'll be confronted by a Brute attack party that includes a Chieftain with a Fuel Rod Gun, a Prowler, and some assorted Brutes. If you drive rashly around the corner at speed, you can reasonably expect to be immobilized by a Power Drain and find your vehicle transformed into scrap metal within seconds. Instead, inch forward gradually, blasting each enemy in turn, and you'll pass this trap set for less vigilant players unscathed. (Incidentally, if you're lacking a suitable second ranged weapon, you should hop out and collect the Fuel Rod Gun dropped by the Chieftain.)

The rest of the journey continues in similar vein, with the most tricky encounter being the last one, when you round a corner to face a Wraith, usually supported by a Shade turret, and a Brute with a Fuel Rod Gun standing on the floating platform behind it. Eliminate the secondary targets first, and you can simply charge at the Wraith with all guns blazing.

P: To take down the Scarabs, you first need to establish air superiority by aggressively clearing the skies of Banshees. Get to a reasonable height, and fly in wide circles to avoid the many guns aimed in your direction as you blast your targets with both weapons systems. Once this threat is removed, pick which Scarab you would like to destroy first, then follow each of these steps in turn.

• **1:** Fly around your chosen target in a wide circle to avoid incoming projectiles (you should have the undivided attention of both über-tanks by now, so the air will be thick with plasma fire), and bombard its front deck to clear it of Brutes. This isn't necessary on Normal, but it's better to err on the side of caution on Legendary – especially when, as can be the case in this battle, checkpoints are few and far between.

• **2:** Pick one of its legs, and smash the shielding to disable the Scarab.

• **3:** Strafe around and smash the armor that covers the engine core. With combined cannon fire and missiles, this shouldn't take more than five seconds or so – well within the time it takes you to fly around it in a broad circle.

• **4:** Here's the tricky part. Once the armor plating is removed, you need to fly at a low level to get a clear shot at the exposed engine core. You really can't afford the luxury of staying in one position while you line up the perfect missile shot – if the top cannon of the Scarab you're attacking doesn't get you, the main cannon of the other Scarab will. For that reason, don't rush. If the Scarab gets up before you manage to hit its weak spot with bullets or by squeezing a missile through, so be it. It's no great inconvenience to knock it down again – but being sent back to the start of the battle for a moment of foolishness *would* be.

Once the first Scarab falls, several Covenant vehicles will arrive to support the second. Destroy these straight away, then repeat all four of the steps above to end the confrontation. If you're feeling brave, try landing on the deck after clearing it of adversaries, then blow the engine core at close quarters. It's hard to define quite why, but we find that disabling Scarabs this way is far more satisfying than using a vehicle. Plus, it looks *great* on saved films.

- The Mauler may be superb against most Combat Forms, but it's rather less impressive against the variety derived from former Elites. When you face these in numbers, it can pay to dual wield it with a Plasma Rifle to rapidly disable their shields.

- While driving down the slope in a Scorpion, you'll notice a ferocious aerial battle taking place overhead. There are two low-flying Banshees that you can shoot with the turret, saving you the trouble of dealing with them in the Hornet later.

[THE COVENANT V]

On the first bridge section, there are two Grunts in the distance armed with Fuel Rod Guns. Kill these, and the rest of the fight gets instantly much easier. Collect their weapons as you pass – they'll enable you to dispatch many of the Brutes in the second area with ease.

Watch out for the Chieftain positioned here – he may activate an Invincibility device as he bears down on you. Collect his Gravity Hammer before you leave – it's the perfect weapon for dealing with the enemy that lies ahead...

Pick up a Shotgun (see map) as you escape, and stick close to the Arbiter to benefit from his assistance. Use grenades to destroy distant Combat Forms, and try to stem the tide of Infection Forms in quieter moments to prevent them from occupying corpses. At the end of the Ring Room, drop through the hole behind the elevator to end the mission.

CITADEL: BOTTOM FLOOR

(Return journey only)

(Return journey only)

CITADEL: RING ROOM

(Return journey only)

(Return journey only)

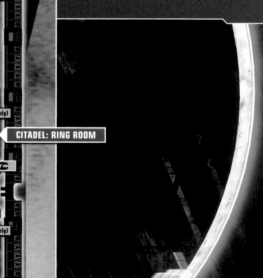

D. It's at this point that you'll fully appreciate the wisdom of bringing ranged weapons along. Grunts with Fuel Rod Guns will unleash a relentless barrage of missiles from the far end of the corridor, and it's supremely difficult to pick your way through the explosions. Fortunately, you don't have to. You're safe at the top of the ramp for now, so snipe them from here, then help your eerie Flood allies dispatch the nearby infantry. As you move forward, additional Grunts with Fuel Rod Guns may appear; another Grunt will run out to set up a Plasma Turret, too. Again, dispatch these from behind solid cover before they have a chance to cause too much chaos. When you make it to the door, collect a Fuel Rod Gun and a complete supply of ammo, then pick up the turret before you press forward.

R If you were curious as to why the first bridge section featured such a paucity of Brutes, the answer lies directly in front of you: they're all *here*. Operating from the best cover available, focus on dispatching the Jump Pack Brutes that

arrive (and their peers on the ground) with your Plasma Turret. Once you have advanced approximately a third of the length of the bridge section, two Grunts with Fuel Rod Guns will emerge from the far exit. Hit them with headshots immediately.

A Brute Chieftain with a Gravity Hammer awaits you at the very end of the bridge. As you should have a Fuel Rod Gun with more than enough ammunition to spare, you really shouldn't need our help with this one. Take his Gravity Hammer to go with your FRG, and collect ammunition for the latter should you need it.

S. The return route is crawling with Flood, but a fully-loaded Fuel Rod Gun will enable you to vaporize them as you run. Should any get too close for comfort, switch to the Gravity Hammer to contemptuously swat them aside. Even though a few Combat Forms may carry deadly weapons such as Shotguns or Brute Shots, there's nothing that should unduly trouble you. If fighting the Flood really isn't your forte, you can choose to follow in the Arbiter's wake, contributing a few shots but allowing him to bear the brunt of Gravemind's fury.

BASICS

CAMPAIGN

EXTRAS

MULTIPLAYER

USER INSTRUCTIONS

PREFACE

MISSION 1

MISSION 2

MISSION 3

MISSION 4

MISSION 5

MISSION 6

MISSION 7

MISSION 8

MISSION 9

THE COVENANT: DEBRIEFING

[SPARTAN LASER]

It's the ultimate laser pen, writ large — and you really *can* blind someone with it. Permanently.

- The Spartan Laser must power up before it can fire, with the gauge inside the reticle indicating how long that will take.
- Release the trigger at any time to cancel the firing process — there is no battery penalty for doing so.
- You can begin "priming" a Spartan Laser shot before you actually line the target up in your sights. This enables you to remain safely behind cover until the very last moment. It takes time to perfect the skill, but you'll appreciate practical experience accrued in Campaign mode when you get to use it in multiplayer matches.
- In the Master Chief's hands, the Spartan Laser is a super-powerful solution to a variety of vehicle, turret and Chieftain-related woes. In the hands of an AI-controlled ally on Legendary, however, it's a fabulously destructive weapon with infinite ammo.

[HORNET]

Banshees are, like, *so* last season…

- Piloting a Hornet is a little unusual at first, but you'll soon become accustomed to it.
  You increase or decrease altitude with **R**; you can also reverse, strafe, and hover on the spot by releasing all controls.
- The Hornet has two weapons systems: a machine gun, and homing rockets. The latter will only track a target if fired when the targeting reticle is red.
- While the homing function of the missiles is invaluable when you fight against airborne adversaries, it's less important against infantry or ground-based vehicles — it's safer to bombard them from distance.
- When pitted against Banshees, the Hornet's ability to fly sideways enables you to evade some of the incoming fire, yet the Covenant vehicle generally has the advantage at close range. In short, it's better to fight them from distance.

CORTANA

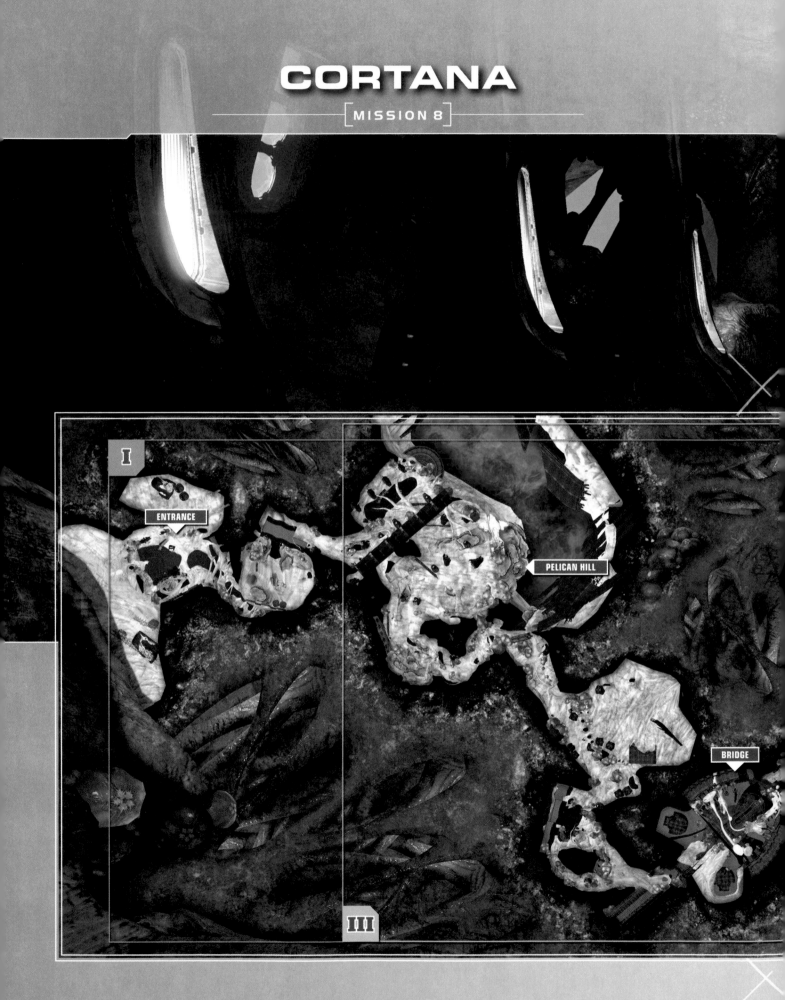

ENTRANCE

PELICAN HILL

BRIDGE

I

III

BASICS

CAMPAIGN

EXTRAS

MULTIPLAYER

USER
INSTRUCTIONS

PREFACE

MISSION 1

MISSION 2

MISSION 3

MISSION 4

MISSION 5

MISSION 6

MISSION 7

MISSION 8

MISSION 9

REACTOR ROOM

THE HIVE

II

ENTRANCE

PELICAN HILL

BRIDGE

A Drop down and pop the swarm of Infection Forms with the Assault Rifle before they can reach the corpses. Collect grenades and a Plasma Rifle to replace the Assault Rifle prior to moving on – it's better against shielded Combat Forms, should you encounter any. Throughout this mission, take care not to accidentally shoot the fleshy sacs on the walls – they will release Infection Forms if hit with anything other than a direct burst from the Flamethrower.

B As you round the corner, a few sacs containing Infection Forms will automatically explode, spewing forth their perpetually irritating contents. These will revive any bodies they can reach, so eliminate them quickly. Head up the sloped path to reach the upper level of this chamber, where you'll find grenades and a second Plasma Rifle to dual wield with the first. You can also replace your Shotgun with an Energy Sword.

[MISSION 8 NOTE]

The Flood-infested High Charity is a very different environment to the one visited in Halo 2, and it's disturbingly easy to lose your way while negotiating its predominately flesh-covered tunnels and chambers. For that reason, we have opted for a rather more visual type of walkthrough for the Cortana level. Though you may face fewer and less aggressive enemies on Normal, the strategies we offer here are equally applicable for all difficulty levels.

Beating this mission is very much a matter of measured, careful progression, and picking the best position to make a stand when you encounter Flood in numbers. On Heroic and Legendary, your choice of weaponry is equally pivotal. A great configuration is to have a Brute Shot, with an Energy Sword or Gravity Hammer for up-close-and-personal encounters; if these aren't available, they can be replaced by a Needler for ranged fights, and a Shotgun to fill in as a melee weapon. The two Flamethrowers you find are indispensable, so try to conserve their limited fuel to make them last. There's no reason why you can't grab other firearms temporarily when required (such as a Plasma Rifle or Spiker to deal with a Ranged Form, for example), but you should definitely aim to collect and use the weapons recommended above whenever possible.

BASICS

CAMPAIGN

EXTRAS

MULTIPLAYER

USER
INSTRUCTIONS

PREFACE

MISSION 1

MISSION 2

MISSION 3

MISSION 4

MISSION 5

MISSION 6

MISSION 7

MISSION 8

MISSION 9

When you reach the porta in the floor (these unpleasant sphincter-like orifices are what pass for doors in the refurbished High Charity), drop through it and immediately take cover in the corner as illustrated here. After a suitably pregnant pause, Combat Forms will move into the open. Blast these in turn with your two Plasma Rifles, ducking back into cover to recuperate as required. After the Combat Forms withdraw, destroy the Carrier Forms that waddle towards you with grenades – the plasma and incendiary varieties work best. If you can find a Brute Shot here, take it in place of the Plasma Rifles.

At the top of the slope here, you'll encounter several Infection Forms in a small chamber filled with dead Elites, Brutes and – this is the important part – littered with loose grenades. Without leaving the narrow path, use short bursts of flame to prevent the reanimation of too many Combat Forms. Throw a grenade in to set off a chain reaction that will weaken or dismember those that do rise. In the next tunnel, grab a fresh Gravity Hammer or Energy Sword (whichever one you prefer), then drop through the hole to continue.

There are many Pure Forms and Combat Forms on top of the metal and flesh hill, so the best tactic is to run over to the crashed Pelican straight away. The journey is a little fraught, but you'll find useful equipment there (particularly the Flamethrower) that will make this whole battle much less difficult, especially on Legendary. If you're lucky, the Flood won't follow. Make occasional sorties back inside, luring Combat Forms and Pure Forms towards you; the latter are easy prey for the Flamethrower. On more than one occasion we've enjoyed the simple task of dispatching Stalker Forms exclusively, picking them off as they run by in search of their misplaced quarry.

As soon as you pass through the entrance, head straight to the left (as illustrated above). This area provides cover from the damnable Ranged Forms as you pick off the first wave of Combat Forms. Operate from here, drawing all Flood to your position. When the flow of adversaries dwindles to a trickle, you can either wait in the hope that the Ranged Forms will mutate and come in search of you as Stalkers, or collect the nearby Needler and make careful attacking forays from your hiding spot.

Be cautious as you leave your position by the Pelican – Combat Forms or Pure Forms may still be lurking around, though you can generally just give Carrier Forms a wide berth as you press forward. Run to the other side of the fleshy hill, and make your way to the chamber exit. Note that a slope to the left of this porta leads to an upper level where you can acquire two Plasma Grenades and an Incendiary Grenade. The next corridor is empty, and easy to find your way through.

A Terminal is hidden in the lower level of this chamber; it differs from others you have encountered, as you'll realize when you access it. There are many interesting weapons and equipment items, too, so take what you need. A slow but constant trickle of Infection Forms will enter the area throughout, so be prepared to face a few additional Combat Forms before you depart. Be wary as you enter the next corridor – Carrier Forms may be awaiting your arrival.

- A single Brute Shot blast will dislodge a Ranged Form from its position on a wall. It won't necessarily kill it outright (the number of shots required depends on your chosen difficulty level), but it will give you a moment's respite from the relentless rain of projectiles.

- When Pure Forms don't know where you are, they tend to revert to the Stalker body type to conduct a search. If you have plenty of patience, try to take advantage of this.

THE HIVE

REACTOR ROOM

I This room has a design that is oddly redolent of a honeycomb, but don't feel alarmed by its apparent complexity – it's actually, in essence, a straightforward corridor. Staying behind cover at the entrance, be prepared for plenty of Combat Forms to lead the initial attack, and for Ranged Forms to fire from awkward positions on walls. Projectiles from both will inevitably hit the sacs on the walls, which spew forth Infection Forms, so keep your Flamethrower close to hand.

J In this blocked corridor (to your right as you enter the chamber), you can grab a fresh Flamethrower. We advise that you wait until your first model is running dangerously low on fuel before you pick it up, though – these are the only two available, and you need to make them last.

M When all is quiet, carefully venture into the chamber and attempt to lure any lurking Pure Forms and Combat Forms from hiding. Once you're absolutely confident that none remain, climb the slope pictured here and follow the path around, but don't switch off just yet – despite your best efforts, you'll usually encounter Combat Forms as you head upwards. Collect and activate one of the two Cloaking devices (you can then carry the second in reserve) to avoid any nasty surprises.

BASICS

CAMPAIGN

EXTRAS

MULTIPLAYER

USER INSTRUCTIONS

PREFACE

MISSION 1

MISSION 2

MISSION 3

MISSION 4

MISSION 5

MISSION 6

MISSION 7

MISSION 8

MISSION 9

K Be cautious: though it may seem as if you have stemmed the tide in this room, a further group of Flood will attack as you press forward. Backpedal quickly, using grenades to halt their advance. You should also note that Ranged Forms sometimes affix themselves to walls in hard-to-reach locations. Move slowly and carefully, being ready to bolt back the way you came if necessary.

N From this position, jump across the gap and continue on your way upwards. You'll need to make another jump when you arrive at the top of the chamber, but the exit is clearly apparent on the opposite platform.

- As you'll note after a swift perusal of the area maps, there are quite a few Cloaking devices inside High Charity. If you're aiming to make a super-fast speed run, or simply don't enjoy fighting the Flood, you can activate them tactically to avoid certain battles entirely.

- Note that weapons and items encountered on your way through High Charity will generally be unavailable when you make your escape run.

L As soon as you move through the porta you'll notice that, bar the relatively flimsy space crate containing Carbines, this chamber offers very limited cover. There is a tunnel to your right, but it's too easy to be surrounded if you use it. Far better, then, to hang back in the corridor outside, gradually enticing targets towards you by making darting attack runs when it's safe to do so. Ranged Forms are, once again, a seemingly omnipresent irritant, and lethally so on Legendary – but when are they anything less?

O After passing through the porta, you'll arrive in High Charity's reactor core. There are Brute Shots in the nearby dispenser, so stock up on ammunition. Methodically clear the room, firing from positions that shelter you from Ranged Forms, then make your way over to the door on the opposite side of the room. Go through it and follow the corridor to fulfill your objective.

PELICAN HILL

REACTOR ROOM

THE HIVE

Rally Point Alpha

BRIDGE

Hold to swap for

Pull up your Mjolnir armored pants in readiness as you head back to the reactor core, as a fresh collective of Flood are drumming their distended fingers in anticipation of your return. This battle plays out in much the same way as the first. Deal with foes in the immediate vicinity first, then focus on Combat Forms; hurling instructive biological epithets in the direction of the Ranged Forms is optional, but you may find it helps a little.

Access the control panel in the center of the room to expose the reactor pylons, then destroy all three with Brute Shot blasts. The route that you arrived by is now blocked, but a new entrance will be revealed and marked by a waypoint – it's actually directly ahead as you cross the bridge. Pick up Brute Shot ammunition and an Energy Sword if you can find one, then drop through the hole in the floor pictured above to continue.

BASICS

CAMPAIGN

EXTRAS

MULTIPLAYER

USER
INSTRUCTIONS

PREFACE

MISSION 1

MISSION 2

MISSION 3

MISSION 4

MISSION 5

MISSION 6

MISSION 7

MISSION 8

MISSION 9

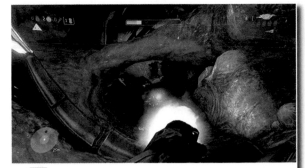

R The route back cuts through areas that you have previously traversed, but a couple of mandatory shortcuts (such as the hole you've just leapt through) make it far less torturous. As you land, several extremely testy Combat Forms will rush to attack. Pull back into cover, and try to slow their advance with grenades and Brute Shot blasts.

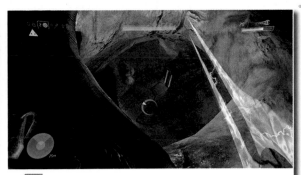

T You will land in the small area that was filled with grenades and corpses earlier, though both are noticeably absent now. There are a few Combat Forms and Carrier Forms through the next porta, but nothing that you can't handle. If possible, try running past the latter while maintaining your distance to avoid triggering their detonation sequence.

S Expect to meet yet more Combat Forms as you enter the Bridge room where you found the Terminal earlier. You will usually encounter several that are shielded and carrying Energy Swords; attempt to stick these with grenades from a distance. When you make it to the corridor directly ahead, a Tank Form will burst through the wall, conveniently creating a much-needed exit. Follow the subsequent tunnel until you find a hole in the floor, then drop through it.

U In this final chamber you'll encounter Combat Forms and Pure Forms, with the latter generally being the Ranged variety. Unless you're aiming for a high score, just make a break for the Pelican outside – simply run into the back of it to end the mission.

If you're the inquisitive type, and like to leave the beaten path to explore, the "Brute Shot jump" is a close cousin to the classic grenade jump. Simply look at the floor, and then shoot the ground as you leap to reach ledges or platforms that would otherwise be out of reach.

CRASH SITE

DROP PATH

EXIT PATH

ZIGGURAT

CONTROL ROOM

TRENCH RUN

I

II

HALO

[MISSION 9]

BASICS

CAMPAIGN

EXTRAS

MULTIPLAYER

USER
INSTRUCTIONS

PREFACE

MISSION 1

MISSION 2

MISSION 3

MISSION 4

MISSION 5

MISSION 6

MISSION 7

MISSION 8

MISSION 9

You can access a hidden Forerunner building by climbing the short slope here. The final Terminal of the Campaign is located inside. If you've diligently visited all the others prior to this point, you'll receive the Marathon Man Achievement as a reward when you access it. The story doesn't end here, though – play through again on Legendary, and you'll get to read different parts of the tale...

As you make your way to the sloped bank of snow on the right-hand side of the Ziggurat, Flood dispersal pods will deploy Combat Forms. It may initially seem that these appear at random, but they are actually limited in number – you can hold back and dispatch each group methodically if you wish. There are Rocket Launchers and Fuel Rod Guns to collect; on the first level of the Forerunner structure, you can also pick up a Flamethrower.

As you follow the route to the Control Room entrance, use a Brute Shot and a Fuel Rod Gun (or a Needler, once the latter runs out of ammunition) to exterminate the Flood. Be wary of attacks from behind – it pays to move slowly, dealing with all targets as they arrive. When you reach the top level, deploy the two Auto Turrets, then get ready to repel a furious Flood onslaught. Don't conserve ammunition – employ every resource at your disposal to hold your position.

After you leave the main Control Room, dispatch the nearby Combat Forms and Infection Forms as you race back outside. When you pass through the door, collect the best weapons you can find, then head up the snow-covered slope that leads to the exit (pictured here). Sentinels, Combat Forms and Carrier Forms abound on the path and through the next door. Though the mood is certainly urgent, you don't actually need to rush as you fight these.

In the climactic battle in the Control Room, dodge the energy beams (be careful not to fall from the platform) and wait until Johnson intervenes. Grab his Spartan Laser, then exact devastating retribution by landing three direct hits.

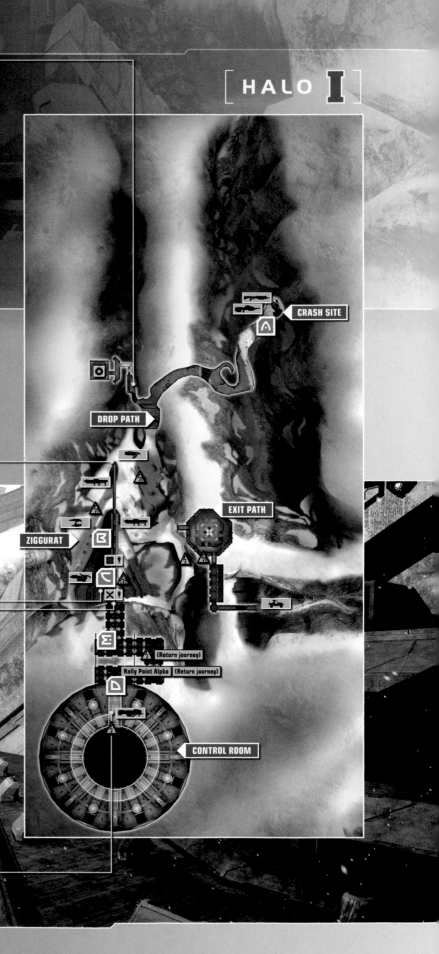

CRASH SITE

DROP PATH

EXIT PATH

ZIGGURAT

CONTROL ROOM

(Return journey)

Rally Point Alpha (Return journey)

BASICS

CAMPAIGN

EXTRAS

MULTIPLAYER

USER INSTRUCTIONS

PREFACE

MISSION 1

MISSION 2

MISSION 3

MISSION 4

MISSION 5

MISSION 6

MISSION 7

MISSION 8

MISSION 9

A Certain weapons can sometimes be carried forward to this mission if you've arrived directly from the Cortana level, but the default kit if you start this level anew is a Rocket Launcher and an Assault Rifle. Trade the latter for a Battle Rifle. There are two amidst the debris behind the crashed Pelican.

When you approach the Ziggurat, hold back as the first Flood dispersal pods touch down. The Combat Forms that emerge will slaughter all but the most fleet-footed, accurate and downright lucky players at close range, so attempting to fight them on the fly is not recommended. Instead, pull back and knock them down from distance with the Battle Rifle. Shielded varieties are a drain on your ammunition reserves, so try to hit them with your Rocket Launcher if you have one; if you don't, dash over to the nearby Fuel Rod Gun during a quiet moment (see map for location) and use that instead. You don't need to worry about destroying their bodies, as

there are no Infection Forms in the opening part of this mission.

Systematically work your way around the snow-covered landscape, triggering the arrival of all new dispersal pods, then engaging their foul payloads from a safe distance. The most efficient weapons combination is a Fuel Rod Gun and a Brute Shot, so aim to pick these up, and then grab ammunition for both whenever you can find it. Thrift is important: you should ensure that practically every shot hits its intended target.

When you approach the walkway on the right-hand side of the building, run into the corner at the very top of the slope to take cover. A much larger force of Combat Forms will attack at this point, and they'll cut you down in seconds if you engage them over open ground. Once the last one falls, run over to collect the Flamethrower.

B Though the same tactic of steady, cautious progression will serve you well as you climb your way to the entrance above, from this point on you will rarely have the luxury of engaging Combat Forms from a safe distance. Worse still, Pure Forms also enter the fray; expect to encounter each body variant during your journey.

For Pure Forms, the Flamethrower is vital, though you'll need to drop it quickly to use the Brute Shot or Fuel Rod Gun against Combat Forms as they arrive. The dispersal pods will deploy Flood both in front of and, less commonly, behind your position. Take

things slowly, and be absolutely sure that there are no hidden adversaries closing in from behind when you press forward. The Sentinels offer a degree of assistance, but you can't rely on their support for long.

Should you run out of ammunition for the Fuel Rod Gun, a Needler is probably the best replacement — but be warned that it takes longer to kill individual enemies with this weapon. Melee weapons may be tempting, but they're not particularly practical here; your objective should be to destroy Flood before they draw near, not to actively seek out close-quarters engagements.

C Take advantage of the brief moment of respite as you reach the entrance to deploy the two Auto Turrets at either side of the doorway. When the Flood attacks in force, the pace and ferocity of the battle will become increasingly relentless as they accumulate in numbers. At first, you can run over to the side and blast Combat Forms as they land; once their ranks swell, it's better to make a stand in front of the doorway. Even though there's no real cover to hide behind, this at least reduces the likelihood that you will be surrounded. Keep your Flamethrower near to hand to eradicate Pure Forms when they attack, and aim to replenish your stock of ammunition and reload whenever possible — the "dead man's click" almost always foreshadows a return trip to the previous checkpoint.

Although the fight only lasts a few minutes in total, it feels much longer. Concentrate on slaying Ranged Forms and the Combat Forms that pose the most immediate danger (particularly those carrying weapons such as the Brute Shot, Shotgun and Mauler), and watch out for nasty surprises at the end: you may encounter Combat Forms armed with a Fuel Rod Gun or Rocket Launcher.

Once the grizzly melee draws to a close, swap your weapons for the most basic guns you can find — the wisdom of this will become apparent later.

D The tactics offered for Normal mode work just as well on Legendary in this brief showdown. Note that you don't actually need to open fire before Johnson makes his vital contribution. Just focus on dodging laser fire (which causes more damage on higher difficulty levels, of course), and take care not to fall from the platform. When you acquire the Spartan Laser, three shots will still suffice.

Σ You'll face Combat Forms (and, for the first time, a swarm of Infection Forms) as you leave the Control Room, but you can safely wait for the Arbiter to dispatch these. Unless the Halo 3 engine's invisible clean-up gremlins have stolen them, the weapons you left behind earlier should be available to collect. If not, a Sentinel Beam (there should be one nearby) will suffice. The only taxing battle occurs when you go through the door to the next building, as the Combat Forms inside are usually of the shielded variety. Smash their bodies once they fall to prevent Infection Forms from reviving them.

- Once the coast is clear, you can use non-essential weapons — that is, anything other than the Brute Shot, Fuel Rod Gun or Needler — to shoot the Stalkers climbing to the upper portion of the Ziggurat building for extra points if you are playing with Campaign Scoring active.

- If you can bear the infamy, it's actually possible to hide entirely from the battle that takes place before the doors to the Control Room open, leaving Johnson and the Arbiter to fight without your assistance. This might be useful if you are determined to complete a playthrough with the Iron skull activated.

- You're unlikely to encounter the following, but a word of advice, just in case: don't use an Auto Turret during or after the confrontation inside the Control Room — the Forerunner device can get a little cranky once the ring has been activated...

TRENCH RUN

A You can use the Mongoose positioned here instead of the Warthog, should you feel so inclined. It makes the final drive more difficult, but it's amusing (and challenging) to attempt it during a later playthrough, or in co-op games.

B Once you drive onto the metal platforms, large explosions indicate where floor panels have dropped into the abyss. These occur more frequently on Legendary, so it's actually better to set a slightly slower pace. The entire structure will be collapsing behind you, though, so you really can't cruise along leisurely without a care in the world.

C Watch out for Infection Forms, Carrier Forms and Sentinels as you follow the path in an anticlockwise direction. As a rule, try to avoid large jumps when there are Sentinels nearby – their beams can tip the Warthog over as it flies through the air.

D Though it may seem solid, this enclosed tunnel is also collapsing, so keep the pedal firmly on the metal. Unless you're actively seeking a high score, avoid the Combat Forms when you encounter them.

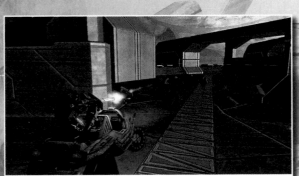

BASICS

CAMPAIGN

EXTRAS

MULTIPLAYER

USER INSTRUCTIONS

PREFACE

MISSION 1

MISSION 2

MISSION 3

MISSION 4

MISSION 5

MISSION 6

MISSION 7

MISSION 8

MISSION 9

Σ This area is packed with Sentinels and Combat Forms. Drive around it in a clockwise direction. You can gain extra points by running down the Combat Forms if you have Campaign Scoring activated, but be wary of slowing down — Combat Forms can and will board your vehicle to hit you with melee attacks.

G The second "tunnel run" is a little more dangerous than the first. There is a large group of Combat Forms armed with Fuel Rod Guns approximately midway through it, so take the path underneath their position to avoid the missiles. Jump off the right-hand side of the ramp when you reach the end.

F This area is populated by Pure Forms, particularly the Ranged variety. Drive around in an anticlockwise direction. You can score big points (and perhaps exorcize a few demons) by hitting some of these on your way through.

- If you're playing with Campaign Scoring activated, run over Combat Forms and Pure Forms to boost your points total during the Warthog run, but steer well clear of Carrier Forms. This is obviously inadvisable if you chose to make the journey in the Mongoose...

- Note that there is an exclusive final cinematic sequence that only occurs when you have completed every Campaign level on Legendary.

H The final approach to the Dawn features undulating slopes that make it hard to see the route ahead, so it's wise to slow down just a little. Try to avoid jumping — you really never know which panel sections might fall down before you land.

I As the Warthog hits the bottom of the ramp behind the Dawn, the final cutscene will kick in. Don't wander off as the final credits roll, as there's an additional sequence once they end. Congratulations! If you're playing on Normal or Heroic for the first time, rest assured that there's plenty more to see and do in Campaign mode, as we reveal in the Extras chapter that follows.

EXTRAS

WARNING! Spoiler alert! Offering in-depth analysis and revealing some of the game's most confidential features, this chapter is primarily designed to further extend and improve your knowledge of Halo 3. However, we *strongly* recommend that you do not read it until you have finished the final level of Campaign mode.

LEGENDARY PRIMER

Okay: so you've just beaten the final level for the first time on Normal or Heroic. Think it's all over? Guess again. Over the following pages, we'll introduce you to additional features that make Halo 3 infinitely replayable (particularly hidden Skulls, Achievements, and the Campaign Scoring system), and we also provide an overview of all enemies, equipment and vehicles, with a bias towards expert "insider" information.

Before we move on to such matters, though, we'd like to offer a few helpful words for players looking to graduate from Heroic to Legendary.

Legendary is *special*. There's really nothing else like it.

Playing Halo 3 on Legendary is like being invited to sleep with the celebrity of your choice, only to find out – *too late!* – that their libido is the timing mechanism for an elaborate bomb positioned under the bed; or riding into the middle of a shootout on a white stallion and saving the day, only to realize – *too late!* – that the horse is a bomb; or being forced to disarm a bomb, choosing to cut the blue wire after anxious, panicked deliberation, only to discover – *too late!* – that the scissors curiously left beside the device were actually the detonation switch.

In short, you tend to explode a lot.

The point is, though, the bits where you aren't actually in bits are absolutely magnificent: challenging, savagely hard in places, yet the sense of satisfaction you get from beating a level on Legendary for the first time is, in our humble opinion, a gaming experience that is almost incomparably sweet.

There's no denying that Bungie's design team take a certain sick satisfaction in occasionally confounding players with ostensibly overwhelming odds. There are several set-piece battles that caused us to coin at least 43 new expletives (which, alas, we can't actually

HALO 3

BASICS

CAMPAIGN

EXTRAS

MULTIPLAYER

LEGENDARY
PRIMER

SKULLS

SCORE SYSTEM

ACHIEVEMENTS

BESTIARY

INVENTORY

VEHICLES

repeat in a family guide for an M-rated game), and we don't doubt that there may be a few battles that could leave you disheartened, disgruntled and discouraged — which are, let's face it, three of the least pleasant things you can be that begin with the letter "d". But these feelings pass, usually in the time it takes you to collect your controller from whichever corner of the room it landed in. The beauty of Legendary, you see, is that once it gets under your skin, you'll not rest until you've beaten it soundly.

So: to help you get started, we've prepared a list of general tips that we'll call The Seven Fundamental Skills of Successful Legendary Veterans. Absorb them and put them into practice and you'll be all set for life on Legendary.

USE COVER

Beating Legendary isn't just a matter of being accurate with weapons, or having fast reactions, or even possessing a solid knowledge of enemy behaviors and weaknesses. These are extremely useful attributes, of course, but the most important skill of all is the ability to pick, and use, solid cover. On Legendary, the rate at which enemies fire is much, much faster, and their accuracy is greatly improved, too. Linger in the open for a split-second too long during large battles, and you'll be contemptuously cut down; even small groups of enemies are deadly if you charge blindly into the fray. You may think, "Oh, it's only a couple of Grunts and a Jackal" as you boldly leap forward to do battle, but next thing you know, the Marine coroners are picking the Chief's boots out of a nearby tree. Fools rush in; survivors choose a good hiding spot and wear their opponents down gradually.

PATIENCE IS A VIRTUE

At first, it may seem that Legendary involves spending 52.7% of your time cowering behind cover, 34.16% watching the "swirling death camera of doom", and the remaining period chewing the furniture out of sheer frustration. After months of constant play, we could stand with our backs to the screen while someone else plays and recite exactly what enemies will do, but even *we* still die once in a while. And sometimes, repeatedly. There's no doubt about it: Legendary is hard. The surprising thing, though, is that you'll find that you improve very quickly. And that's when the fun really starts.

DIVIDE AND CONQUER

Given the sheer number of foes pitted against you, frontal attacks are often suicidal. For that reason, it's better to be smart and sneaky. Try to lure individual enemies towards you, or attack from unexpected directions. On Legendary, discretion really is the better part of valor. But don't worry — it's not all creeping around in the shadows. Passing a checkpoint is usually your cue to put gung-ho tactics to the test, and it's genuinely rewarding when they actually work.

KNOW YOUR ENEMY

Prioritize. Unless you face an opponent that demands your immediate attention (such as a rampaging Chieftain), pick on the little guys first. Grunts are individually weak, but collectively pose a massive threat. If you kill them straight away, you can reduce

the number of weapons pointing in your direction with the least amount of effort. The same applies to the less damage-resistant Brute varieties (see page 130 for more information on Brutes, and page 136 to study a table that reveals which ones you can dispatch with the greatest ease), and Jackals. Of course, when you fight the Flood, your priority is to destroy whichever parts of the teeming, festering multitude are most likely to kill you first.

AIM FOR THE HEAD, AND THE HEART WILL FOLLOW

Players on Normal can get away with a "spray and pray" approach to marksmanship, inexpertly taking down opponents with a lucky shot to the leg or wrist. On Legendary, you really don't have that luxury. The quickest way to kill all Covenant enemies (with the obvious exception of the Hunter) is to aim for the head; with the Flood, hitting the embedded Infection Forms has a similar effect.

USE THE RIGHT WEAPONS

If you study the table on page 136 of this chapter, you'll get a clear idea of which weapons work best on Legendary. As a rule of thumb, though, get used to carrying a Battle Rifle or Carbine at all times. The Magnum/Plasma Pistol dual-wield pairing is the Brute-killing combo that all true Halo artists will favor; if your inner barbarian demands a more immediate cudgel, you can keep a Needler at the ready for a similar purpose. You'll also need to hone your ability to make grenades count — being able to stick enemies with consistent accuracy is an absolute must.

PLAN AHEAD

Having the right weapons, vehicles and (to a lesser extent) equipment to hand as you enter each battle is often the difference between victory, and Mr. and Mrs. Jub-Jub having a war souvenir that makes them the envy of *all* their non-Spartan-helmet-owning Grunty friends. Some fights are maddeningly tricky if you attempt them with low ammo, for example, or if you have short-range weapons when distance sniping is required, and vice versa. Fortunately for you, we always take the time to prepare readers for upcoming fights in each Legendary walkthrough. You're welcome to ignore these suggestions and pick your own weapons and wheels, of course — but on your own (severed) head be it...

SKULLS

Halo 3 features 13 hidden "skull" collectables which, once obtained, are added to the Campaign Options screen. When activated, these add a variety of interesting new effects that can have a profound influence on how you play Campaign mode in both single-player and co-op sessions.

Bungie is almost notoriously reticent when it comes to revealing or explaining secrets and undocumented features in its games, and has explicitly requested that we do not disclose the locations of the skulls in this guide. There are 13 skulls in total: one "gold" skull hidden in each of the nine Campaign missions (which are revealed and discussed here), and a further four that are so secret Bungie won't even let us mention them by name. As a general rule, all skulls are rather well hidden. To find them, you will often need to venture off the beaten path, exploring hard-to-see ledges or reaching ostensibly inaccessible areas. Basically, the secret to skull hunting is to visit areas where there is usually no call for you to set foot, and pay attention to seemingly inconsequential details. If there's no reason for you to be looking in a particular place, that's usually an indication that there might, just *might*, be a reward at the end of that particular platform, precipice or innocuous corner of the map.

Visit the forums at **www.bungie.net** if you'd like to join the hunt to find all 13 of the secret skulls.

SKULL BASICS

- Skulls are available in each Campaign mission from the first time you play them.
- Though the challenge varies in each instance, activating skulls makes Halo 3 more difficult.
- Unlike in Halo 2, collecting a skull simply unlocks it, but doesn't trigger any immediate effect.
- Once found, skulls can be activated at the Campaign Options screen. There is no limit on the number of skulls that can be switched on at any given time, but only expert players should consider activating more than one or two simultaneously.
- Activated skulls add multipliers to points earned during Campaign Scoring sessions. Turn to page 117 to learn more about this feature.

ACTIVATING SKULLS

From the Campaign Lobby, press ⓧ to visit the Campaign Options screen. Initially, you'll find a wall of 13 blank skull outlines, but these are gradually filled in as you collect each one (Fig. 1). To activate a skull, highlight it and then press Ⓐ to turn it on. However, note that doing so will erase your current Campaign save; a confirmation window will remind you of this fact.

SKULL EFFECTS & TIPS

BASICS

CAMPAIGN

EXTRAS

MULTIPLAYER

LEGENDARY PRIMER

SKULLS

SCORE SYSTEM

ACHIEVEMENTS

BESTIARY

INVENTORY

VEHICLES

Iron

Location: Sierra 117

Effect: In single-player Campaign sessions, death leads to a penalty of... drum roll... being sent back to the very beginning of the mission (or a Rally Point, if you chose to start at one). In co-op sessions, the death of one player will cause all participants to be returned to the previous checkpoint.

- The Iron skull is excellent for adding a little zest to co-op games, especially if you're playing in a group where everyone is comfortable with Legendary-grade combat and would like to increase the difficulty level. In solo games, its appeal is pretty much limited to those seeking to test their abilities to their limits in Campaign Scoring sessions.

- And no, before you even think it, you can't just revert to the previous checkpoint when things look grim. In solo games, Bungie has actually removed the option entirely.

Black Eye

Location: Crow's Nest

Effect: You must hit enemies with melee attacks to restore your shield energy. No melee attacks = no shield recharge = death.

- When you strike an enemy, the Master Chief's shield bar will begin to recharge. However, its progress will halt immediately should he sustain damage.

- Using the primary trigger-activated attack of the Energy Sword and Gravity Hammer counts as a melee hit.

- Naturally, missions that contain protracted vehicle sections that don't feature enemy infantry (namely Tsavo Highway, The Storm, The Ark, The Covenant and Halo) are not suited to play with the Black Eye skull activated. However, you should note that hijacking vehicles counts as a melee attack, and will recharge the Chief's shield.

- There are two pieces of equipment that you can employ to recharge your shield. The first, naturally, is the Regenerator. The second is the Invincibility device, which restores the Chief's shield bar once its effect ends.

Tough Luck

Location: Tsavo Highway

Effect: Enemies become much more adept at diving away from grenades and certain other projectiles.

- This skull doesn't mean that you can't stick opponents with grenades, or harm them when you throw them at their feet — it just makes your foe better at avoiding them.

- The most noticeable effect when Tough Luck is active is that Frag Grenades are much less efficient unless you're fighting in extremely cramped quarters. Plasma Grenade and Spike Grenade tags are still possible, especially at close range.

- This skull makes it much harder to use the Needler and charged Plasma Pistol shots.

- Tough Luck has no impact on Hunters and Ranged Forms — but then, these two enemies are hardly distinguished by their dodging ability under normal circumstances.

Catch

Location: The Storm

Effect: Boosts the frequency at which Grunts and Brutes throw grenades by a considerable degree, as well as the number of grenades they drop when they die.

- On higher difficulty levels, the number of grenades thrown by both Grunts and Brutes can be utterly insane. The results can be extremely amusing, especially when your Covenant foes accidentally tag their allies in their haste to blow you back to the previous checkpoint.

- Just to complicate matters further, your allies will also throw grenades on a more regular basis.

- As the number of grenades dropped increases, you will frequently encounter awe-inspiring chain reactions in larger battles.

- If you're playing to survive (and not just to admire the pyrotechnics and spectacular deaths), maintaining a safe distance when you face Grunts and Brutes is of paramount importance.

- Catch has no effect on Flood.

Fog

Location: Floodgate

Effect: Deprives you of a tool all good players take for granted: the Motion Tracker.

- The Motion Tracker doesn't even appear onscreen when Fog is active.

- If you're extremely familiar with a mission and the behavior of its inhabitants, activating Fog isn't a problematic penalty. However, even the best players will miss it during fights against the Flood and in missions that involve vehicular combat.

- On the plus side, you now can laugh derisively when Brutes deploy Radar Jammers.

Famine

Location: The Ark

Effect: All weapons dropped by enemies or allies contain much less ammunition or battery power than usual.

- This skull makes it really hard to save a number of key weapons for later skirmishes, and forces you to improvise with whatever you have to hand. This is particularly tough if you favor battery-powered Covenant firearms such as the Plasma Pistol, Beam Rifle, Energy Sword or Gravity Hammer.

- Famine doesn't just reduce the amount of ammunition in the weapons you can collect from beside corpses — it also has an effect when you exchange firearms with allies, or collect many "scripted" weapons from preset locations.

- Some weapons are exempt from Famine's hunger for clips, batteries and missiles. Firearms in dispensers (both space crates and Marine cabinets) do not fall under its influence, and certain fixed weapons are arbitrarily excused from its parsimonious rationing. Some turrets can be found with the standard supply of ammunition; others can be cut by half. We don't have the space to document each instance here, but a little exploration (particularly while under pressure in Campaign Scoring sessions) will reveal which guns, melee weapons and turrets can be trusted to last the course.

- It's a tricky penalty to bear on all missions, but Famine can be especially harsh during fights against the Flood on higher difficulty levels.

Thunderstorm

Location: The Covenant

Effect: "Promotes" Covenant to higher levels in their hierarchy. For instance, a Brute Captain in blue armor would become the superior variety clad in gold armor. In missions that feature Flood, the number of shielded Combat Forms is increased.

- Naturally, this skull raises the difficulty level of all missions where you encounter large numbers of Brutes by a notable degree.

- Its effect is especially apparent during missions that involve plenty of vehicular combat. As enemy pilots, drivers and passengers are tougher, it takes more shots to stop them.

- Thunderstorm is a great choice if you'd like to enliven co-op games. If Legendary alone just isn't challenging enough, this skull can help tip the balance back in the favor of your enemies.

Tilt

Location: Cortana

Effect: Heightens natural resistances and weaknesses of each enemy type, which means that your choice of weapons requires a great deal of thought and forward planning.

- Broadly speaking, Tilt creates a situation where you really must use plasma weapons against shielded enemies, switching to ballistic weaponry to finish them off. Let's use a gold Brute Captain as an example. With Tilt active, it will take two entire Battle Rifle clips or five Sniper Rifle shots to remove his power armor; once unprotected, a single headshot will suffice to finish the fight. A Plasma Rifle, conversely, will divest him of his power

armor within a second, but will take an absolute age to kill him.

- Chieftains are an utter torment with Tilt active, as they enjoy a resistance to practically everything. The best weapon you can use against them in many situations is the Beam Rifle, but these aren't always available.

- To survive confrontations against large groups of Brutes, you'll generally need to use specific weapons. You should aim to have a Plasma Pistol or Plasma Rifle combined with a Magnum, Battle Rifle or Carbine whenever you face them. Needlers still work well, though.

- Shielded Combat Forms are also difficult to fight against, especially on Legendary. Use grenade sticks or melee weapons when you face them.

Mythic

Location: Halo

Effect: After Legendary comes Mythic. When this skull is active, all enemies have double the usual allocation of health points.

- While you can still knock down Grunts and Jackals with headshots, Brutes provide a much sterner test of your mettle when Mythic blesses them with twice their usual stamina. You'll see Captains surviving grenade tags, and even rank-and-file Brutes withstanding four melee attacks before they fall.

- Combat Forms are made of sterner stuff, making certain staple weapons (particularly the Brute Shot) much less effective against them. They can still be knocked down immediately if you hit the Infection Form embedded in their chests with a precision firearm, though. The shielded variety will be a constant thorn in your side on Heroic and Legendary.

- Pure Forms also become much hardier — it's alarming to see even the weaker Stalker Form survive a grenade tag. The Flamethrower should be your constant companion.

- Screams completely lack potency when written down, but on the subject of Ranged Forms under the influence of Mythic we'd like to say "Aaaaargh!", "Aaaaargh!" and, moreover, "Aaaaaargh!"

THE SCORE SYSTEM

BASICS

CAMPAIGN

EXTRAS

MULTIPLAYER

LEGENDARY
PRIMER

SKULLS

SCORE SYSTEM

ACHIEVEMENTS

BESTIARY

INVENTORY

VEHICLES

SCORING BASICS

Before we reveal the magic numbers behind Campaign Scoring and offer guidance on how to maximize your scoring potential in each mission, here's a quick explanation of how this engrossing meta-game works.

Getting Started

To activate Campaign Scoring, press ❎ at the Campaign Lobby screen. Highlight the entry above the skulls display, and press Ⓐ. If you have a current saved game, you will be asked for confirmation before you can adjust the Campaign Scoring setting, as doing so will delete saved progress in the last mission you played.

There are three settings you can choose from. "Off" is the default setting, "Team" activates Campaign Scoring, and keeps a running tally for all participants in co-op sessions. "Free For All", by contrast, keeps a separate total for each player, which lends itself perfectly to cooperative play with a uniquely competitive edge. Both options activate Campaign Scoring for solo play, so you can pick either if you're playing alone.

Scoring Mechanics

When you play a mission with Campaign Scoring active you score points for every kill you make, with a running total appearing in the bottom right-hand corner of the screen. All enemies and vehicles with a driver have a "value", which is immediately added to your total once you dispatch or destroy them.

So far so simple, right? It gets a little more complicated. The feature that makes the Campaign Scoring system so endlessly enjoyable is the inclusion of varied "multipliers", which reward players for their prowess.

- The **Difficulty Multiplier** is governed by your choice to play on Easy, Normal, Heroic or Legendary. If you play on Easy, you will receive a quarter of the usual "base" total for every kill. Therefore, a Brute that would net you 20 points on Normal will only be worth 5 on Easy.

- **Skull Multipliers** can be activated once you find the nine "gold" skulls hidden in Halo 3's Campaign mode (see page 115). Each one introduces handicaps that can make the process of completing a mission far more demanding. As a rule, the tougher the challenge is, the larger the multiplier will generally be.

- **Style Multipliers** are awarded on a per-kill basis, and reward techniques such as grenade sticks, headshots and stealth attacks. It's not just a matter of dispatching all adversaries you encounter — it's *how* you do it that enables you to achieve the highest scores. Note that a small medal will appear near to the score display whenever a Style multiplier is applied.

- A **Time Bonus** is added if you can complete a mission before a set deadline, with the available multiplier decreasing from a maximum 3x (which will triple your total score) to 1x (no bonus at all).

- Finally, note that **Penalties** are imposed every time you die, revert back to a previous checkpoint, or kill an ally. These take your Difficulty and Skull multipliers into account, and are subtracted from your score immediately.

Difficulty, Skull and Style multipliers are all calculated and applied instantly during play; any potential Time Bonus is only awarded once the level ends. If you're wondering how individual kills are scored, the process goes like this:

Points scored for each kill = Unit's base scoring value x (style multiplier + possible second style multiplier) x (difficulty multiplier + skull multipliers)

While you only receive points for enemy deaths that you are directly responsible for when you are on foot, this changes once you jump behind the wheel of a vehicle. Every time a passenger or gunner dispatches an enemy or destroys an occupied Covenant vehicle, you will score points.

Carnage Report

When Campaign Scoring is activated, a Carnage Report screen appears once the mission ends. This provides a more detailed breakdown of your performance in the level (and, if you're playing with friends, how you all fared in relation to each other). You can cycle through the main information pages with 🇱🇧 and 🇷🇧.

Results: Reveals your final score, all active multipliers, and adds a Time Bonus if you have cleared the level within one of four potential deadlines.

Carnage: Details the total number of kills made, plus figures that show how many Betrayals you were responsible for. The K/Friendly column documents how many allies you killed (see the Penalties table to learn how many points you stand to lose), while the Deaths section is fairly self-explanatory — though note that instances where you reverted back to a previous checkpoint also count towards this figure.

Enemy Kills: Offers a more detailed breakdown of the adversaries you have slain. See table Enemy Classes to learn how the "class" categories work.

Enemy Vehicle Kills: Like Enemy Kills, but specific to vehicles. See table Enemy Vehicle Classes for information on vehicle classes.

Points Breakdown: "Medals" reveals the number of times you have been awarded Style Points for killing opponents in specific ways, while "Medal Points" details how many additional points your prowess has earned you. "Normal Pts" is your score minus Style Points, and Points is your total score, but without penalties.

ENEMY CLASSES

Infantry	Most Brute types, Drones, lower-ranking Grunts, shield-bearing Jackals, Carrier Forms, Combat Forms, Sentinels
Specialist	Jump Pack Brutes, Brute Trackers, Brute Stalkers, Brute Bodyguards, Grunts (Heavy & Ultras), Jackal Snipers, Pure Forms
Leader	Brute Captains
Hero	Brute Chieftains

ENEMY VEHICLE CLASSES

Light	Chopper, Ghost, Shade
Standard	Banshee, Prowler
Heavy	Phantom, Wraith
Giant	Scarab

SCORES & MULTIPLIERS

ENEMY SCORES

TYPE	CLASS	BASE VALUE
Brute	Infantry	20
Brute (Jump Pack)	Specialist	30
Brute Bodyguard	Specialist	30
Brute Captain	Leader	50
Brute Chieftain	Hero	150
Brute Stalker	Specialist	30
Brute Tracker	Specialist	30
Drone	Infantry	10
Grunt	Infantry	10
Grunt (Heavy & Ultra)	Specialist	10
Hunter	Specialist	150
Jackal	Infantry	15
Jackal Sniper	Specialist	20
Carrier Form	Infantry	10
Combat Form	Infantry	15
Combat Form (shielded)	Infantry	20
Pure Form: Ranged	Specialist	30
Pure Form: Stalker	Specialist	20
Pure Form: Tank	Specialist	50
Sentinel	Infantry	5

ENEMY VEHICLE SCORES

TYPE	CLASS	BASE VALUE
Banshee	Standard	100
Banshee (ambient)	Standard	50
Chopper	Light	100
Ghost	Light	100
Prowler	Standard	150
Shade	Light	50
Wraith	Heavy	200

DIFFICULTY MULTIPLIERS

SETTING	MULTIPLIER
Easy	0.25
Normal	1.0
Heroic	2.0
Legendary	4.0

SKULL MULTIPLIERS

SKULL	MULTIPLIER
Iron	3
Black Eye	1.5
Tough Luck	1.5
Catch	1.5
Fog	1.5
Famine	2
Thunderstorm	1.5
Tilt	2
Mythic	2

STYLE MULTIPLIERS

TYPE	MULTIPLIER	NOTES
Grenade Stick	1.25	Only counts for the "stuck" enemy, though a Multi-Kill bonus may be awarded if others are taken out by the blast.
Headshot	1.25	Applies to Brutes, Grunts, Jackals, and Combat Forms when you hit the Infection Forms embedded in their chests. Cumulative with EMP.
Stealth Kill	1.25	Only applies if your adversary is completely oblivious to your presence when you land a melee attack.
Road-Kill	1.25	Applied when you dispatch an enemy by slamming them with a vehicle.
Multi-Kill	1.25	Awarded when you kill 3 or more enemies within 1.5 seconds.
Needler Superdetonation	1.25	End an opponent's life with a satisfyingly large Needler-fueled bang, and this bonus is just the icing on the cake.
EMP	1.25	Awarded for killing a Brute or shield-bearing Jackal within 3 seconds of destroying their shields with a charged Plasma Pistol shot or Power Drain.

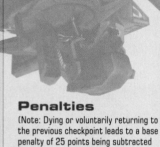

ALLY	BASE PENALTY
Arbiter	50
Elite	50
Marine/Civilian	50
ODST	100
Marine Sergeant	100
Sentinel	5
Hornet	150
Mongoose	50
Pelican	200
Scorpion	200
Warthog	150
Gauss Warthog	100

Penalties

(Note: Dying or voluntarily returning to the previous checkpoint leads to a base penalty of 25 points being subtracted from your score. This total, like those in the table on the right, is subject to the effects of Difficulty and Skull multipliers.)

CAMPAIGN SCORING STRATEGIES & TIPS

If you'd like to score points totals that would inspire a passing googolplex to bow, scrape and tug its forelock in deference, the advice and guidance we offer over the next nine pages will make a good starting point. Before you begin reading, though, here's a quick explanation of the sections you'll encounter.

Achievement Milestone: How many points you'll need to score to unlock that mission's Campaign meta-game Achievement.

Recommended Multiplier: The total multiplier you should aim for to unlock that Achievement. Don't forget that Style multipliers only work on a kill-by-kill basis, whereas the others apply throughout the entire level. Thus, your overall multiplier is mainly the result of the following formula: Total multiplier = (Difficulty multiplier + Skull multiplier) x Time Bonus.

Time Bonus: How quickly you'll need to finish the level to win one of the four possible Time Bonuses.

General Tips: A collection of thoughts, observations, tactics and tricks that can help you maximize your score. We've arranged these in sequential order, beginning at the very start of the mission.

Skull Recommendations: Details (for all four difficulty settings) which skulls work particularly well on each mission (and when they should be avoided), with a three-star rating system providing an at-a-glance guide. The more stars in a cell, the easier it is to play with that skull on the relevant difficulty level. Note that recommended skulls are highlighted for maximum clarity.

SIERRA 117

BASICS

CAMPAIGN

EXTRAS

MULTIPLAYER

LEGENDARY
PRIMER

SKULLS

SCORE SYSTEM

ACHIEVEMENTS

BESTIARY

INVENTORY

VEHICLES

**Guerilla
Achievement Milestone:**
15,000 points

**Recommended
Multiplier:**
4+

TIME BONUS	
0-15 min	3x
15-20 min	2.5x
20-25 min	2x
25-30 min	1.5x

General Tips

• The Marines that fight with you at the start will "steal" a lot of kills. This isn't a massive problem on Legendary, though – you can simply hold back and let the Covenant do their job.

• On Legendary, you have immediate access to Plasma Grenades – and, therefore, grenade stick bonuses.

• The opening battles along the river bank are definitely the most awkward, as you don't have access to a ranged weapon. Though the attraction of EMP/headshot bonuses against the Brutes is high, it's really not worth the penalties if you're subsequently blown back to the previous checkpoint by a crowd of Grunts. On higher difficulty levels, it's probably better to play it safe.

• In the Grunt Camp area, be sure to tap out the Grunt "sleepers" on lower difficulty levels, then focus on gaining Needler and EMP/headshot bonuses for the rest of the fight. On Legendary, dispatch all Grunts and Jackal snipers with Carbine headshots, then use the Plasma Pistol/Magnum combo on the remaining Brutes and Shield Jackals. Be quick – the Arbiter is a veritable points thief in this battle.

• Be sure to make an EMP/headshot kill on the Brute Captain interrogating the Marine, but watch out for the Jackal sniper on Legendary.

• When you reach the Sub-station area, you can run over and try to dispatch the two nearest Brutes for EMP/headshot bonuses. On Legendary, this is much more risky – you'll need to get back behind cover and dispatch the Jackal snipers before the Pelicans are attacked by Banshees.

• Kill all Grunts with headshots before you move over to the second part of the Sub-station area. Once the Brutes pull back around the corner leading to Sniper Alley on Legendary, err on the side of caution – they have Brute Shots, and are protected by a distant sniper with a Beam Rifle.

• In the area that follows the sniper duel, there is a Chieftain riding aboard the Phantom that hovers briefly beside Johnson's crashed Pelican. If you still have Beam Rifle ammunition, it's possible to kill him – though attempting this is a real gamble on higher difficulty levels.

• At the dam, you can focus on dispatching snipers and Grunts, then drop down to maximize your points by engaging Brutes and shield-bearing Jackals with EMP/headshot kills. It's prudent to kill the Chieftain with your Sniper Rifle before you drop down, though…

• After freeing Johnson and the Marines, run into position at the end of the dam and try to kill as many enemies as you can before the Pelican arrives.

SKULL RECOMMENDATIONS

SKULL	RECOMMENDATIONS				TIPS
	EASY	NORMAL	HEROIC	LEGENDARY	
Iron	★★★	★★	★	★	The opening battles are tough, yet it's definitely possible on Legendary. The snipers that appear from the Sub-station area onwards are the principle danger.
Black Eye	★★★	★★★	★★	★	Though torturously difficult on Legendary, this is probably the best Covenant-oriented level to use it on.
Tough Luck	★★★	★★★	★★★	★★	A strongly recommended choice (and especially so on lower difficulty levels, given that you can't use grenades until a third of the way through the mission). You have access to all the weapons you need after the opening battles, and there are no large packs of Brutes to worry about.
Catch	★★★	★★	★★	★★	The opening battles on Legendary are extremely chaotic, but you can usually dispatch all Grunts from distance in subsequent fights. As an added bonus, Brutes don't use Spike Grenades until the second mission.
Fog	★★★	★★★	★★★	★★	It definitely makes a couple of confrontations more difficult (particularly the opening fracas along the river bank and the fight that takes place as you approach Johnson's crashed Pelican), but Fog is another good choice for Sierra 117.
Famine	★★★	★★	★★	★★	The presence of Covenant dispensers throughout the mission helps, but the reduced ammunition for key weapons (particularly the Battle Rifle, Sniper Rifle and Magnum) means that you'll need to make every shot count.
Thunderstorm	★★★	★★★	★★★	★★	Though the thrill of a field promotion fills Grunts with an alarming enthusiasm for their work, most Brutes on this level are already Captains. If you focus on EMP/headshot kills against them, Thunderstorm offers significant points dividends.
Tilt	★★★	★★★	★★	★★	As there are plenty of Plasma Pistols and no large groups of Brutes, this is one of the better missions to play with Tilt activated. You'll need to secure a Beam Rifle to take down the Chieftain when you reach the Dam, however.
Mythic	★★★	★★★	★★	★★	As you should be aiming exclusively for lethal headshots, Mythic doesn't have a massive effect during Sierra 117. That said, the battles along the riverside at the start are much tougher.

Demon
Achievement Milestone:
15,000 points

Recommended Multiplier:
4+

TIME BONUS	
0-20 min	3x
20-25 min	2.5x
25-30 min	2x
35-40 min	1.5x

General Tips

- When you face the large group of charging Grunts in the road corridor en route to the South Hangar, try making a deft thumbstick flick as you fire the Battle Rifle to take down three at once for a welcome bonus.

- Kill the first two Jackals in the South Hangar with the Magnum/Plasma Pistol combo. Survival is more important than multipliers in the battle that follows on higher difficulty levels – if you don't concentrate on efficient crowd control, you'll be quickly overwhelmed. That doesn't mean that you shouldn't attempt to make every kill a headshot (or, in the case of nearby Brutes, a grenade stick), though.

- There are two Plasma Pistols in the Motor Pool area, so put them to good use. When Brutes rush forward, it's safer to kill the first couple with a grenade stick on Legendary. You can usually fight the remaining foes one at a time after that point.

- Take a Plasma Pistol with you to the Barracks, and be sure to secure the two held by the Jackals on the upper walkway as soon as you can. The concentration of Brutes here means that you need to be patient, and carefully make EMP/headshot kills.

- This is a morbid tip, but if you wait for the Brutes to execute their Marine captives, you won't have to worry about them stealing your targets during the Barracks battle or the Landing Pad Bravo

confrontation that follows. In single-player sessions, you already have to worry about the Arbiter busying himself with the process of reducing your potential point total.

- If you're confident in your abilities, take the two Plasma Pistols dropped by the second pair of Jackals in the Barracks into the elevator rather than the Chieftain's Plasma Turret. You'll have to be patient to secure EMP/headshot kills on the Jump Pack Brutes, and the Arbiter will be a nuisance throughout, but the multipliers soon stack up.

- As you make your way back to the Ops Center to rearm the bomb, grab a fresh Plasma Pistol – the shield-bearing Jackals you encounter are a ready source of EMP and headshot multipliers, though be careful not to fall afoul of the Grunt turret operators. (When you finish the Ops Center battle, take the Chieftain's Fuel Rod Gun – we'll tell you why in a moment.)

- After rearming the bomb, speed run aficionados will find that they can sprint to the final elevator without stopping to fire a single shot on lower difficulty levels. You'll need to pick both your fights and your route through the roadway and final South Hangar battle more carefully on Legendary, though – the Grunts and Jackals are much more aggressive.

- The panicking Grunts in the room where you fought the Drones earlier can be tricky to kill with headshots as they run back and forth. If you have your heart set on a speed multiplier, it may be better to just kill those you can get a clear shot at as you run through.

- If you took our advice and brought the Fuel Rod Gun along, you can use it to annihilate the group of Drones that fly by as you reach the roadway during the final journey to the Hangar.

- When you reach the Hangar, you could squeeze a few final points out of this mission by aiming to secure an EMP/headshot bonus with each Jackal.

SKULL RECOMMENDATIONS

SKULL	RECOMMENDATIONS				TIPS
	EASY	NORMAL	HEROIC	LEGENDARY	
Iron	★★★	★★	★	★	It's definitely worth an attempt on Normal. If you're crazy or gifted enough to try on higher difficulty levels, watch out for the two snipers when you visit the Ops Center for the third time.
Black Eye	★★	★	★	★	There are a number of battles in the Crow's Nest level that make Black Eye an extremely poor choice on Heroic and Legendary – particularly the swarm of Drones on the journey to the Ops Center after clearing the South Hangar.
Tough Luck	★★★	★★★	★★★	★★	It's a minor inconvenience for a 1.5 multiplier. You may as well activate it as standard, though you'll miss "easy" grenade sticks on Legendary.
Catch	★★	★★	★	★	Enclosed spaces + Catch = explosive headaches. It's always amusing, of course (the very first fight against the Grunts on the roadway is but a taste of things to come), but it's just not practical if you're looking for big scores. Plus, playing with Catch active slows your progress to a crawl, so you can kiss time multipliers goodbye.
Fog	★★★	★★★	★★★	★★★	If you know the level well, Fog should be on as standard. You'll need to be vigilant while fighting in the Motor Pool and Barracks (especially against their respective Chieftains), but there are no real instances where you're likely to be attacked from behind without prior warning.
Famine	★★★	★★★	★★	★★	Crow's Nest bulges at the seams with Marine weaponry on dispensers that are exempt from the Famine effect, but you'll miss having full Plasma Pistols in the Motor Pool, Barracks and on Landing Pad Bravo. If you're lousy at securing EMP/headshot bonuses but fully at home with the Battle Rifle, this is an excellent choice.
Thunderstorm	★★★	★★★	★★	★★	Thunderstorm is generally less appropriate on levels that feature a heavy Brute presence, but it's definitely a skull you can deal with on Crow's Nest.
Tilt	★★	★★	★★	★	With a Plasma Pistol or Plasma Rifle and a Magnum, the numerous Brutes you face aren't a problem. With a Battle Rifle in reserve, neither are Grunts and Jackals. The first two Chieftains you face, however, are overwhelmingly tough – especially the one in the Motor Pool. On Legendary, you'll need to use the Grav Lifts cleverly to even stand a chance of surviving.
Mythic	★★★	★★	★	★	If you're accomplished at using a Plasma Pistol with a Magnum or Battle Rifle, it's certainly worth a try on higher difficulty levels. Again, though, the fights against the Chieftains are extremely demanding.

TSAVO HIGHWAY

BASICS

CAMPAIGN

EXTRAS

MULTIPLAYER

LEGENDARY PRIMER

SKULLS

SCORE SYSTEM

ACHIEVEMENTS

BESTIARY

INVENTORY

VEHICLES

Cavalier Achievement Milestone:
15,000 points

Recommended Multiplier:
4+

TIME BONUS	
0-15 min	3x
15-20 min	2.5x
20-25 min	2x
25-30 min	1.5x

General Tips

- Up to and including the battle in front of the crashed Phantom, all enemies are easy meat for Road-Kill multipliers. Skilled players will use handbrake turns for additional Multi-Kill bonuses where possible. If you're aiming for thoroughness over speed, collect grenades as you find them — they'll come in useful later.

- If you're on a speed run, you can drive straight from the beginning through to the Pelican Crash Site area in one continuous drive. Naturally, the challenge increases in accordance with your chosen difficulty level.

- Though you can cause havoc on Easy and Normal, the Covenant blockade at the dry lake bed is extremely dangerous on Heroic and Legendary. Instead, you'll need to barge your way through as quickly as possible, park behind the small dam to give your shields a moment to recharge, then hop out to clear the area with a stolen Beam Rifle (and, with the Shade turrets, grenades). It's a dangerous fight, but worth every last point.

- When you reach the crashed Pelican, the Fuel Rod Gun-wielding Chieftain is your absolute priority. If you're worried about your Marine companions stealing valuable points, you can leave your Warthog in the open before dashing for cover. Just pray that no witnesses survive to report the event...

- Once you've dispatched the Chieftain from range (you did remember to bring a fresh Beam Rifle, didn't you?), be content with headshots against the assorted snipers and infantry in this area. In the Campaign chapter, we advise players to capture one of the two Choppers to make later battles much easier on Legendary, but there's no reason why you can't destroy both if you're searching for maximum points throughout. If you do, use the Fuel Rod Gun or grenade tags to destroy the Shade turrets.

- On speed runs, you definitely need to secure a Chopper at this point; you can boost it over the broken road section and choose to bypass later enemies entirely on lower difficulty levels.

- The huge set-piece battle just off the highway can be exceedingly tough on Heroic and Legendary. If you're determined to secure every last point in this lengthy confrontation, try stockpiling Plasma Pistols in the buildings before the Phantom bearing the first batch of reinforcements arrives.

- On the final stretch of road use the Chopper to divest Brutes of their power armor, then jump out and finish them off with headshots. If you planned ahead and brought a Plasma Pistol along, you can also aim to make some valuable EMP/headshot kills.

SKULL RECOMMENDATIONS

SKULL	RECOMMENDATIONS				TIPS
	EASY	NORMAL	HEROIC	LEGENDARY	
Iron	★★★	★★	★	★	It's just about possible on Heroic, but any sane individual wouldn't even want to *think* about attempting an Iron playthrough on Legendary.
Black Eye	★★	★	★	★	Black Eye really isn't compatible with vehicle-oriented missions. You can enjoy a degree of success up until the fight against the Choppers just before you reach the Roundabout area, but you'll need to play perfectly to reach the next group of melee-friendly infantry. Is the stress and hardship worth a 1.5 multiplier? We think not.
Tough Luck	★★★	★★★	★★	★★	Grenades don't figure highly in this mission. The only time you might need them is during the main battle just off the highway, and only then on Legendary or Heroic.
Catch	★★★	★★	★★	★★	It's fun on all difficulty settings, but you'll definitely benefit by taking a Chopper to use in Tsavo Highway's main battle. If you're looking for a high score, though, leave this firmly and resolutely disabled.
Fog	★★★	★★★	★★	★★	The big fight in the center of the level is much harder without the Motion Tracker, and combat involving Choppers is also filled with fraught moments. You can address these issues by using the Chopper-related tips (how to get one over the break in the highway, and long-distance cannon shooting at the Roundabout area) in the walkthrough.
Famine	★★★	★★	★★	★★	If you favor the Chopper-oriented strategy for the second half of Tsavo Highway (see above), having Famine active is no great hardship.
Thunderstorm	★★★	★★	★	★	It makes Choppers and Wraiths more difficult to neutralize, and the main battle is a nightmare. We suggest you leave Thunderstorm off for this one unless you're prepared for a really stiff challenge.
Tilt	★★★	★★	★	★	You really need a Chopper for the latter half of the level if you activate Tilt on Heroic or Legendary. Keep a Beam Rifle at the ready to deal with the Chieftains.
Mythic	★★★	★★	★	★	If a Tsavo Highway playthrough filled with adamantine Choppers, and Brutes that shrug off previously withering attacks with stamina to spare sounds like a good time, then good luck to you.

<table>
<tr><td>**Askar**
Achievement Milestone:
15,000 points</td><td colspan="2">**TIME BONUS**</td></tr>
<tr><td rowspan="4">**Recommended**
Multiplier:
4+</td><td>0-15 min</td><td>3x</td></tr>
<tr><td>15-20 min</td><td>2.5x</td></tr>
<tr><td>20-25 min</td><td>2x</td></tr>
<tr><td>25-30 min</td><td>1.5x</td></tr>
</table>

General Tips

- You can pick up a few easy Multi-Kill points with a well-placed grenade when you encounter the first group of Jackals and Grunts viewing the Prophet of Truth's sermon.

- Unless you plan to drive the Warthog or operate its turret, keep the gates closed to minimize the number of kills taken by Marines. On Heroic and Legendary, dispatch the Grunts with your Battle Rifle, but use the Plasma Pistol/Magnum combo on Jackals and Brutes whenever you can.

- Not dying is more important than style multipliers at Lake Bed A, especially on Legendary. Simply hijack and use the Wraith in the far corner.

- With a little forward planning, you can save Missile Pod ammunition to destroy the two Banshees that arrive before they are shot down by the Hornet.

- If you're willing to take the risk, it's possible to secure EMP/headshot combo bonuses against the Jackals and Brutes just inside Factory B, but stay out of the Chieftain's line of fire.

- If you pick up a Rocket Launcher before the Drones arrive, you might be able to use it to score additional Multi-Kill points against the swarm. The Drones retreat through the broken skylight after a set period, so be ready to fire after them with a Battle Rifle to gain a few extra kills.

- On lower difficulty settings, drive the Mongoose aggressively when you reach Lake Bed B to reach targets (especially the Wraiths) before the other drivers can catch up. You should then swing around and head for a Missile Turret to target Banshees and the vehicles that are deployed later. On Legendary, there's too much scope for random, unavoidable deaths if you drive around the lake bed, so it's better to head straight for a turret.

- When the Scarab arrives, take the elevator to the top of the crane nearest the door and use the Sniper Rifle there to secure as many headshots as you can. Once its crew has been eliminated, jump on board to destroy its engine core.

- If you plan ahead by locating and carrying a couple of Plasma Pistols from Lake Bed B into the Warehouse area, you can use them to win massive style points against the Brutes you face there. It's tougher on Heroic and Legendary, of course, but the rewards are considerable.

- Marines are an issue inside the Warehouse, but the Arbiter's presence means that there's little point in waiting for the Brutes to slaughter them before you attack. Speed and accuracy is the solution, though it won't hurt to look the other way should a Marine need your help. It's also beneficial to callously stand by as the Hunters slaughter everyone when they enter. If you can shoot at their unprotected backs as they make jam out of their doomed quarry, all the better.

- In the final battles, it's better to be satisfied with headshot multipliers on higher difficulty levels — it's often too risky to try for anything more.

- If you're willing to make the effort, you can haul a Missile Pod all the way from Lake Bed B to the final battle to use against the "ambient" Banshees circling overhead.

SKULL RECOMMENDATIONS

SKULL	RECOMMENDATIONS				TIPS
	EASY	NORMAL	HEROIC	LEGENDARY	
Iron	★★★	★★	★	★	As usual: you have almost no hope on Legendary, but it's eminently achievable on Normal.
Black Eye	★★	★★	★	★	It's worth a shot on Normal — the Lake Bed A and (to a lesser extent) Lake Bed B fights are tough, but there are ways and means at your disposal to get through them.
Tough Luck	★★★	★★★	★★★	★★	Sacrificing the full potential of your grenade arsenal in return for an increased multiplier is a savvy move, though EMP/headshot kills will be tougher to win.
Catch	★★★	★★	★★	★★	Factory A and the Warehouse are more difficult, but Catch is an invigorating addition if speed isn't of the essence.
Fog	★★★	★★	★★	★★	The battles on Lake Bed A and B can be awkward, and you'll need to be extremely methodical during the final battle to hunt down and destroy Grunts and Jackals.
Famine	★★★	★★★	★★	★★	There are quite a few Marine weapon dispensers to find, but having reduced ammunition in certain important weapons is a real handicap.
Thunderstorm	★★★	★★★	★★	★	The Lake Bed A and B battles are obviously more painful with Thunderstorm active, and the Warehouse fights against Brutes are also more demanding. You'll particularly learn to loathe the Ghosts and Choppers on Legendary.
Tilt	★★★	★★	★	★	As long as you can keep a Plasma Pistol or Plasma Rifle with you at all times, Brutes (particularly those in the Warehouse) aren't much harder than usual to beat. The Chieftains, by contrast, can be *very* tough.
Mythic	★★★	★★	★	★	Again, the principle issues you face with Mythic are that vehicles are harder to destroy, and marauding Chieftains can take much longer to wear down. You'll need to make the most of the Sniper Rifles you can find to beat the last two.

FLOODGATE

BASICS

CAMPAIGN

EXTRAS

MULTIPLAYER

LEGENDARY PRIMER

SKULLS

SCORE SYSTEM

ACHIEVEMENTS

BESTIARY

INVENTORY

VEHICLES

Exterminator Achievement Milestone: 15,000 points	TIME BONUS	
	0-10 min	3x
Recommended Multiplier: 6+	10-15 min	2.5x
	15-20 min	2x
	20-25 min	1.5x

General Tips

- You can actually kill a few of the Combat Forms fighting Marines in the distance shortly after the mission begins.

- When the Combat Forms first attack, attract their attention and aim for successive Multi-Kills with the Gravity Hammer. You need to dispatch as many of them as you can this way before the Arbiter gets involved.

- Inside the Warehouse, stand at the top of the steps to the right of the office and use the Battle Rifle to score "headshot" bonuses. Dispatch large groups with Frag Grenades or the Gravity Hammer to reap Multi-Kill rewards.

- Stick to the Battle Rifle in the next Warehouse area, and allow Infection Forms to reanimate Combat Forms. The more targets you have to shoot, the better. Don't bother taking the Flamethrower – it's of no use to you until you encounter Pure Forms.

- The Combat Form ambush in the rusty, winding corridor is an easy Multi-Kill opportunity if you still have the Gravity Hammer.

- When the Elites land, view the ensuing fight from afar and utter a silent prayer that the Flood get the upper hand.

- At the bottom of the slope that leads out of the dry lake bed, again concentrate on "headshot" bonuses. You'll need to be quick – the Arbiter and any surviving Elites won't hesitate to steal your kills. With any luck, the Infection Forms released by the two Carrier Forms when they topple will revive a few additional Combat Forms.

- Accurate long-range marksmanship will enable you to restrict the Arbiter to a few "lucky" kills in the first area of Factory B. In the confrontation that follows, a group of Combat Forms will drop down from above, providing a clean and simple Multi-Kill bonus.

- Collect the Flamethrower before you head outside – short of grenade sticks, there really is no better way to kill Pure Forms during this mission.

- If Elite reinforcements arrive, there's nothing you can do about it. Just grit your teeth and make all the kills you can.

- If you're close enough to make an easy throw, grenade sticks are the most profitable way to dispatch the Ranged Forms as you work your way over to the crashed Flood vessel.

Flood Scoring Tips

- The Battle Rifle should be your constant companion throughout Flood-oriented missions, as it's the key to high scores. You achieve "headshot" multipliers by shooting the Infection Form inside a Combat Form's chest.

- There is no score for shooting Infection Forms. They're a nuisance, but try to lead them towards corpses they can reanimate.

- As with later missions that feature the Flood, scoring highly with Pure Forms is a matter of balancing ambition and greed with the need to be practical. Ideally, you will always hope to face Tank Forms, as these yield the most points and are easily slain with a Flamethrower. However, if you purposefully avoid shooting the least-valuable Stalker Forms, they are just as likely to transform into the excruciatingly irritating (and lethal) Ranged Forms. On Legendary, it's usually best to just make the kill and live to fight another day.

- Shielded Combat Forms (most commonly encountered on Legendary and Heroic) should be dispatched with a secondary weapon – just accept the lower points total, and don't waste Battle Rifle ammunition on their shields. Unlike with other Combat Forms, you should ensure that their bodies are destroyed before you move on.

SKULL RECOMMENDATIONS

SKULL	RECOMMENDATIONS				TIPS
	EASY	NORMAL	HEROIC	LEGENDARY	
Iron	★★★	★★★	★★	★★	This is arguably the easiest mission to complete on Legendary with Iron active. You'll need to be extremely cautious, move at a snail's pace at all times (bar the moments where you choose to run away, of course), and let the Arbiter (plus Elites, if they survive) do the hard work for you.
Black Eye	★★★	★★★	★★	★★	Floodgate seems almost tailor-made for the Black Eye skull. There are times when caution is important (Lake Bed B, Factory B and Lake Bed A in particular), but you can make your way through the entire mission with a Gravity Hammer and an Energy Sword. Naturally, you should use the Battle Rifle to score headshot multipliers when it's practical to do so, especially during the early encounters before Combat Forms begin wielding weapons.
Tough Luck	★★★	★★★	★★★	★★★	You may lose a few Multi-Kill bonuses, but grenades really aren't a vital part of your arsenal in the Floodgate mission. Note that the Tough Luck skull has no effect on Ranged Forms.
Catch	★★★	★★★	★★★	★★★	As Flood don't use grenades, Catch is effectively a way to collect "free" points. Activate it as standard once you locate the skull in Campaign mode.
Fog	★★★	★★	★★	★★	With Infection Forms insinuating their way into corpses all over the battlefield, and Combat Forms capable of leaping into the fray from all directions, the loss of your Motion Tracker definitely hurts more than usual. You'll miss it most during the final approach to the Flood ship.
Famine	★★★	★★★	★★	★	You need very specific weapons to deal with the Flood on higher difficulty levels, and Famine's effect can be quite devastating, particularly during the second half of the mission. On Legendary, this is a skull you should only activate if you know the Floodgate level extremely well.
Thunderstorm	★★★	★★★	★★	★★	Thunderstorm increases the number of shielded Combat Forms you encounter, but they don't tend to enter the fray until very late in the mission. Enable it for all Floodgate high score attempts.
Tilt	★★★	★★★	★★	★★	Shielded Combat Forms are far more difficult to deal with, and there's no doubting that Pure Forms (particularly Ranged Forms and Tank Forms) are more difficult to kill with anything but the best weapons.
Mythic	★★★	★★	★★	★★	If you're going to attempt any Flood mission with Mythic active, make it this one. You don't encounter Pure Forms until the end, and Combat Forms can be dispatched in the usual Campaign Scoring style (that is, with a Carbine or Battle Rifle) with little effort.

Demon
Achievement Milestone:
50,000 points

Recommended Multiplier:
4+

TIME BONUS	
0-20 min	3x
20-30 min	2.5x
30-40 min	2x
40-50 min	1.5x

General Tips

- Once you have reduced enemy numbers during the first sniper battle, it's possible (though dangerous) to move closer and collect a Plasma Pistol to kill Brutes with EMP/headshot combos.

- If you're well versed in the art of fighting Hunters, try to finish off the pair you face after the second sniper battle by sticking them with grenades. It takes a fairly intimate understanding of their total stamina on your chosen difficulty level to pick the right moment (especially on Heroic and Legendary), but even a wild guess is worth a try.

- Have a couple of Plasma Pistols at the ready when the two Prowlers arrive. The Brutes dropped off are a relatively easy source of EMP/headshot bonuses.

- Follow the guidance on page 74 to, with the help of a few Marines, turn a Prowler into an intimidating weapons platform. The rewards are significant, especially if the Marine with the Rocket Launcher can get enemy vehicles in his sights.

- After Johnson arrives in his Pelican, set off immediately — if you dawdle, the Sentinels will attack the two Ghosts that race to intercept you.

- Once you acquire a Scorpion, aim to stay ahead of the other vehicles at all times. You should definitely be able to destroy the enemy vehicles and the pair of Hunters that attack as you drive down the slope.

- Don't take the short-cut of leaping over the edge when the Gauss Warthog arrives. For top scores, you really need to dispatch the Ghosts on the cliff path and the infantry at the bottom. This is most easily accomplished if you take control of the Gauss cannon, but you'll need to be lethally precise and enjoy a little fortuity on Legendary.

- The journey down the main slope is packed with high-scoring targets (particularly Wraiths), but be cautious on higher difficulty levels — even in a Scorpion, a solitary Ghost or Chopper can be your undoing if you drive with careless haste towards your targets.

- After "tapping out" the Grunts and stealth-killing the Brutes in the two rooms inside the Cartographer building, take a Plasma Pistol with you to the next chamber. On Heroic and Legendary, you can score an impressive number of EMP/headshot bonuses against the Brutes and Jackals located there.

- On the return journey through the same room, EMP/headshot kills are still possible as you fight the reinforcements, but the presence of a Chieftain makes it much more hazardous.

- You can score EMP/headshot kills against the camouflaged Brute Stalkers, but you'll need to fire the charged Plasma Pistol shot at close range to hit them.

- Take the two Plasma Pistols dropped by the Jackals into the final confrontation. If you deal with the Chieftain first, you can really boost your points total by killing the Jump Pack Brutes for EMP/headshot bonuses.

SKULL RECOMMENDATIONS

SKULL	RECOMMENDATIONS				TIPS
	EASY	NORMAL	HEROIC	LEGENDARY	
Iron	★★★	★★	★	★	Being one of the longest missions in Halo 3 (it's second only to The Covenant in this respect), The Ark is a real challenge for connoisseurs of the Iron skull. Hardcore experts will definitely feel they have a chance of beating it on Legendary, but certain battles later in the level — specifically the section leading up to and including the fight against the Scarab — make it a task suited to the type of flaming ninja that all other flaming ninjas discuss in hushed tones.
Black Eye	★★	★	★	★	Not recommended. Seriously: the combination of Black Eye and vehicular combat is bad at the best of times, but it's ridiculous in a mission where you spend much of your time in a slow-moving tank with no infantry in sight.
Tough Luck	★★★	★★★	★★★	★★★	There is one battle in a cramped room inside the Cartographer building where you might lament the fact that your opponents are more inclined to scatter on cue as you throw a grenade — but only for an extremely fleeting moment. Given the lack of potential for Plasma Pistol/headshot kills, this is an excellent choice.
Catch	★★★	★★★	★★	★★	This only really has an effect on the battles that take place before you get your hands on a vehicle, and the final section inside the Cartographer building (which can be quite unpleasant on Legendary). Catch is definitely a reasonable choice on The Ark.
Fog	★★★	★★★	★★	★★	You probably won't even notice that the Motion Tracker isn't there until you pass through the Shield Wall. At that point onward, you'll miss its presence quite keenly.
Famine	★★★	★★★	★★	★★	With a little forward planning, Famine's effect is really quite negligible during this mission — indeed, it's probably worth activating on all Campaign Scoring playthroughs once you know the level well.
Thunderstorm	★★★	★★	★	★	On higher difficulty levels it's clearly a struggle during the vehicle-oriented battles, and you'll need to make every shot count in the early sniper battles.
Tilt	★★★	★★	★★	★★	As it can take half-a-dozen Sniper Rifle shots to take down a Brute Captain on Legendary, you'll need to play the opening confrontations in an entirely different way, dispatching Grunts and Jackals before moving in to fight the Brutes at close quarters. Thereafter, you always have access to plasma weaponry, and there are tricks and techniques you can use to dispatch both Chieftains with relative ease. If you're playing to secure maximum EMP/headshot bonuses, this skull is a must.
Mythic	★★★	★★	★★	★	If you read the entries for both Thunderstorm and Tilt, you'll get a fairly clear idea of what to expect with Mythic enabled (though, admittedly, your Sniper Rifle ammo will last a little longer). Only Plasma Pistol specialists should activate this skull on higher difficulty levels.

HALO 3

BASICS
CAMPAIGN
EXTRAS
MULTIPLAYER

LEGENDARY PRIMER
SKULLS
SCORE SYSTEM
ACHIEVEMENTS
BESTIARY
INVENTORY
VEHICLES

THE COVENANT

Vanguard Achievement Milestone:
50,000 points

Recommended Multiplier:
4+

TIME BONUS	
0-20 min	3x
20-30 min	2.5x
30-40 min	2x
40-50 min	1.5x

General Tips

- Remaining in one piece is of paramount importance during the opening battle on higher difficulty levels. It's definitely possible to dispatch the first Brute for an EMP/headshot bonus, but you'll need to hurry to kill Grunts before your allies can take them down, though.

- As per the tip on page 86 of the Campaign chapter, arming the Marine riding shotgun in the Warthog with your Spartan Laser on Legendary is a vital tactic. If you want to secure maximum points for destroying the Wraith in front of the first tower, though, you should take a Fuel Rod Gun along as well.

- You can score a few grenade stick and Multi-Kill bonuses against the Covenant troops inside the entry hall.

- After clearing the way to the elevator, ensure that you have a Magnum (they're available in the drop pods just outside the tower) to go with a Plasma Pistol, with a Beam Rifle in reserve. You can use the latter to dispatch the Chieftain in the upper tower room, then switch to the dual wield combo to take down Brutes for maximum points.

- Fight aggressively in the aerial engagement to prevent your allies from reducing your potential points. Don't forget to destroy the Anti-Air Wraith (and, on higher difficulty levels, the Brutes) when you fly over the small island.

- The landing pad zone is packed with easy points, but be very careful when the Elite dropship lands – you should avoid friendly kills at all costs.

- When the Brutes run out from inside the tower, it's possible to plant a Power Drain through the entrance and follow it up with a Frag Grenade for a Multi-Kill bonus. There's no room for error, though – if you're not superlatively swift, you'll lose the potential EMP bonus. You may prefer to run in front of the door (though out of the blue field, of course) and try to get a few headshots instead.

- On Heroic and Legendary, stand back and let the Hunters bludgeon and blast the Elites into oblivion before you step in to kill them. They'll generally knock the Arbiter unconscious too.

- The Brutes that you face as you make your way to the elevator are ripe for Plasma Pistol/headshot takedowns.

- If you're following the strategy suggested in the Campaign chapter, and have brought a Beam Rifle along to use against the Chieftain in the top tower room, you'll be interested to note that the soldier that usually rides as a passenger on your Hornet carries a Magnum. If you can find him – or, more likely, his corpse – and grab the gun, you can kill the Chieftain with ease with the Beam Rifle, and also score EMP/headshot bonuses against the Brute Stalkers.

- When the Flood arrive, aim for "headshot" and Multi-Kill bonuses; against shielded Combat Forms, grenade tags work best. As in most Flood battles, wait for Infection Forms to reanimate corpses to increase your score.

- There are a couple of "ambient" Banshees that you can destroy as you make your way down the snowy slope in the Scorpion.

- Be thorough in the Scarab battle – don't miss a single enemy, and watch out for the vehicle reinforcements that arrive once the first Scarab falls.

- The confrontations in the Ring Room leading to the Prophet of Truth are too hectic on higher difficulty levels to make EMP/headshot multipliers worth the risk. Instead, favor a ranged weapon for headshots, and a Needler for Superdetonation rewards, especially in the second section.

- When the Flood attacks, use a ranged weapon against standard Combat Forms to score "headshot" multipliers, and a melee weapon (or, ideally, grenade tags) against shielded varieties. If ammunition is an issue, you can try for Needler bonuses instead. Try to extend the battle for as long as you can – the more that Infection Forms reanimate bodies, the better.

SKULL RECOMMENDATIONS

SKULL	EASY	NORMAL	HEROIC	LEGENDARY	TIPS
Iron	★★★	★★	★	★	It's the longest mission of all, but there are no flashpoints where regular deaths could be described as a certainty for elite players, even on Legendary. We'd single out the fight against Hunters and Drones in the second tower as the most potentially dangerous encounter.
Black Eye	★★	★	★	★	It's possible on the lower difficulty levels, but we wouldn't care to try it.
Tough Luck	★★★	★★★	★★★	★★★	The inconvenience is a small price to pay for the 1.5 multiplier on this vehicle-heavy mission.
Catch	★★★	★★	★★	★	It makes the first part of the opening battle quite hellish on Heroic and Legendary, and all indoor sections are extremely unpredictable. Not recommended if a high score is your objective.
Fog	★★★	★★★	★★	★★	Until you know the level like the back of your hand, it's better to leave this skull disabled.
Famine	★★★	★★★	★★	★★	The second of the two towers you visit is definitely harder, especially on Legendary, but the rewards are worth the additional effort and forward planning.
Thunderstorm	★★★	★★	★★	★★	A good choice for skilled players – it slows your progress to a crawl in places, but the extra points are more than adequate compensation.
Tilt	★★★	★★	★★	★★	If you use Plasma Pistols or Needlers against Brutes, and Beam Rifles against the first two Chieftains, you'll barely notice that the skull is active during most confrontations.
Mythic	★★★	★★	★★	★	As above, but enemy vehicles are also tougher to destroy. The fight against the two Hunters and the swarm of Drones is a decidedly unpleasant experience on Legendary.

Orpheus
Achievement Milestone:
15,000 points

Recommended
Multiplier:
6+

TIME BONUS	
0-15 min	3x
15-20 min	2.5x
20-25 min	2x
25-30 min	1.5x

General Tips

- In the first two areas, allow the Infection Forms to reanimate the corpses, though be wary of shielded Combat Forms on Heroic and Legendary. Collect a Carbine if you can find one for headshot bonuses.

- When there are no nearby threats and you find standard (that is, not shielded) Combat Form corpses nearby, pop the nearest wall-mounted sac filled with Infection Forms — they'll hopefully revive the cadavers if you lead the way towards them.

- In the Pelican Hill area, it's difficult to manage the Flood in a way that enables you to maximize your points total. You should still set up your base of operations in the outside area beside the Pelican, but try to lure enemies in gradually, and don't take unnecessary risks. A Needler yields the highest scores when you use it against Ranged Forms and Tank Forms. If you're willing to push your luck a little, topple the Carrier Forms near the exit and lead the Infection Forms to corpses before you push forward.

- In the small chamber littered with grenades, leave the Infection Forms alone, and prepare yourself for the mini onslaught of Combat Forms that ensues.

- In the Bridge area, a constant trickle of Infection Forms will enter once you have neutralized the initial Flood occupants. Lead them to corpses to "recycle" Combat Forms.

- There are a number of Cloaking devices situated in and between the Bridge and the Reactor Room. You can employ these during speed runs to skip lengthy confrontations.

- The Hive is difficult enough to pass through at the best of times, but you can use the Carbines on the dispenser by the door to increase the number of points gained by shooting unshielded Combat Forms.

- In the Reactor Room, be careful not to knock any Flood into the abyss unless you kill them with the shot that propels them over the edge.

- During the escape run, you should again lure Infection Forms over to prone Combat Forms to revive them.

- When you return to Pelican Hill, a more aggressive and direct approach will prevent the Arbiter from reducing your potential points tally. This may not be worth the risk on Heroic or Legendary when you are pitted against Ranged Forms, though.

SKULL RECOMMENDATIONS

SKULL	EASY	NORMAL	HEROIC	LEGENDARY	TIPS
Iron	★★★	★★	★	★	We would rather set fire to our feet and dance a tango than bother with an attempt on Legendary.
Black Eye	★★★	★★	★	★	It's achievable, for certain, but Ranged Forms become an even greater torment. If you think you can endure the stress and frustration they cause, give it a try – but don't say we didn't warn you...
Tough Luck	★★★	★★★	★★★	★★★	You may lose a few potential Multi-Kill points, but the effect is negligible. In the close confines of certain tunnels and small chambers, it's also worth noting that the Flood doesn't really have anywhere to dive to.
Catch	★★★	★★★	★★★	★★★	It's a consequence-free multiplier. Activate it.
Fog	★★★	★★	★	★	When it can be hard enough to know where *you* are at times while grinding your way through the Flood labyrinth, disabling the Motion Tracker is only something you should do if you're attempting to achieve an absurdly high score.
Famine	★★★	★★	★	★	As you rely heavily on weapons lost and found during the Cortana mission, Famine's effect limits your ability to use certain essential firearms. It's a fairly poor choice for high score attempts on Legendary, in spite of the 2x multiplier.
Thunderstorm	★★★	★★★	★★	★★	The additional shielded Combat Forms can make your life very frustrating on higher difficulty levels.
Tilt	★★★	★★	★	★	Shielded Combat Forms become a real menace, and Pure Forms (especially the Ranged variety) are an incessant trial unless you can engage them with very specific weapons. You'll need the patience of a saint on Legendary.
Mythic	★★★	★★	★	★	As above.

HALO

BASICS

CAMPAIGN

EXTRAS

MULTIPLAYER

LEGENDARY PRIMER

SKULLS

SCORE SYSTEM

ACHIEVEMENTS

BESTIARY

INVENTORY

VEHICLES

Reclaimer Achievement Milestone: 15,000 points	TIME BONUS	
	0-15 min	3x
Recommended Multiplier: 6+	15-20 min	2.5x
	20-25 min	2x
	25-30 min	1.5x

General Tips

- When the dispersal pods land, save Battle Rifle ammunition for headshot bonuses against standard Combat Forms, and make every shot count. The Rocket Launcher and the nearby Fuel Rod Gun should be used to destroy the shielded variety.

- Without wasting ammunition for essential weapons, you can use firearms that you don't need to kill the Stalker Forms climbing to the upper levels of the tower.

- Grenade sticks or Needler explosions are the most profitable way to dispatch Pure Forms, but keep the Flamethrower at hand for emergencies.

- Use Frag Grenades to score Multi-Kill bonuses against groups of Combat Forms as you make your way to the upper floor.

- On higher difficulty levels, don't concern yourself with multipliers in the battle that takes place while you wait for the door leading to the Control Room to open. Follow the advice offered in the Campaign chapter, and focus on using weapons that destroy Flood with a minimum of fuss.

- To eliminate the maximum number of Combat Forms and Sentinels as you run for the Warthog, you'll need to hurry — pause for a second, and you'll lose valuable points as they wipe each other out.

- You can secure extra points when you face the Carrier Forms by allowing the Infection Forms they release to reanimate any surviving Combat Form bodies, though this probably isn't worth the effort at this stage.

- When you encounter Sentinels during the Warthog run, you can usually afford to slow down just a little as the Arbiter shoots them with the turret.

- The three "roundabout" structures yield additional points. The first is the least profitable (the Infection Forms are worthless, the Carrier Forms too hazardous to hit, and the Sentinels aren't worth a great deal), but the second is packed with Combat Forms. The third structure features Ranged Forms and Tank Forms. Though risky on Heroic and Legendary, try to hit as many of these as you can.

- The tunnel areas feature fewer Combat Forms, but there are definitely some that you can hit if you pick the correct route. Steer well clear of those armed with Fuel Rod Guns in the second tunnel, though.

[SKULL RECOMMENDATIONS]

SKULL	RECOMMENDATIONS				TIPS
	EASY	NORMAL	HEROIC	LEGENDARY	
Iron	★★★	★★	★	★	If you can drive the final Warthog run blindfolded, Iron is worth a try — even on Legendary. You'll need to take every precaution, though, and advance very slowly as you follow the route to the entrance. The fight outside the main doors is ungovernably chaotic on Heroic and Legendary, so you'll almost certainly need to sacrifice the points gained there in favor of safety and security in some hidden, Flood-free corner far away. Don't return until Johnson and the Arbiter eventually clear the area — it usually takes around ten minutes on Legendary.
Black Eye	★★	★	★	★	The Warthog run is abysmally hard. Not recommended.
Tough Luck	★★★	★★★	★★★	★★	It's a tactical disadvantage, especially during the main battle outside the entrance on Heroic and Legendary. As skull forfeits go, though, it's fairly minor.
Catch	★★★	★★★	★★★	★★★	Consider it an oblique apology from Bungie for every death you've suffered at the hands of the Ranged Forms.
Fog	★★★	★★	★★	★	While you can keep track of most Combat Forms prior to setting foot on the imposing Forerunner structure, the journey to the entrance is very difficult, especially on Legendary. And as for the battle when you get there — well, it's truly a backs-to-the-walls encounter without a Motion Tracker. Reach the Control Room, and it's plain sailing thereafter.
Famine	★★★	★★★	★★	★	You rely explicitly on weapons dropped by enemies for the first half of the Halo mission, so it's an extremely tough task to reach the Control Room in one piece on Legendary.
Thunderstorm	★★★	★★★	★★	★	Shielded Combat Forms — need we say more? These aren't so bad on the way up, when you can set your own pace, but if you have a penchant for Sisyphean trials, the battle outside the main entrance is deeply unpleasant.
Tilt	★★★	★★	★	★	Shielded Combat Forms and Pure Forms will be the bane of your life before you get inside the Control Room.
Mythic	★★★	★★	★	★	As above, but arguably worse. Even standard Combat Forms will often survive single Brute Shot blasts.

ACHIEVEMENTS

There are 49 Achievements in Halo 3, with a total of 1000 points available overall. The following table reveals which conditions you need to fulfill to unlock each one of them, and of course how many points they're worth.

ACHIEVEMENT	NAME	CONDITION	G	TIPS
I	Landfall	Finish the first mission of the Campaign on Normal, Heroic, or Legendary.	20	These Achievements are simple sequential milestones. Besides, if you're reading this table, then you should have already unlocked them all. If you haven't, leave this chapter and don't come back until you've beaten Halo 3's final level – this chapter is absolutely packed with spoilers, and we'd hate for you to see anything you shouldn't know about yet.
II	Holdout	Finish the second mission of the Campaign on Normal, Heroic, or Legendary.	20	
III	The Road	Finish the third mission of the Campaign on Normal, Heroic, or Legendary.	20	
IV	Assault	Finish the fourth mission of the Campaign on Normal, Heroic, or Legendary.	30	
V	Cleansing	Finish the fifth mission of the Campaign on Normal, Heroic, or Legendary.	30	
VI	Refuge	Finish the sixth mission of the Campaign on Normal, Heroic, or Legendary.	30	
VII	Last Stand	Finish the seventh mission of the Campaign on Normal, Heroic, or Legendary.	40	
VIII	The Key	Finish the eighth mission of the Campaign on Normal, Heroic, or Legendary.	40	
IX	Return	Finish the final mission of the Campaign on Normal, Heroic, or Legendary.	50	
X	Campaign Complete: Normal	Finish the Campaign on Normal.	125	Follow the guidance offered in the main Campaign chapter to unlock these Achievements.
XI	Campaign Complete: Heroic	Finish the Campaign on Heroic (unlocks Achievement for Normal, if not earned).	125	
XII	Campaign Complete: Legendary	Finish the Campaign on Legendary (unlocks Achievements for Normal and Heroic, if not earned).	125	
	Iron	Finish the Campaign on Normal, Heroic, or Legendary, then find and claim this skull.	10	Halo 3's gameplay-altering collectable skulls are discussed on page 114 of this chapter. Refer to that section for more information.
	Black Eye	Finish the Campaign on Normal, Heroic, or Legendary, then find and claim this skull.	10	
	Tough Luck	Finish the Campaign on Normal, Heroic, or Legendary, then find and claim this skull.	10	
	Catch	Finish the Campaign on Normal, Heroic, or Legendary, then find and claim this skull.	10	
	Fog	Finish the Campaign on Normal, Heroic, or Legendary, then find and claim this skull.	10	
	Famine	Finish the Campaign on Normal, Heroic, or Legendary, then find and claim this skull.	10	
	Thunderstorm	Finish the Campaign on Normal, Heroic, or Legendary, then find and claim this skull.	10	
	Tilt	Finish the Campaign on Normal, Heroic, or Legendary, then find and claim this skull.	10	
	Mythic	Finish the Campaign on Normal, Heroic, or Legendary, then find and claim this skull.	10	
	Graduate	Earn 5 EXP or finish 10 games to complete the requirement for basic training (Online).	10	Time, patience and a certain amount of skill are required to unlock these three multiplayer Achievements. See page 148 to learn more about Ratings, and the EXP you need to earn to advance.
	UNSC Spartan	Earn your Sergeant rating to be recognized as a true Spartan (Online).	15	
	Spartan Officer	Advance to the Spartan Officer ranks (Online).	25	
	Two for One	Score a Double Kill with a single Spartan Laser shot in a ranked free for all playlist (Online).	5	If you move as you fire the Spartan Laser, it can create a "fan effect" which can kill multiple opponents simultaneously. Use this technique to unlock this Achievement.
	Too Close to the Sun	Destroy an enemy Banshee with the Spartan Laser or Missile Pod in a ranked playlist or in Campaign.	5	You can unlock this Achievement by playing The Storm in Campaign mode. In the area where Marines attack the Covenant on Mongooses, there are Missile Pods against the long wall, and you shouldn't need to look far to find a Banshee.

HALO 3

BASICS

CAMPAIGN

EXTRAS

MULTIPLAYER

LEGENDARY PRIMER

SKULLS

SCORE SYSTEM

ACHIEVEMENTS

BESTIARY

INVENTORY

VEHICLES

ACHIEVEMENT	NAME	CONDITION	G	TIPS
	Triple Kill	Kill 3 enemies within 4 seconds of one another in a ranked free for all playlist (Online).	5	These two Achievements may seem daunting, but they'll probably happen sooner than you think. It's just a question of being on a map you feel comfortable with, wielding a suitably powerful weapon, and having Lady Luck beam bounteously in your direction.
	Overkill	Kill 4 enemies within 4 seconds of one another in a ranked free for all playlist (Online).	5	
	Lee R Wilson Memorial	Score 5 grenade sticks in any ranked free for all playlist (Online).	5	You have two choices: endeavor to pick this up during general play, or specifically aim to kill with grenade sticks alone, accepting the hit to your Skill level growth if you subsequently have a terrible match.
	We're in for some Chop	Destroy an enemy vehicle with equipment in a ranked playlist or in Campaign.	5	This isn't too difficult – just get creative with Trip Mines, for example during the third Campaign mission.
	Killing Frenzy	Kill 10 enemies without dying in any ranked free for all playlist (Online).	5	For most players, acquiring a vehicle is the key to unlocking this one. A careful, considered rampage in a Banshee, Chopper or Ghost should work, but be prepared to wait – there's no shortcut to bagging this Achievement.
	Steppin' Razor	Score a Triple Kill with an Energy Sword in a ranked free for all playlist (Online).	5	You'll obviously need to be playing on a map that features the Energy Sword, such as Construct or The Pit, to win this one. There's no foolproof way to fulfill the requirement, but being first to arrive at the Energy Sword spawn point at the beginning of a match is a good start.
	Mongoose Mowdown	Splatter an enemy with a Mongoose in a ranked free for all playlist (Online).	5	High Ground and Isolation are good hunting grounds for people seeking this Achievement. You'll need to be driving at top speed, and to hit your target squarely. Oh, and it helps if they don't see you coming – look out for an opponent engaged in a firefight, and ensure your aim is true.
	Up Close and Personal	Kill 5 enemies via melee or assassination in a ranked free for all playlist (Online).	5	If you don't pick this up during your first few weeks of play, it's a warning sign that you're neglecting the melee attack – often the quickest and cleanest way to win close-quarters battles in multiplayer matches. Snowbound and High Ground are good maps to focus on if you're looking to unlock this Achievement. Stay indoors, weaken your opponents with weapons fire while running towards them, then aim to finish each fight with a thundering body blow.
	Fear the Pink Mist	Kill 5 enemies with a Needler in a ranked free for all playlist or in Campaign.	5	Many players will already have this from their first Campaign playthrough. If not, visit the Grunt Camp area of the opening Sierra 117 mission. You'll find a few Needlers and the required number of enemies there.
	Headshot Honcho	Kill 10 enemies with headshots in a ranked free for all playlist or in Campaign.	5	This is obviously much easier to unlock in Campaign mode. Start at Rally Point Bravo on Sierra 117, grab a Sniper Rifle and Battle Rifle from the crashed Pelican, then set up camp on the ledge above the dam area. Take your time, and this one will be extremely simple.
	Used Car Salesman	Destroy a vehicle that has three enemies in it in a ranked playlist or in Campaign.	5	Again, this is easier to complete in Campaign mode. There's a battle on The Ark where two groups of Brutes arrive on Prowlers (see page 75). Playing on Normal (it's less tricky that way), grab the Rocket Launcher from underneath the crashed Pelican, and be ready for their arrival.
	Marathon Man	Locate and access all Terminals in the Campaign.	40	As we document the locations of all Forerunner Terminals in the Campaign chapter, you should have already unlocked this. If not, their locations are highlighted in three mission walkthroughs – The Ark, The Covenant, and Halo.
	MVP	Earn the MVP in any ranked playlist (Online).	5	Being an accolade that acknowledges a truly excellent performance, we can't offer any specific tips on unlocking this Achievement. You'll get your moment of glory eventually. Hopefully, it will be the first of many to come…
	Maybe Next Time Buddy	Board the same vehicle within 10 seconds after being boarded in any free for all playlist (Online).	5	You'll need quick wits to unlock this Achievement. When an opponent hijacks your vehicle, hit the ground running and immediately hold down the "board" button (default RB) as you give chase. It takes a little luck, but you'll crack it one day.
	Guerilla	Score over 15,000 points in the Campaign meta-game on the first mission.	10	Turn to page 116 to learn more about Halo 3's scoring system, including tips on how to unlock these Achievements.
	Demon	Score over 15,000 points in the Campaign meta-game on the second mission.	10	
	Cavalier	Score over 15,000 points in the Campaign meta-game on the third mission.	10	
	Askar	Score over 15,000 points in the Campaign meta-game on the fourth mission.	10	
	Exterminator	Score over 15,000 points in the Campaign meta-game on the fifth mission.	10	
	Ranger	Score over 50,000 points in the Campaign meta-game on the sixth mission.	10	
	Vanguard	Score over 50,000 points in the Campaign meta-game on the seventh mission.	10	
	Orpheus	Score over 15,000 points in the Campaign meta-game on the eighth mission.	10	
	Reclaimer	Score over 15,000 points in the Campaign meta-game on the final mission.	10	

BESTIARY

BRUTES

1 When you destroy its power armor, a Brute's head is its principle weak spot — a single shot from a precision weapon guarantees an immediate kill. Accuracy is everything if you are using a Magnum, though — if you hit a Brute's shoulder (which can happen fairly frequently), the impact will spin it around, making a follow-up shot difficult until it turns to face you again. You can score quicker Brute takedowns with sniper weapons by aiming exclusively for the head.

2 No matter which weapon you use to remove the power armor, it's prudent to have a Magnum, Battle Rifle or Carbine in reserve to end the exchange with a headshot — Brutes can endure massive damage to their bodies before they fall.

3 If a Brute's lower body is unprotected (as is the case with some varieties, and with all types when the power armor is destroyed), you can drop them briefly to their knees by shooting one of their legs with certain weapons — particularly the Magnum, Shotgun and Sniper Rifle. A point-blank Shotgun blast can achieve this even when the power armor is still active. While a Brute is stunned, you can finish it off with a headshot or grenade tag. (You should note, however, that this does not work on berserk Brutes.)

4 Rank-and-file Brutes are equipped with a wide variety of weapons. Spike Rifles and Brute Shots are the most common, but you'll also encounter many Brutes that favor Plasma Rifles, Carbines and, later in the game, Maulers. They throw Spike Grenades frequently, and will intelligently use them to flush you from cover.

5 Brutes use bone-crushing melee attacks at close range, which can disable the Chief's shields in a single blow on Legendary.

6 Don't forget that a single melee attack to a Brute's back is an instant kill.

BRUTE CHIEFTAINS

1 The power armor used by Brute Chieftains is stronger than that used by other Brutes, so you'll also need to shoot their helmets off before you can end a battle with a headshot.

2 Unlike other Brutes, you cannot stick grenades to the bodies of Chieftains, and they're quicker to dive when you throw explosives. To kill them in this way, you need to aim specifically for their weapon. A Plasma Grenade stuck to a Chieftain's Gravity Hammer or Plasma Turret can result in an instant kill — but it's an art that few players will master. Additionally, the Needler — that usually trusty Brute killer — is practically useless against them.

3 Brute Chieftains don't become pack leaders via civilized political intrigue and careful canvassing of grassroots support — these are unrelentingly vicious warriors, the physical elite of the Brute race, so you'll find they are extremely strong, aggressive and agile. You'll need to backpedal furiously if they charge, and ideally find a suitable hiding spot if you lack weapons capable of stopping them in their tracks quickly.

BASICS

CAMPAIGN

EXTRAS

MULTIPLAYER

LEGENDARY
PRIMER

SKULLS

SCORE SYSTEM

ACHIEVEMENTS

BESTIARY

INVENTORY

VEHICLES

Brute Minors are similar to the standard blue-armored Brutes, but weaker.

Extremely strong senior pack members, Brute Captains can even survive being "stuck" with a Plasma Grenade on Legendary.

Jump Pack Brutes are difficult to track while in motion, but they tend to stay in one position when they land — which is their principle weakness.

Don't fight Brute Stalkers in the open — find a safe hiding spot, and try to pick them off one by one. Shooting them reduces the efficiency of their camouflage.

Any Brute can potentially go berserk at any time. Arms outstretched, they'll aim to bludgeon all enemies in sight to death, and may fire their weapons wildly as they charge. The quickest (and most advisable) way to stop them is with a headshot.

Chieftains armed with a Gravity Hammer will run inexorably at the Master Chief, swinging their weapon as they draw near; attacks where they strike the ground also cause "area effect" damage. If you're quick and remarkably accurate, you can stick a grenade (Plasma or Spike) to the Gravity Hammer for an instant kill.

The Plasma Turret's sheer rate of fire means that it's often difficult to get a clear shot at the Chieftain wielding it. Battles against these foes tend to be protracted unless you have powerful weaponry at the ready — it's often patience, rather than remarkable instances of skill or bravery, that enables you to beat them.

The blast radius of shots from the Fuel Rod Gun makes this type of Chieftain extremely dangerous, so being able to take refuge behind solid cover is essential. As with Chieftains armed with Plasma Turrets, beating them is generally a matter of wearing them down without taking any risks.

GRUNTS

1 A single headshot from a Magnum, Battle Rifle, Carbine or either of the sniping weapons will immediately topple Grunts of all types. Smart Spartans will always have one of these at the ready for this very purpose.

2 Grunts can be surprisingly resilient on Legendary, as you'll find if you attempt to tackle a group of them with automatic weapons such as the SMG, Spike Rifle or Assault Rifle. Every second spent shooting at a Grunt's torso is a window of opportunity for one of his Covenant allies to expedite your return to a previous checkpoint.

3 The backpacks worn by Grunts can be destroyed, but there's no tangible benefit from doing so deliberately (unless, of course, you derive a certain sadistic satisfaction from it).

4 The majority of Grunts carry Plasma Pistols, but some wield Needlers; the latter should generally be your first choice targets. Lest you momentarily forget, Grunts are also prolific in their use of Plasma Grenades. The trick to avoiding these (in addition to being vigilantly watchful, of course) is to listen for audio cues. Chatty Grunts can't help but foreshadow certain actions, and often thoughtfully provide spoken clues as they pull an arm back to throw. Even if they don't, the distinctive hissing of a primed Plasma Grenade is your prompt to be elsewhere, quickly.

Rarely encountered on lower difficulty settings, yet fairly common on Legendary, grey Grunt Ultras are a hardier breed than their cousins clad in other colors.

JACKALS

1 The shields carried by certain Jackals are impervious to many weapon types, particularly those used by Marines, though the Plasma Rifle and charged Plasma Pistol shots can temporarily disable them. Shield-bearing Jackals are not individually very dangerous (unless holding a charged Plasma Pistol shot at the ready – look out for the distinctive green glow), but dealing with them safely can often slow your progress to a crawl.

2 The firing embrasure on a Jackal's shield is a small yet significant weak point. If you don't have a Plasma Pistol or Plasma Rifle, firing a Battle Rifle or Magnum at this gap can cause sufficient damage to send a Jackal reeling backwards, creating a brief opportunity for a headshot.

3 A single shot to the head with a precision weapon (such as the Magnum, Carbine or Battle Rifle) is the quickest way to kill a Jackal, but it's a challengingly small target to aim for. As Jackals can withstand a surprising number of direct hits on Legendary, we suggest you perfect the art of Jackal-felling headshots as soon as you can.

4 Jackals move extremely quickly. When they start sprinting, it's better to focus your attention on another target, rather than wasting ammunition on an unlikely headshot.

Armed with Carbines or Beam Rifles, Jackal snipers will become the bane of your life in certain Legendary battles unless you first methodically pick them off from a safe position. Aim for the head – ideally before they have noticed your arrival.

DRONES

1 Drones are, in terms of physical endurance, probably the weakest members of the Covenant military ranks, but their sheer weight of numbers and maneuverability make them deadly when encountered in swarms.

2 Drones use Plasma Pistols and Needlers, with the latter variety being particularly dangerous. Surviving a Drone swarm is generally a matter of finding the best possible cover, then darting out to pick off targets of opportunity before retreating once again.

Drones are vulnerable to melee attacks at close quarters, even when flying.

HUNTERS

1 When a Hunter lunges at you, dodge to the left. As they always lead with their left arm (from your view, on the right-hand side of the body; the one bearing the fearsomely solid shield), this is the easiest way to avoid harm.

2 While the small patch of writhing pink flesh is a sufficiently large target for expert marksmen to hit, you should note that you can destroy the armor on the upper portion of a Hunter's back more quickly by sticking grenades to it.

3 As well as an eerie glow, you'll notice that there's a distinct sound effect that can be heard as a Hunter's weapon is powering up. This warning will often save your life when you are fighting two Hunters at once. If you're supremely confident, you could try to repeatedly engineer situations where one Hunter will inadvertently shoot his partner while aiming for you, in order to achieve an impressive no-shots kill.

BASICS

CAMPAIGN

EXTRAS

MULTIPLAYER

LEGENDARY
PRIMER

SKULLS

SCORE SYSTEM

ACHIEVEMENTS

BESTIARY

INVENTORY

VEHICLES

INFECTION FORMS & CARRIER FORMS

1 Individually, Infection Forms are barely worth the effort it takes to shoot them (as long as there are no bodies, dead or alive, that they can take control of, that is). As a swarm, though, they can strip your shield in the blink of an eye on Legendary, and make it very hard to find effective cover. Automatic weapons and the Flamethrower are the best way to destroy them.

2 There's a degree of strategy to how you deal with Carrier Forms. Knocking them over is easy; dealing with the Infection Forms that emerge after the blast, less so. When you're given the opportunity to safely avoid Carrier Forms and move on before you're forced to destroy them, do just that – dispatching the tenacious Infection Forms is a big drain on your ammo supply. On other occasions, you can use their explosive nature to your advantage to disrupt the charge of massed hordes of Combat Forms.

COMBAT FORMS

1 Forget headshots: the torso is the weak spot on a Combat Form. You should aim specifically for the regions marked here on the three different types, as killing the Infection Form located inside the chest cavity will stop them immediately. Quantity, not quality, is the true danger posed by this variety of Flood.

2 Combat Forms are not truly "dead" until their body has been destroyed, as they can otherwise be reanimated by a nearby Infection Form. Make sure you destroy prone Combat Form bodies with melee attacks whenever the opportunity arises. (Carrying a Flamethrower around purely for this purpose works well too.)

3 Combat Forms may carry many different weapon types, with those that wield Brute Shots, Shotguns and Magnums often being the most dangerous. You can actually destroy their arms to cause them to drop carried weapons, but it's generally advisable to just knock them down in the most direct way possible. As Combat Forms use fierce melee attacks at close range, you should keep moving at all times when you face them.

PURE FORMS

1 The "Stalker" uses melee attacks when close to the Master Chief, but is rarely a threat unless faced in large numbers. This is the weakest and least dangerous variety of Pure Form – kill them in this guise every time you have a chance to do so, as they'll be swift to move away and transform into other, far more annoying forms if you don't.

2 The "Ranged" type is deeply irritating, and thoroughly deadly when left unchecked. You can force it to stop firing temporarily by making a few shots at its "mouth" area with a ranged weapon. This will usually give you sufficient time to get closer to use a Flamethrower, Shotgun or melee attack. If you're having difficulty telling when they're dead, here's a tip – they generally topple over to one side when fatally injured.

3 The "Tank" spits out Infection Forms as it lumbers forwards, and can be astonishingly robust unless you have the right weapons to deal with it. If you don't have a Gravity Hammer, Energy Sword or Flamethrower, aim for its face – this is its weak spot. As a fringe benefit, shots that hit that area also tend to stun it momentarily.

SENTINELS

Sentinels only briefly feature as adversaries in Halo 3. As in previous episodes, they're vulnerable to plasma-based firearms, and their broken shells can be collected and used as the Sentinel Beam weapon – something they're also weak against.

INVENTORY

EQUIPMENT

NAME	USAGE TIPS	ENEMY USAGE TIPS
Deployable Cover	• Not particularly strong on Legendary – in a large firefight, don't be surprised to see it cut out rapidly under pressure. • Can be used to block doorways and narrow corridors, for example to slow a pursuing horde of Flood.	• Melee attack base unit to destroy it. • A charged Plasma Pistol shot or sustained Plasma Rifle fire will quickly disable it. • Brutes will sometimes use a Deployable Cover unit as you attack them to cover a retreat.
Bubble Shield	• A Bubble Shield effectively offers two barriers to hide behind – you're not obliged to stay in the centre.	• Strike the base unit to destroy it. • Brutes are vulnerable to melee attacks while hiding inside a Bubble Shield.
Grav Lift	• It's not just a tool for reaching higher ground – you can also use Grav Lifts to deflect charging Brutes, Chieftains, and even onrushing vehicles.	• Not used. However, watch out when Brutes and Grunts throw grenades in your direction when you are standing near an active Grav Lift – if one passes through the energy field, the results can be unpredictable.
Power Drain	• Its effects last for approximately six or seven seconds. • Though there is a momentary pause as it activates, a Power Drain operates even while airborne. • Throw one at a large group of Brutes, and quickly follow up with an explosive or a volley of shots for maximum effect. • Power Drains can be used to deter Covenant from giving chase.	• Brutes toss Power Drains regularly, so it's a good idea to get used to the sound they make as they activate, and be prepared to move immediately. • Don't get too close to Brutes when you're driving a vehicle – they won't hesitate to throw a Power Drain to disable your ride. • Shoot the unit to destroy it.
Regenerator	• Remember: you're not invulnerable while it is active – a Regenerator only increases the speed at which your shield recharges. • Regenerators are best used when you have good cover to work from. You'll still need to duck out of sight when hurt, but only for a moment.	• Regenerators last for around fifteen seconds. • Brutes tend to use Regenerators to protect Chieftains. Don't be misled, though – you can still kill them with a suitably powerful weapon.
Flare	• Brutes regard Flares as dangerous, and may jump out of the way when you throw them. However, it's only a temporary distraction – and you'll find that you cause more damage to your vision than to theirs.	• The moment a Brute activates a Flare, turn away and get behind cover until it explodes. • The device auto-destructs after five seconds.
Radar Jammer	• Brutes may enter their berserk state when you deploy a Radar Jammer in their direction, and Grunts may panic. Generally, though, you're better off choosing a different piece of equipment. Brutes hunt primarily by sight, so using one will often only inconvenience you.	• Shoot unit to destroy it. • Radar Jammers cause interference on your Motion Tracker for twenty seconds. • This device is especially dangerous when used by Brute Stalkers. If you can't destroy it safely, withdraw to a secure hiding spot until its effects end.
Trip Mine	• If they are not triggered, Trip Mines usually auto-destruct after approximately a minute and a half.	• The sound generated by an active Trip Mine makes it easy to detect. Unless you're daydreaming, you'll hear one well before you see it.
Cloaking	• Cloaking lasts for around twelve seconds, but fades over the last two. • While firing weapons and incurring damage affects your visibility, melee attacks and grenade throws do not. It's best to keep moving after you use them, though.	• Cloaking units used by Brute Stalkers do not have a time limit. • When you destroy a Stalker's power armor, he will remain fully visible until he is killed.
Invincibility	• Invincibility lasts for approximately ten seconds. During that time, you are completely impervious to all forms of damage, but falling from a great height will still kill the Master Chief.	• Invincibility units are used by Chieftains only. When they activate one, don't bother attacking them: just run or hide.
Auto Turret	• The Auto Turret has a very short range, and really doesn't pose a threat to an organized Covenant attack group. However, it *will* distract them – and that's never a bad thing. Note that there is a short delay before its weapon system activates.	• N/A

GRENADES

FRAG GRENADES

Frag Grenades are ideal to kill or disrupt large groups of low-ranking infantry (Grunts and Jackals especially), to blast an advancing horde of Combat Forms and Infection Forms, or to distract enemies as you beat a hasty retreat to cover. While they can be used to kill weakened Brutes, it's generally wasteful to try to do so.

PLASMA GRENADES

These colorful, sticky globes of doom are an absolutely pivotal part of your arsenal on Legendary. As they're plentiful wherever Grunts are found, you can regularly use them to kill Brutes (and, with practice, from surprisingly long range). They're less effective when thrown at the ground as their blast radius is smaller than that of Frag Grenades – but, at a pinch, they can be used for similar purposes. They're extremely efficient for dealing with certain small vehicles and Shade turrets, too.

HALO 3

BASICS
CAMPAIGN
EXTRAS
MULTIPLAYER

LEGENDARY
PRIMER
SKULLS
SCORE SYSTEM
ACHIEVEMENTS
BESTIARY
INVENTORY
VEHICLES

SPIKE GRENADES

Spike Grenades may share a key characteristic with Plasma Grenades, but don't make the mistake of thinking that the similarities stretch beyond their sticking qualities. The different trajectory of a thrown Spike Grenade means that it's much less suited to tagging enemies or vehicles from greater distances; additionally, its razor-sharp payload is only lethal at point-blank range (or, of course, when "stuck"). These are best saved for taking out Brutes at close proximity or, if necessary, shield-bearing Jackals.

INCENDIARY GRENADES

Incendiary Grenades cause their target to burst into flames, and will burn anything that comes in contact with them. It's a one-shot kill weapon against all opponents bar Chieftains, though their relative scarcity means that you should save them for use in emergencies, or against powerful opponents. As they are hugely effective against the Flood, these are worth their weight in gold during the Cortana level...

WEAPONS

When you play Halo 3 on Heroic or Legendary, having finely honed reactions will only get you so far if you're artlessly indiscriminate in your choice of weapons. Knowing which firearms are suitable for specific enemies – and situations – is absolutely vital.

The table that you'll find overleaf is designed to illustrate the efficiency of each weapon against the main enemy types based on the chosen difficulty level. The more stars in a weapon's cell, the more effective it is against the corresponding foe. While you'll notice that some columns state the patently obvious – for instance, the fact that only a guileless simpleton or a gaming madman would attempt to take down a Brute Chieftain with an Assault Rifle on Legendary – you'll find that it pays to study how the efficiency of many weapons decreases as you play on higher difficulty settings.

Of course, the table's guidance reflects each weapon's approximate worth under optimum conditions. It assumes that you are within the ideal range boundary (see "Weapon Range"), that your weapon

sights track your opponent with unerring accuracy, and that you aim for the most vulnerable part of each enemy's body.

The information offered in the table is fairly self-explanatory, but you should note that the following "Analysis" section is generally skewed towards examining how effective weapons are on Legendary.

Weapon Range

If you've ever found yourself wondering: "At what distance does an Assault Rifle become less efficacious than a potato gun?", then cry a lusty halleluiah and clap your hands in giddy anticipation, because we've prepared a diagram to show you. Beyond the marks specified on this diagram – which, to aid easy range recognition, is a top-down view of the Dam in the Sierra 117 mission – the power and/or accuracy of all featured weapons can be said to decrease by a notable degree. The reduction in efficiency thereafter is sometimes sudden and severe (as with the Shotgun and Needler); with other weapons, such as the Carbine and Battle Rifle, you'll notice a more gradual decline.

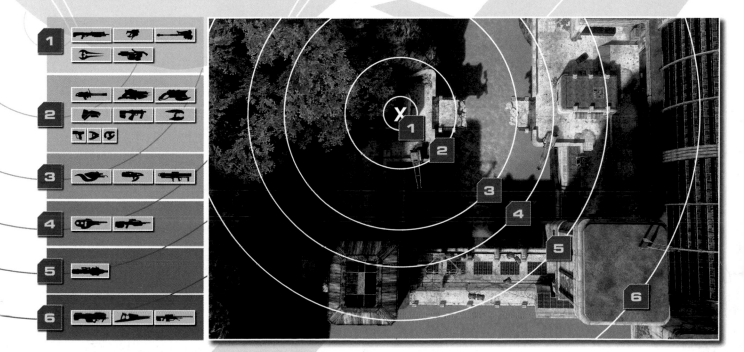

WEAPON EFFICIENCY

Weapon	Reload / Cooling Time	Ammo [Clip/Max]	Difficulty	Grunts	Jackals	Brutes	Brute Chieftains	Hunters	Combat Forms	Combat Form [Shielded]	Pure Form [Tank]	Pure Form [Stalker]	Pure Form [Ranged]	Infection Form
Assault Rifle	1.8	32 / 352	Easy/Normal	★★★	★★	★★★	★	★	★★★	★★	★★	★★	★★	★★★★
			Heroic/Legendary	★★	★★	★★	★	★	★★	★	★	★★	★	★★★★
Battle Rifle	2	36 / 108	Easy/Normal	★★★★	★★★★	★★★★	★★★	★★	★★★	★★	★★★	★★	★★	★★
			Heroic/Legendary	★★★★	★★★★	★★★	★★	★★	★★★	★	★★	★	★	★★
Beam Rifle	2.9	100	Easy/Normal	★★★★	★★★	★★★★	★★★★	★★	★	★	★	★	★	★
			Heroic/Legendary	★★★★	★★★	★★★★	★★★★	★	★	★	★	★	★	★
Brute Shot	3	6 / 12	Easy/Normal	★★★	★★★	★★★	★★★	★★★	★★★★	★★★	★★	★★★	★★★	★★★
			Heroic/Legendary	★★	★★	★★	★★	★★	★★★★	★★	★	★★	★★	★★★
Carbine	2.4	18 / 72	Easy/Normal	★★★★	★★★★	★★★★	★★★	★★	★★★	★★	★★★	★★	★★	★
			Heroic/Legendary	★★★★	★★★★	★★★	★★	★★	★★★	★	★	★★	★	★
Energy Sword	N/A	100	Easy/Normal	★★★	★★★	★★★	★★	★★★★	★★★★	★★★★	★★★★	★★★★	★★★★	★
			Heroic/Legendary	★★	★★	★★	★★	★★★★	★★★★	★★★★	★★★★	★★★★	★★★★	★
Flamethrower	N/A	200	Easy/Normal	N/A	N/A	N/A	N/A	N/A	★★★★	★★★	★★★★	★★★★	★★★★	★★★★
			Heroic/Legendary	N/A	N/A	N/A	N/A	N/A	★★	★★	★★★★	★★★★	★★★★	★★★★
Fuel Rod Gun	3	5 / 25	Easy/Normal	★★★★	★★★★	★★★★	★★★★	★★★★	★★★★	★★★★	★★★★	★★★★	★★★★	★★★
			Heroic/Legendary	★★★★	★★★★	★★★★	★★★	★★★★	★★★★	★★★	★★★	★★★	★★★	★★★
Gravity Hammer	N/A	100	Easy/Normal	★★★★	★★★★	★★★★	★★★	★★★	★★★★	★★★★	★★★★	★★★★	★★★★	★★★★
			Heroic/Legendary	★★★★	★★★★	★★★	★★	★★	★★★★	★★★	★★★★	★★★★	★★★★	★★★★
Machine Gun Turret	N/A	200	Easy/Normal	★★★★	★★★	★★★	★★	★★★	★★★★	★★★	★★★	★★★	★★★	★★★
			Heroic/Legendary	★★★	★★★	★★★	★★	★★	★★★★	★★★★	★★	★★★	★★	★★★
Magnum	1.9	8 / 40	Easy/Normal	★★★	★★★	★★	★	★★	★★	★	★	★	★	★
			Heroic/Legendary	★★★	★★	★	★	★	★★	★	★	★	★	★
Mauler	2.4	5 / 20	Easy/Normal	★★★★	★★★	★★★	★★	N/A	★★★★	★★★	★★	★★	★★	★★★★
			Heroic/Legendary	★★★★	★★	★★	★	N/A	★★★★	★★	★★	★★	★★	★★★★
Missile Pod	N/A	N/A	Easy/Normal	★★★★	★★★★	★★★★	★★★★	★★★★	N/A	N/A	N/A	N/A	N/A	N/A
			Heroic/Legendary	★★★★	★★★★	★★★★	★★★	★★★★	N/A	N/A	N/A	N/A	N/A	N/A
Needler	1.1	19 / 76	Easy/Normal	★★★	★★	★★★★	★	★	★★★★	★★★★	★★★★	★★	★★★★	★★★
			Heroic/Legendary	★★★	★	★★★★	★	★	★★★★	★★★	★★★	★	★★★	★★★
Plasma Pistol	2.1	10 / 100	Easy/Normal	★	★★★	★★★★	★	★	★	★	★	★	★	★★
			Heroic/Legendary	★	★★★	★★★★	★	★	★	★	★	★	★	★★
Plasma Rifle	2.6	100	Easy/Normal	★★★	★★★★	★★★★	★★	★★★★	★★★★	★★★★	★★★	★★★	★★★	★★★
			Heroic/Legendary	★★	★★★	★★★	★	★★★★	★★★★	★★★	★★	★★	★★	★★★
Plasma Turret	N/A	200	Easy/Normal	★★★	★★★★	★★★★	★★	★★★★	★★★★	★★★	N/A	N/A	N/A	★★★
			Heroic/Legendary	★★	★★★	★★★	★★★	★★★	★★★★	★★	N/A	N/A	N/A	★★★
Rocket Launcher	4.3	2 / 6	Easy/Normal	★★★★	★★★★	★★★★	★★★★	★★★★	★★★★	★★★★	★★	★★★★	★★★	★★★
			Heroic/Legendary	★★★★	★★★★	★★★★	★★★★	★★★★	★★★★	★★★	★★	★★★★	★★★	★★★
Sentinel Beam	2.4	100	Easy/Normal	★★★	★★★	★★★	N/A	N/A	★★★★	★★★	★★	★★★	★★	★★★★
			Heroic/Legendary	★★	★★	★★	N/A	N/A	★★★	★★	★★	★★	★★	★★★★
Shotgun	2.0/4.5*	6 / 30	Easy/Normal	★★★★	★★★	★★★★	★★★	★★	★★★★	★★★	★★★	★★★★	★★★	★★★
			Heroic/Legendary	★★★	★★	★★★	★		★★★★	★★★	★★	★★★	★★★	★★★
SMG	1.4	60 / 180	Easy/Normal	★★★	★★	★★★	★★	★★	★★★★	★★	★	★★	★	★★★★
			Heroic/Legendary	★★	★	★★	★	★★	★★	★	★	★★	★	★★★★
Sniper Rifle	2.6	4 / 20	Easy/Normal	★★★	★★★	★★★★	★★★★	★★★	N/A	N/A	N/A	N/A	N/A	N/A
			Heroic/Legendary	★★★	★★	★★★★	★★★	★★	N/A	N/A	N/A	N/A	N/A	N/A
Spartan Laser	2.4	100	Easy/Normal	★★★★	★★★★	★★★★	★★★★	★★★★	N/A	N/A	N/A	N/A	N/A	N/A
			Heroic/Legendary	★★★★	★★★★	★★★★	★★★★	★★★★	N/A	N/A	N/A	N/A	N/A	N/A
Spiker	1.6	40 / 120	Easy/Normal	★★★	★★★	★★★	★★★	★★★	★★★	★★	★★	★★	★★	★★★
			Heroic/Legendary	★★	★★	★★	★★	★★★	★★★	★★	★	★	★	★★★

* One cartridge/full reload
Highlighted cells indicate recommended weapon types per enemy during an average Campaign playthrough.

LEGENDARY WEAPON ANALYSIS

HALO 3

BASICS
CAMPAIGN
EXTRAS
MULTIPLAYER

LEGENDARY PRIMER
SKULLS
SCORE SYSTEM
ACHIEVEMENTS
BESTIARY
INVENTORY
VEHICLES

WEAPON	STRENGTHS	WEAKNESSES
Assault Rifle	There's certainly no shortage of ammunition on most missions, and the "stun" effect when you spray individual Grunts and Brutes at close range usually prevents them from returning fire.	It's just not a practical choice on Legendary – it takes too long to stop enemies in their tracks, and it's woefully inefficient against shielded opponents.
Battle Rifle	It's the ultimate headshot weapon, and its bursts of three bullets make it very accurate; you can also take down multiple targets with each shot. With the exception of Flood-oriented missions, you should have one to hand at all times.	Not great against shields – it is best to combine it with a Plasma Pistol or Plasma Rifle for maximum effect.
Beam Rifle	Enables you to engage foes from a safe distance (well, obviously), and it's excellent against Brutes and Chieftains.	Overheats far too easily – you really need to acquire the knack of spacing out multiple shots during sniping sessions.
Brute Shot	It's outstanding against Combat Forms (though not the shielded type), and ammunition is plentiful on Legendary.	Not very convincing against Covenant enemies – even Grunts can usually withstand two shots. Use it only as a last resort or ammunition-saving temporary measure.
Carbine	It's a precision firearm, so swift headshots are its principle strength. We prefer the Battle Rifle as a rule, and use the Carbine only when the former is not available, though the Covenant weapon has the undisputed benefit of a faster fire rate.	As is the case with the Battle Rifle, it's not tremendous against shields.
Energy Sword	Quick and deadly against Flood; rarely encountered during battles against Covenant foes. Astonishingly good against Hunters if you make an accurate lunge at their unprotected backs.	You'll need a ranged weapon as a backup (ideally a Needler or Brute Shot) to deal with situations where Combat Forms or Ranged Forms attack from afar.
Flamethrower	Kills Pure Forms with a single burst, and is superb for managing large groups of Infection Forms.	It destroys Combat Forms – but only after a protracted delay while they attempt to beat you down with flaming melee attacks. The usual turret mobility penalties apply.
Fuel Rod Gun	It has great stopping power, and is even more devastating when you give it to your allies.	Only suitable for medium-range combat – over long distances, it's just too easy to dodge its missiles.
Gravity Hammer	Solid against Covenant troops if the locale you are fighting in offers enough cover for you to approach them, and absolutely lethal against massed hordes of Combat Forms.	The ability to hit multiple opponents is excellent, but it's painfully slow in comparison with the Energy Sword.
Machine Gun Turret	It's not ideal against shields, yet its ferocious rate of fire means that it's still a reliable choice against Brutes – they drop quickly once their power armor cuts out.	As with all turret weapons, you lose the ability to dodge effectively.
Magnum	It's a precision weapon suitable for headshots alone. Combined with a Plasma Pistol (or, failing that, Plasma Rifle), this is the king of Brute-killing tools.	Utterly useless without a plasma weapon to dual wield with it – which is why we give it such a low rating in the table to the left.
Mauler	Brilliant against Combat Forms as they draw near, especially if you use two at once.	Its pitiful range and relative scarcity counts against it; generally, it's better to favor an Energy Sword or Gravity Hammer during Flood missions.
Missile Pod	The best anti-vehicle weapon in the game, bar none.	As with the Spartan Laser, you only encounter it during a handful of specific set-piece battles. Don't waste it against infantry!
Needler	Outstanding against Brutes, Pure Forms and Combat Forms.	Eats through its ammo supply in a flash unless you're careful. Use something – *anything!* – else when you face Chieftains, Hunters, or, though to a lesser extent, shield-bearing Jackals.
Plasma Pistol	Combine it with a precision weapon (Magnum, Battle Rifle or Carbine) for the ultimate solution to all your Brute problems. Its EMP effect on vehicles makes hijacking a breeze.	Utterly worthless when employed as a weapon in its own right
Plasma Rifle	Solid enough against most infantry, great for destroying Brute power armor – and an absolute revelation if dual wielded against a Hunter.	Once a Brute's power armor is destroyed, they can withstand a large amount of Plasma Rifle fire before they fall.
Plasma Turret	Better against shields and power armor than the Machine Gun Turret, but less efficient against flesh and bone.	Grunts are surprisingly resistant to its effects on Legendary.
Rocket Launcher	Satisfying, and enormously destructive.	Rarely encountered. It has rather lengthy reloading times, and its missiles are easy for enemies to dodge over long ranges.
Sentinel Beam	Strips Brute power armor rapidly, and is much more powerful than the models encountered in previous Halo games.	On the rare occasions that you find one, you generally have better options at your disposal.
Shotgun	Massive close-range damage.	A good choice against the Flood, but no longer the best. It also takes too long to dispatch Brutes on Legendary.
SMG	It has a withering fire rate when used in a dual wield configuration, and is undoubtedly powerful at close range...	...but it's hard to recommend the SMG for any purpose on Legendary. Use it for the sheer fun of doing so – there's not a single instance we can think of where you won't have a better option close to hand.
Sniper Rifle	Same as the Beam Rifle – save it for fights against Brutes and Chieftains.	Obviously unsuited to close-range combat. If you systematically take the time to reload before you attack a target, four bullets should always be sufficient.
Spartan Laser	It appears no more than twice in Campaign, and on only one of those occasions do you have a varied choice of targets.	Has a long charge time and low ammo. In Mission 7, it makes sense to wipe out the Chieftain and Shade turrets with it, then hand it to a Marine.
Spiker	When dual wielded, it's pretty effective against most enemy types (with the exception of Pure Forms), and finding ammunition is rarely a problem.	Low range and slow projectile speed are the main issues. Generally speaking, there tend to be faster ways to take down enemies on Legendary.

VEHICLES

WARTHOG M12 LRV

1 The Warthog's hood shields the driver and front seat passenger from incoming projectiles, but it's also a weapon in its own right.

2 The windshield protects the Master Chief (and, to a lesser extent, the passenger riding shotgun) from harm, but shatters under sustained fire. Once it breaks, head-on charges towards enemy forces become more dangerous.

3 Passengers tend to be more vulnerable to incoming fire due to their sitting position. If you're riding with Marines, it pays to give them powerful weapons that you can easily spare, or that you find after battles. Sniper Rifles and Beam Rifles are both good choices.

4 With the two Warthog models that carry onboard weapons, the person manning the turret enjoys a small degree of protection from incoming non-explosive projectiles. The machine gun variant is very effective against infantry, though it's also capable of taking down small vehicles. Both can pack a punch even on Legendary, but only when driven by an expert wheelman.

The Warthog M12 LAAV is armed with an anti-vehicle Gauss cannon. It's much the same as its cousin with the machine gun, though less effective against infantry.

The Warthog M831 TT is a general-purpose troop carrier, but you can still wreak havoc with it if you arm the Marines on board with the best weapons available — and, of course, drive quickly and aggressively.

SCORPION

1 The Scorpion's armor is pretty much impervious to small arms fire from infantry, but you become a large, slow-moving target whenever you drive one. The principle threats to the driver's safety are Wraiths, Shade turrets, Banshees, Ghosts (especially in groups), and Brutes armed with Fuel Rod Cannons. Note that the Scorpion's ability to protect its driver is linked to its physical appearance — the less pristine its condition, the more damage suffered by the Chief.

2 While you may need to hit a Brute Chieftain a few times to score a kill on Legendary, the Scorpion's main cannon is still an enormously powerful weapon. Don't underestimate the extent of "splash damage" — even though a near miss will not kill the driver of a small vehicle, it may tip it over and put it temporarily out of commission.

3 Unlike in previous Halo games, the Scorpion's driver has no control over the secondary machine gun turret, which must now be manned by an ally. The turret operator is generally well-shielded from harm (snipers and explosives aside), and plays his part by dealing with crowd control or secondary targets (such as Ghosts) while the driver targets more dangerous adversaries.

BASICS

CAMPAIGN

EXTRAS

MULTIPLAYER

LEGENDARY
PRIMER

SKULLS

SCORE SYSTEM

ACHIEVEMENTS

BESTIARY

INVENTORY

VEHICLES

MONGOOSE

1 There's a slight reduction in damage from small arms fire when you drive a Mongoose, but you're still extremely exposed. Only speed, evasive maneuvers and a healthy dose of luck will keep you alive during pitched battles.

2 Passengers riding pillion on a Mongoose won't be harmed by shots to the front of the vehicle, but are susceptible to damage from all other directions.

3 The Mongoose is prone to rolling when the driver misjudges bumps in the road, or when caught in the blast radius of nearby explosions. Don't be too quick to jump out unless it's absolutely necessary, though – the odds are usually favorable that it will come to rest on its wheels.

HORNET

1 The Hornet isn't particularly sturdy, so you'll need to make use of its superb maneuverability to avoid incoming fire.

2 The Hornet's rockets have an excellent rate of fire, but there's a definite knack to getting the best out of their homing function (activated when the target reticule is red). From longer range, the homing ability is inactive, and rockets fire in a straight line. This is great for bombarding troops and vehicles on the ground, but lousy for air-to-air combat.

3 Two passengers can ride on the ledges either side of the Hornet cockpit but, being completely open to the elements, they rely on the pilot to keep them out of harm's way. In co-op games, it's great fun to use this feature to drop a partner on top of a Scarab, or near to a vehicle that you'd particularly like to hijack.

BANSHEE

1 The Banshee's body offers limited protection against smaller weapons, so it's prudent to keep a sensible distance from groups of enemy infantry.

2 While the Banshee's main plasma cannons are powerful, you'll generally find that its limited range and accuracy mean that it is best used in air-to-air dogfights only; strafing runs on vehicles or infantry can be risky and inefficient. The Fuel Rod Gun is much more powerful, but has a slower fire rate and is difficult to aim.

3 Lest you forget, the Banshee's true strength is its speed – its unlimited boost feature enables the pilot to immediately escape dicey situations, but at the cost of disabling the weapons systems. You can also use aeronautical trickery (default Ⓐ plus a direction on Ⓛ) to evade incoming fire, or just for the sheer fun of it.

GHOST

1 The hood and extended "wings" of a factory-issue Ghost offer more protection from incoming bullets than you might initially think, but this shielding is greatly reduced when the vehicle sustains damage to its bodywork.

2 The dual cannons have an extremely high rate of fire, but are not enormously powerful (particularly against larger vehicles). That said, the Ghost's superb speed and maneuverability enables pilots to duck behind cover between volleys.

3 As in Halo 2, you can melee attack the Ghost's "wings" to destroy them, which may enable you to squeeze the vehicle into places it is not, at least *technically*, supposed to be in.

4 The Ghost's speed boost feature is great for accelerating out of situations that have that distinct "near death" feel to them, and also makes it a powerful battering ram when driven purposefully at enemy infantry.

WRAITH

1 The Wraith, like the Scorpion, protects the driver from most weapons used by enemy infantry, but its slow speed often makes it an easy target for turrets and explosive projectiles. Once the hatch covering the driver's compartment is destroyed, the pilot is vulnerable to well-aimed shots. The Wraith's limited "speed boost" feature can turn its large armored hood into a crude but deadly battering ram.

2 The Wraith's main cannon is one of the most powerful weapons you can use in Halo 3, but this is offset by its slow delivery. During combat, the "Space Invaders Principle" reigns supreme — aim at where an opponent *will* be, not where they actually are.

3 The Wraith's plasma turret is primarily used to deal with nearby infantry, but also acts as a deterrent to would-be hijackers. The gunner is exposed to arms fire, with snipers being a particularly potent threat. (In Campaign mode, you can sometimes score easy Brute kills this way — snipe one gunner from a safe distance, and another Brute will often foolishly run to take his place.)

4 As you should already be aware, the Wraith has an Achilles heel — an exhaust port on its back end, which is concealed by a protective shield that can be destroyed. As a driver, it's vital that you are facing your enemy at all times.

The Anti-Aircraft Wraith has a powerful dual Fuel Rod Gun-based weapons system in place of the standard mortar. Its fast rate of fire makes it extremely dangerous at close range.

HALO 3

BASICS

CAMPAIGN

EXTRAS

MULTIPLAYER

LEGENDARY PRIMER

SKULLS

SCORE SYSTEM

ACHIEVEMENTS

BESTIARY

INVENTORY

VEHICLES

CHOPPER

1 The cruel and ugly Chopper is designed to plough through infantry and small vehicles, so its front end is resistant to a wide variety of weapons. That said, a well-aimed Plasma Grenade thrown through the gap between its wheels can still kill (or severely weaken) its driver. Facing one on foot, your ability to jump aside at the right moment to avoid an onrushing Chopper is the difference between a triumphant cry of "Olé!", and a valedictory "Ol-*argh*!"

2 Chopper drivers have very little protection at the rear and on either side — damage is reduced, but not by a significant amount. After ploughing through an enemy position, you'll need to either make a swift getaway, or turn the vehicle around to bring the "business end" to bear on your foes immediately.

3 The Chopper's forward-firing dual cannons make it extremely dangerous — when you face them on foot, it's vital that you find cover. When driving a vehicle such as a Warthog, the trick is to stay behind them at all times and hope your gunner can do his job before the Brute gets a clear shot...

4 The speed boost feature can be used to escape incoming fire or pursuing vehicles, but its principle function is to help the driver smash through flesh and metal. It only works briefly, though, so timing is everything.

PROWLER

1 As with the Chopper, the Prowler's large front end shields the driver from the effects of many smaller weapons, but a well-aimed Spike or Plasma Grenade can cause problems for all on board. Again, damage from projectiles is reduced around the driver's seat, but not by a great deal.

2 The Prowler's powerful turret can be turned a full 360 degrees. If you have a driver who has the ability to lead you safely through enemy lines, this feature can enable you to wreak havoc. Facing a Prowler, your best bet is to hide until it passes by, or to encourage the Brutes to abandon ship with a grenade.

3 The Prowler can carry two extra passengers in addition to a driver and gunner, but they're sitting targets unless the wheelman can deftly steer through firefights.

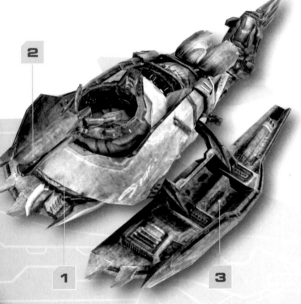

SHADE TURRET

1 The Shade's front armor plating protects the gunner from most infantry weapons, which can make it an extremely awkward target to deal with when you're on foot. If you manage to get close enough, sticking a grenade on it will disable it immediately. The metal plating at the side of the Shade can be partially destroyed, and its gunner is completely vulnerable to attacks from behind. (In co-op games, a good tactic is to have one player draw the turret's fire in one direction, while a second lines up a shot on the Grunt manning it from elsewhere.)

2 The dual plasma cannons on the Shade fire very powerful but slow-moving projectiles. On foot, you can usually jump and dodge to avoid these with ease, though this becomes more difficult as you approach the turret.

MULTIPLAYER

From co-op Campaign sessions to epic team-based Slayer battles, Halo 3 is an extraordinarily varied and feature-packed multiplayer game. In this chapter, we'll teach you how to become a much better player, offering expert guidance and considered analysis (including tips from elite players and designers at Bungie) to help you to fulfill your playing potential.

PLAYING CO-OP

CO-OP BASICS

Setting up co-op games (in split-screen mode, or via a LAN or Xbox LIVE) is extremely simple, so we're not going to waste words on explaining what the Halo 3 user interface (and, as a second port of call, your manual) already tells you (Fig. 1). However, if you haven't played co-op Campaign in a Halo game before, you'll definitely benefit by reading this short introduction.

Even though you might notice certain sporadic differences, missions played in co-op mode are functionally identical to those enjoyed in solo Campaign sessions. For this reason, it's worth turning up the difficulty level to create a more worthwhile challenge. You should aim to play on Heroic at very least, but co-op is also a great way to get firmly acquainted with Legendary. Even with a companion to watch your back, you'll need an impeccable understanding of Halo strategy to win battles convincingly, and to cooperate fully to survive for more than a minute at a time. If you charge headlong into battle as if playing on Normal, you'll be lucky to have the time to remark "This isn't Kansas anymore, Toto!" before the corpses of the Master Chief and the Arbiter are swarmed by souvenir-hunting Grunts (Fig. 2).

When you play split-screen co-op (Fig. 3), you suffer the obvious drawback of a reduced viewing area, and less audio clarity — is the Grunt you can hear chattering away baiting you, or your companion? That said, you have the benefit of being able to see exactly what your allies are up to at any moment. Via System Link or Xbox LIVE, the opposite applies: you have the luxury of a full screen and speakers to yourself, but it's perhaps harder to keep track of what your teammates are doing.

0   1

0   2

0   3

BASICS

CAMPAIGN

EXTRAS

MULTIPLAYER

PLAYING CO-OP

MULTIPLAYER
BASICS

GAME TYPES

MULTIPLAYER
TACTICS

MULTIPLAYER
MAPS

FORGE

CO-OP STRATEGY

The key to succeeding in and enjoying co-op Campaign to its fullest is **communication** — so important, you'll notice, that we felt obliged to break out the bold font for extra-special emphasis. If you plan ahead, playing to your respective strengths, you'll find that your team is greater than the sum of its parts. It pays to take a more tactical approach to your choice of weapons, rather than simply grabbing favorites as and when they appear. On the first mission, for example, one player can focus on Brutes, dual wielding a Plasma Pistol and a Magnum with a Needler in reserve, while a second player can use a Battle Rifle, Brute Shot and grenades to deal with Grunts and Jackals (Fig. 4).

Ideally, each player should have a specific role, and be ready to adapt to the circumstances at hand. The following list illustrates a selection of tactics and techniques that you can use in co-op games.

- Get into the habit of immediately pulling back a safe distance from enemies when a partner is killed, thus forcing a fast respawn (and reducing the likelihood of being kicked back to a checkpoint).

- In large areas, or if there is more than one floor, players can take different routes in order to divide the enemy forces.

- When you have access to transport, you can have one player act as a gunner (especially if the vehicle has a turret), while another drives. However, it's often more effective to choose individual vehicles to maximize your firepower, particularly when you have the support of nearby Marines.

- One player can seek to draw enemy fire, while another flanks the enemy position with grenades at the ready.

- When you face particularly strong opponents, you can have one player act as "bait" while a second stealthily moves around to attack from behind (Fig. 5).

- One player can flush enemies from behind cover while another acts as a sniper from a safe distance.

- A player who specializes in the use of the Plasma Pistol and Magnum combo can act as a pack mule, using his reserve weapon slot to, for instance, carry Battle Rifle ammunition for a teammate.

This is merely a small list of tactical decisions you can make during combat, but — to hammer the point home — all require regular communication to succeed. Even if you're playing with people you don't know well on Xbox LIVE, don't be bashful. Make suggestions, warn teammates if they're in imminent danger, and be ready to listen to advice from more skilled players. You'll soon find that, no matter how shy you may think you are, there's a common (and often inventively expletive-laden) language that comes naturally to all Halo players in co-op sessions.

The Campaign chapter features assorted tips and tactics for co-op games, but we could not hope to document every possibility — nor do we attempt to. Halo 3 offers boundless opportunities for experimentation and creativity, and the biggest part of the fun is devising unique strategies with friends. More often than not, a crazy, convoluted plan that goes spectacularly, explosively wrong is more enjoyable than a dozen simple tactics that work like a charm...

0 4

0 5

MULTIPLAYER BASICS

Halo 3 offers a wide variety of ways to play with and against other people, from split-screen or LAN co-op sessions, to online multiplayer games and collaborative map editing. With co-op mode introduced on page 144 and the powerful yet intuitive Forge editor discussed on page 206, the primary focus of this chapter is the two main multiplayer options: Matchmaking and Custom Games.

Note: You must have an Xbox LIVE Gold Membership to play online. Refer to your user manual for further details.

MATCHMAKING

Matchmaking is the quickest way to dive into a multiplayer game. You simply choose a Playlist that corresponds to the type of combat you'd like to participate in, and Bungie's servers will then allocate a suitable Game Type and collection of similarly skilled opponents (see "Rating and Skill", page 148). You can form parties to travel together from match to match, sending out invites via your Friends and Recent Players lists. It's also possible to create impromptu parties by pressing ⊗ at the end of a game.

As the choice of Game Type Variant is made by Bungie's servers, you may occasionally encounter instances where a less favored ruleset or map appears. If this happens, you can press ⊗ before a game begins to exercise your Veto (Fig. 1). If the majority of players do the same, a new map and Game Type will be selected. You should note that the Veto can only be used once before each game.

0.1

The Matchmaking Lobby has a few handy settings that you can access by pressing ⊗, which enable you to refine how Halo 3 will search for available matches. "Quickest" offers the fastest and most direct route into a game; "Good Connection", "My Language" and "Close Skill Range" (only in Ranked Playlists) refine the search in obviously useful ways, but at the cost of slower searches.

There are two different types of Playlists: Ranked and Social. It's only a quick summary, but the key differences between these are:

Ranked Playlists:
- Enable you to earn Skill
- Are more competitive
- Free-for-all games do not allow parties

Social Playlists
- Are more laid back
- Allow you to play in large parties
- Allow you to play with guests

CUSTOM GAMES

0.2

While Matchmaking is tailor-made for players looking to dive into the first available game, the Custom Games option (Fig. 2) is designed for parties to play matches of their own choosing. The awe-inspiring array of customizable options means that you can create and refine unique versions of each Game Type, though it pays to have a reasonable knowledge of Halo 3's maps before you do so – for example, Valhalla is perhaps better suited to matches featuring a large number of participants. After minutes, hours or even days of careful adjustments, you can then choose to make your creation available to other Halo 3 players via the Fileshare option if you wish (Fig. 3).

As all options in the Custom Games Lobby and its many sub-menus are explained by onscreen captions, there's little need for us to detail them here (which is actually a blessing, as doing so would increase the size of this guide to telephone directory proportions). However, when you first begin to experiment with the Custom Games option, you can turn to page 151 to learn more about individual Variants, and study available maps from page 160 onwards.

0.3

ONSCREEN DISPLAY

BASICS

CAMPAIGN

EXTRAS

MULTIPLAYER

PLAYING CO-OP

MULTIPLAYER
BASICS

GAME TYPES

MULTIPLAYER
TACTICS

MULTIPLAYER
MAPS

FORGE

The onscreen display in multiplayer mode is effectively identical to the one used for Campaign games, but with a few additional features.

1 The name of the Variant in progress appears in the bottom-right corner of the screen. The score (yours, and the current leader, or team totals) is displayed below, and an arrow highlights your current team if applicable.

2 Each player has a Service Tag (a three-digit code: one letter and two numbers) and a Gamertag to aid easy identification. At close range, a Gamertag will appear above the head of friend and foe alike. The Service Tag will only appear above distant friendly characters in your current field of view.

3 In objective-based Variants, waypoint indicators (see table below) help you to find your way to the relevant target. Objectives may also appear on your radar as a white triangle, as they do in Campaign mode.

4 All significant events that occur during multiplayer matches are acknowledged by onscreen messages. Pay attention to these, as they often impart important information. For example, if the pop-up text tells you that the opposing team has captured your flag, that's your cue to leave your favorite hidden sniping spot and help your teammates to track it down.

ICON	NAME	GAME TYPE
∨	General Waypoint	Various
💣	Bomb	Assault
🚩	Flag	Capture the Flag
☠	Oddball	Oddball
👑	Hill	King of the Hill
★	VIP	VIP
◎	Juggernaut	Juggernaut

RATING AND SKILL

There are two systems in Halo 3 that you can use to gauge the ability of all competitors in Matchmaking games: Rating and Skill. A player's Rating is expressed in the form of a military title (for example, Sergeant or Captain) and a grade (Grade 2, for instance), and gives a "global" indication of how experienced that individual is. A Skill level, by contrast, is unique to individual Ranked Playlists, reflects how good you are "locally" in each Playlist, and is used to set you up with the most appropriate opponents in Matchmaking games. Both are useful for establishing that it's a cold, hard *fact* that you're better than your friends. The opposite, alas, is also true.

If you like to quantify your fun by laughing at the miserable credentials of less capable players, or glaring covetously at the impeccable stats of the Halo 3 elite, you'll be glad to know that you can access the Player Details screen for each participant before and after matches by selecting their Gamertag (Fig. 4).

0 4

Rating: Your Rating is represented both by an icon and a name. It is determined primarily by the amount of Experience Points (EXP) you obtain in Matchmaking games. EXP is awarded when you play well in both Ranked and Social Playlists. You are given EXP when your team wins a team match, and every time you finish in the top half of a free-for-all battle. On the other hand, no matter how miserable your performances may be, EXP will never be deducted from your total – thankfully, Bungie sees no reason to contribute a punitive EXP "insult" to add to the woes of players on an injuriously bad losing streak.

There is only one exception to this rule: an EXP penalty is levied when a player quits a team game, no matter the reason, which can cause someone to drop down a Rating if their EXP total falls below the required level. You may feel hard done by if your broadband connection goes the way of the Forerunners through no fault of your own, but take solace from the fact that it's a system that benefits everyone who plays team-based matches in the long term.

To summarize, a player's Rating gives a broad indication of their general experience, playing time and, if they have an Officer Rating, their ability. As the table to the right shows, all Ratings in the Enlisted class require only EXP. This means that a player who exclusively spends time in Social Playlists (or, indeed, the worst Ranked Playlist player in the world) could eventually reach the dizzy heights of Gunnery Sergeant Grade 4. However, to enter the Officer class, you will need EXP *and* Skill. Which leads us neatly to...

Skill: In each Ranked Playlist you have an individual Skill level, which is expressed as a number. This separation reflects the fact that proficiency in team-based or objective-based games doesn't necessarily translate into Slayer supremacy, and vice versa. Based on your performances in a specific Ranked Playlist, your connected Skill level can go up or down, and therefore offers a clear and accurate indication of how good you are. We won't bore you by explaining the underlying mathematics but, in brief, winning or finishing at the top of the score table helps you to gradually reach higher Skill levels, while a string of lousy last-place finishes might cause you to drop Skill levels. Additionally, the Skill level of other players in matches is also taken into account. You generally gain more points for beating players with a higher Skill level, and fewer for those with a total on a par or below yours; similarly, playing badly in games against players with lower Skill levels has a more adverse affect on your Skill level than when your opponents are at a higher level.

To become an Officer (Captain, Major, et al.), you will first need to reach a "Highest Skill" milestone, as we reveal in the Officer table. Until you reach a Highest Skill of 20 in a Ranked Playlist, for example, you cannot achieve the Rating of Captain – though you will (with time and perseverance) move up through the different Lieutenant Grades. If you subsequently increase your Highest Skill level to 20, the promotion to Captain is instantaneous. Even if you then drop back down to 19, your Highest Skill milestone has been reached and is permanent, so your Rating remains – only repeat "quitters" who decrease their EXP by bailing from team games run the risk of being stripped of their new stripes.

ENLISTED

RATING	GRADE	ICON	EXP	HIGHEST SKILL
Recruit	-	◇	1	N/A
Apprentice	1	◈	2	N/A
Apprentice	2	◈	3	N/A
Private	1	⌒	5	N/A
Private	2	⌒	7	N/A
Corporal	1	⌒	10	N/A
Corporal	2	⌒	15	N/A
Sergeant	1	⌒	20	N/A
Sergeant	2	⌒	30	N/A
Sergeant	3	⌒	40	N/A
Gunnery Sergeant	1	⌒	50	N/A
Gunnery Sergeant	2	⌒	60	N/A
Gunnery Sergeant	3	⌒	150	N/A
Gunnery Sergeant	4	?	300	N/A

REQUIREMENTS

OFFICER

RATING	GRADE	ICON	EXP	HIGHEST SKILL
Lieutenant	1		70	10
	2		85	
	3		200	
	4	?	400	
Captain	1		100	20
	2		150	
	3		300	
	4	?	600	
Major	1	★	200	30
	2	★	300	
	3	★	600	
	4	?	1,200	
Commander	1	★	300	35
	2	★	450	
	3	★	900	
	4	?	1,800	
Colonel	1		400	40
	2		600	
	3		1,200	
	4	?	2,400	
Brigadier	1	?	500	45
	2	?	1,000	
	3	?	2,000	
	4	?	4,000	
General	1	?	600	50
	2	?	1,200	
	3	?	2,500	
	4	?	5,000	

BASICS
CAMPAIGN
EXTRAS
MULTIPLAYER

PLAYING CO-OP
MULTIPLAYER BASICS
GAME TYPES
MULTIPLAYER TACTICS
MULTIPLAYER MAPS
FORGE

• If you're going it alone in team-based Playlists, party up with your teammates after a good match. You'll learn each other's skills as you play, and potentially enjoy much more success over multiple matches by staying together – being forced to learn the idiosyncrasies of new teammates every game really won't help you to reach your potential.

FIELD PROMOTIONS

If a player reaches what appears to be his or her particular Skill peak (or *level of mediocrity*, as "glass half empty" types might call it) in a Ranked Playlist, they still have the opportunity to rise in Grade by accumulating EXP. However, if the same player breaks their personal Skill glass ceiling at a later date, they might experience what Bungie refers to as a Field Promotion – an instant elevation to a superior Grade in their new Rating.

Here's how it works. Let's imagine that you are a Major, and that the Highest Skill level you have achieved is 32. After months of play, you have risen to Major Grade 4 by accumulating over 1200 EXP. If you then subsequently embark upon a winning streak in a Matchmaking Playlist that sees you reach a Skill of 35, you will immediately become a Grade 3 Commander – a quite considerable leap in prestige, but one richly deserved.

MEDALS

Halo 3 awards a wide range of Medals to acknowledge skilful play and noteworthy feats, as the table below and on the following page reveals. You'll hear some of these announced as you play, and can study your medal haul in the post-game Carnage Report.

RATING AND SKILL TIPS

• You can increase your Skill level in Ranked Matchmaking only.

• You can earn EXP in any Matchmaking Playlist, both Ranked and Social.

• Officer Ratings require Skill.

• Many Playlists are designed to cater to specific playing styles and preferences. For example, "Team Slayer" Playlists feature games that require solid tactics where players coordinate to get kills. A "Team Skirmish" Playlist features objective-based games that require coordinated offensive and defensive tactics. Occasionally you will also encounter very specific Playlists, such as "Team Snipers", that focus on a distinctive style of play.

• If you have friends that you play with regularly, learn what you do best as a group, pick a Playlist where you will be most competitive, and concentrate on competing in that Playlist. Don't go in cold, though. If you are serious about increasing your Skill level, warm up with a few social matches to prepare for the more competitive play ahead. Most Ranked Playlists will have equivalent Social Playlists that feature the same style of play.

ICON	NAME	CONDITION
	STANDARD SPREE	
	Killing Spree!	Kill 5 opponents in a row without dying.
	Killing Frenzy!	Kill 10 opponents in a row without dying.
	Running Riot!	Kill 15 opponents in a row without dying.
	Rampage!	Kill 20 opponents in a row without dying.

ICON	NAME	CONDITION
	ROLE SPREE	
	Shotgun Spree!	Kill 5 opponents in a row with a Shotgun without dying (no melee attacks).
	Open Season!	Kill 10 opponents in a row with a Shotgun without dying (no melee attacks).
	Sniper Spree!	Kill 5 opponents in a row with a sniper weapon without dying (no melee attacks).
	Sharpshooter!	Kill 10 opponents in a row with a sniper weapon without dying (no melee attacks).
	Sword Spree!	Kill 5 opponents in a row with an Energy Sword without dying.
	Slice 'n Dice!	Kill 10 opponents in a row with an Energy Sword without dying.
	Splatter Spree!	Splatter 5 opponents in a row with a vehicle without dying (you may switch vehicles).

ICON	NAME	CONDITION
★	Vehicular Manslaughter!	Splatter 10 opponents in a row with a vehicle without dying (you may switch vehicles).
◆	Juggernaut Spree!	Kill 5 opponents in a row as the Juggernaut without dying.
★	Unstoppable!	Kill 10 opponents in a row as the Juggernaut without dying.
◆	Infection Spree!	Kill 5 humans in a row as a zombie without dying.
★	Mmmm Brains!	Kill 10 humans in a row as a zombie without dying.
◆	Zombie Killing Spree!	Kill 5 zombies in a row as a human without dying.
★	Hell's Janitor!	Kill 10 zombies in a row as a human without dying.
◆	Hail to the King!	Kill 5 opponents in a row from inside the hill (without dying and without stepping outside its radius) before it moves.

MULTI-KILLS

ICON	NAME	CONDITION
★	Double Kill!	Kill 2 opponents within 4 seconds.
◎	Triple Kill!	Kill 3 opponents within 4 seconds of one another.
◎	Overkill!	Kill 4 opponents within 4 seconds of one another.
◎	Killtacular!	Kill 5 opponents within 4 seconds of one another.
◎	Killtrocity!	Kill 6 opponents within 4 seconds of one another.

OBJECTIVE

ICON	NAME	CONDITION
◎	Killed VIP!	Kill an opponent's VIP in a VIP game.
◎	Killed Flag Carrier!	Kill an opposing flag carrier.
◆	Flag Kill!	Get a melee kill with the flag.
▽	Flag Score!	Score in a Capture the Flag game.
◉	Killed Bomb Carrier!	Kill an opposition bomb carrier in an Assault game.
▽	Bomb Planted!	Plant the bomb in an Assault game.
✱	Oddball Kill!	Get a melee kill while holding the Oddball.
◎	Killed Juggernaut!	Kill the Juggernaut in a Juggernaut game.
◉	Last Man Standing!	Be the last human in an Infection game.

HEROIC

ICON	NAME	CONDITION
◉	Laser Kill!	Kill an opponent with the Spartan Laser.
✹	Grenade Stick!	Kill an opponent by sticking them with a Plasma or Spike grenade.
▦	Beat Down!	Kill an opponent with a melee attack.
▦	Assassin!	Kill an opponent with a melee attack from behind.
◇	Bulltrue!	Kill an opponent who is in the act of a sword lunge.
⚲	Hijacker!	Board a vehicle by forcibly removing the driver.
⚲	Skyjacker!	Board an aircraft by forcibly removing the driver.
◉	Wheelman!	Be the driver of a vehicle when a passenger kills an opponent.
◈	Splatter!	Hit and kill an opponent with a vehicle.
✸	Death From the Grave	Kill an opponent after you have died.
◎	Killjoy!	End an opponent's spree (any spree, whether Standard or Role based).
⊕	Sniper Kill!	Kill an opponent with a Sniper Rifle or Beam Rifle.
✳	Incineration!	Kill an opponent with a flame-based weapon.

SECRET

ICON	NAME	CONDITION
?	Mystery Medals	You can unlock hidden accolades by performing certain (truly remarkable) multiplayer feats.

CARNAGE REPORT

Don't forget that you can press ◀ at the end of a match to study a statistical review of your performance (and, if you're interested, see how your opponents fared, too). It's often surprising how revealing the information you find in the Carnage Report truly is. For example, a player with a high positive "K/D Spread" (number of kills minus number of deaths) and assorted sniper medals can be immediately identified as the sneaky camping [*expletive deleted*] who was wiping you out every time you respawned near the shore on High Ground.

There are many other stats to view, including which opponent you victimized the most during a game (always helps to add a little spice to post-game banter). The Assists column is perhaps the most consistently interesting piece of data. When you have one of those matches where it seems that everyone in the world is forming an orderly queue to "steal" your kills, you can (*maybe*) vindicate yourself by pointing this stat out to teammates and adversaries alike. (Whether you do so in a whining or heartbreakingly plaintive tone is entirely at your discretion.)

Finally, if you ever feel the urge to revisit past glories, check out **http://www.bungie.net/stats/** to study your online performances in Bungie's powerful Game Viewer.

GAME TYPES

BUILT-IN GAME TYPES

BASICS

CAMPAIGN

EXTRAS

MULTIPLAYER

PLAYING CO-OP

MULTIPLAYER
BASICS

GAME TYPES

MULTIPLAYER
TACTICS

MULTIPLAYER
MAPS

FORGE

Halo 3's multiplayer mode includes nine different Game Types. Each one features a number of Variants – that is, sets of specific rules that alter the way in which a Game Type plays. Some simply require that you kill as many opponents as you can, while others demand that you fulfill objectives.

In Matchmaking mode, Bungie's servers provide a selection of Game Types and Variants for each Playlist, and you can expect these to be rotated and expanded as time goes by. The following section introduces the main built-in Variants, and a collection of tips to help new players get started.

[SLAYER]

Relentless deathmatches in which players score by killing opponents.

VARIANTS	RULES	TIPS
Slayer	Individual Slayer: first player to 25 kills wins.	• If you're experiencing too many deaths, pick different areas to frequent, and study the Multiplayer Maps section (page 160) to learn the locations of notable "power weapons".
Team Slayer	Team Slayer: first team to 50 kills wins.	
Rockets	Standard Slayer game rules, but players wield Rocket Launchers.	• In Rockets mode, it's easier to score kills with a rocket's "splash damage" than with direct hits. Aim for an area of the ground where your (invariably) jumping opponent will land. As you have infinite ammo, reload often and don't hold back: a dead target is worth more than a second rocket in the tube.
Eliminatio	Quick and tactical Team Slayer game played in 5 rounds of 5 kills.	
Duel	Slayer game where the player currently in the lead has a waypoint indicator above their head. First player to 10 kills wins.	• In Eliminatio mode, 5 kills can take place within the blink of an eye if you're careless. Don't take any chances, and never stray too far from cover.
		• When you're in the lead in Duel mode, everyone will be tracking you down, so don't linger in open areas. Try to draw your opponents into narrow tunnels to create deadly bottlenecks, and then pick off the weakened survivors.

[ODDBALL]

Follow the waypoint indicator to find the Oddball, and hold it for as long as you can to score. If the Oddball lies on the ground for too long, it is returned to its initial location.

VARIANTS	RULES	TIPS
Oddball	Whoever holds the Oddball long enough to score 50 points wins.	• When carrying the Oddball, you can't drive or use your weapons. To defend yourself, you must either discard the Oddball temporarily, or melee attack with it. The latter always results in an instant kill, so don't get too close to the Oddball carrier. Equally, don't hesitate to unceremoniously "deck" someone if they approach you while you're holding it.
Team Oddball	First team to reach 100 total points wins.	
Lowball	Every team member must earn at least 25 points for a team to win.	
Ninjaball	The Oddball carrier moves much faster than usual, but is weaker and has a slow-recharging shield. Whoever holds the Oddball long enough to reach 100 points wins.	• In Lowball mode, team members must take turns to protect each other. VIP mode tactics work well here.
Rocketball	Oddball game in which players wield Rocket Launchers.	• If you are in a very close match, consider leaping into an available abyss. You'll gain a few invaluable seconds with the Oddball, which will subsequently be reset.

[CAPTURE THE FLAG (CTF)]

Team-based combat in which teams score by picking up a flag and taking it back to their base. When a flag lies on the ground for too long, it is returned to its initial location.

VARIANTS	RULES	TIPS
Multi Flag	Every team has a flag. First team with 3 captures wins.	• Defend and attack at the same time in Multi Flag. If you launch full-scale attacks, you expose yourself to the possibility of embarrassingly quick defeats.
One Flag	Only one team has a flag. Teams attack and defend in turns. The team with the most points after 4 rounds wins.	• When your flag is stolen, be quick to chase the thieves down. If you manage to kill them, guard the flag until it is returned. You can return a flag more quickly by standing near it, with a progress bar showing how long you need to wait.
Tank Flag	Multi Flag game in which flag carriers can take more damage (though their shield takes longer to recharge) but are slower.	• Use vehicles for fast attacks: this will save precious time and is also a good way to protect a flag carrier (who can only be a passenger). If the map has numerous vehicles, using one as a decoy to distract enemy forces can be an effective strategy.
Attrition CTF	Multi Flag game where respawn times are very long, but teams respawn entirely on flag capture.	• As with the Oddball, a flag melee attack is always a one-hit kill.
		• In Attrition CTF, the long respawn times engender a more tactical, slower-paced style of play. Communication and cooperation are vital, more so than in any other CTF Variant.

ASSAULT

Team-based combat in which teams score by planting a bomb in the opposing team's base, and guarding it until it detonates. If an unprimed bomb lies on the ground for too long, it is returned to its initial location.

VARIANTS	RULES	TIPS
Assault	Every team has a bomb and a base to defend. First team to trigger 3 detonations wins.	• Waypoint indicators guide you to the bomb, and to the enemy base while you're carrying the bomb.
Neutral Bomb	Every team has a base to defend, but there's only one neutral bomb. First team to trigger 3 detonations wins.	• With the default settings, a bomb instantly arms itself when planted. If an arming time is set, though, you must stand near the planting point until the progress bar fills in order to arm it. The opposing team can disarm the bomb before it explodes by taking control of it.
One Bomb	Only one team at a time has a base to defend. Teams defend a base in turns. The team with the most points after 4 rounds wins.	• Make sure you always guard your base, and never send a bomb carrier out alone.
Attrition Bomb	Neutral Bomb game where respawn times are very long, but teams respawn entirely on detonations.	• The carrier can use the bomb to melee attack enemies; however it is often more efficient to temporarily drop the bomb and fight back. • Unless you actively intend to check out in a big, suicidal bang, don't stand too close to your bomb when it is about to detonate.

JUGGERNAUT

One player is the Juggernaut and has stronger attributes. Whoever kills the Juggernaut becomes the Juggernaut.

VARIANTS	RULES	TIPS
Juggernaut	You score only by killing the Juggernaut, or by killing other players while you are the Juggernaut. The Juggernaut has an Overshield and is more powerful, but his shield recharges more slowly. First player to earn 10 points wins.	• When you become the Juggernaut everyone will suddenly attack you – especially the people who were cooperating with you moments before. A good player always has an exit plan in mind to escape his former "teammates" until his shield can charge up.
Mad Dash	The Juggernaut has the same attributes as in Juggernaut mode. Only he can score by reaching certain specified destinations. The first player to earn 5 points wins.	• As the Juggernaut, you're usually tagged with a waypoint indicator, so keep moving to prevent other players from locating you too easily.
Ninjanaut	Normal Juggernaut game in which the Juggernaut moves faster, has Active Camo, and is not marked with a waypoint indicator. The Juggernaut has a weaker shield, but it regenerates at a faster rate.	• Steer clear of open areas – you're an easy target for medium and long-range weapons when you cross these as the Juggernaut. • If you can get sufficiently close while the Juggernaut is distracted by other players, the Energy Sword, Shotgun and carefully thrown Plasma or Spike grenades are all extremely effective.

KING OF THE HILL

Your objective is to conquer a designated area of the map (the "Hill") which is clearly marked by a wall. The longer you maintain control of it, the more you score.

VARIANTS	RULES	TIPS
Crazy King	The Hill regularly changes location. Whoever controls it long enough to earn 100 points wins.	• Standing still inside a Hill is foolish. Instead, try to run around the boundary walls; as a fringe benefit, you'll also find that it's a little easier to spot incoming opponents. Oh, and if there's cover inside a Hill, use it!
Team King	The Hill regularly changes location. The first team that controls it long enough to earn 150 points wins. You only score when the Hill is uncontested by the opposing team.	• Make a note of all entrances to each Hill – this helps you to anticipate the directions that enemies will arrive from. • Before you challenge the Hill, try to collect decent weapons and, above all, pick up grenades.
Mosh Pit	The Hill doesn't move, and all players inside its boundaries are tougher. Whoever controls it long enough to earn 100 points wins.	• It's efficient to weaken opponents inside the Hill boundaries with grenades as you approach, but be careful in team games – you really won't be popular if indiscriminate throws wipe out your allies. • In team games, it is much more effective to have one person gaining time while other players fan out and defend in depth. Clustering on the Hill gives no benefit and makes you vulnerable to grenades.

TERRITORIES

Teams score by taking control of certain Territories. To conquer a Territory, you must occupy it continuously until the gauge at the bottom of the screen is filled.

VARIANTS	RULES	TIPS
Territories	Teams attack and defend Territories in turns. Only the attacking team can score. Once a Territory is captured, it is locked and cannot be taken back. The team with the most points after 4 rounds wins.	• Capture times are reduced to 75% or 66% respectively when two or three teammates occupy a Territory simultaneously. As a general rule, though, it is more practical to have two players on a Territory gaining time, and a third player deterring incoming opponents.
Land Grab	Territories are free and can be taken by every team. Once a Territory is captured, it is locked and cannot be taken back. The team with the most points after 3 rounds wins.	• If you leave a Territory that you are in the process of capturing, the gauge will slowly decrease in your absence. This means that you can dive out to take cover for a few seconds if required. • When a round time limit is up, Sudden Death will start if any Territory is still contested, and last until the Territory in question is either captured or freed.
Flag Rally	Land Grab game where Territories are captured quickly, but can be wrestled from your control by your opponents.	• It's usually far more effective to try to conquer each Territory methodically – with a large group, you can overwhelm divided enemy forces. • When a Territory is being seized by the opposing team, its icon will flash on your screen as a warning. • If an opponent contests a Territory you're trying to capture by stepping inside its boundaries, the gauge will stop filling until you engineer his or her departure from either the Territory, or (ideally) the mortal coil. • In Flag Rally games you must focus simultaneously on attack and defense, as captured Territories are not locked.

BASICS

CAMPAIGN

EXTRAS

MULTIPLAYER

PLAYING CO-OP

MULTIPLAYER
BASICS

GAME TYPES

MULTIPLAYER
TACTICS

MULTIPLAYER
MAPS

FORGE

 [VIP] At least one team has a VIP. Teams usually score by killing another team's VIP.

VARIANTS	RULES	TIPS
VIP	Every team has a VIP who has an Overshield that recharges slowly. When a VIP dies, the next player to die becomes the VIP upon respawning. First team to 10 points wins.	• The key to victory lies in each team's ability to protect their VIP while attacking his enemy counterpart in well-planned raids. • VIPs cannot board vehicles. • VIPs are marked with waypoint indicators, so there's really no point in simply hiding in the nearest dark corner. VIPs should either be always on the move, or protected by their teammates in a suitably fortified position. If you know your current map well, you can pick a solid defensive position to make a stand – but watch out for explosives... • In Influential VIP, teams benefit from moving as groups, though this makes them rather vulnerable to certain power weapons and grenades.
One Sided VIP	Teams take turns in defending their VIP for a set period of time. The team with the most points after 4 rounds wins.	
Escort	Only one team has a VIP, who scores by reaching certain destinations marked by waypoint indicators. Rounds end when the countdown expires, the VIP dies, or all waypoints are reached. The team with the most points after 4 rounds wins.	
Influential VIP	Normal VIP game where all characters are faster, more resistant, more powerful, have fast-regenerating shields and Active Camo when they're close to their VIP.	

[INFECTION] Each player starts either as a zombie or a human, with both species having very different attributes. Zombies score by killing humans, and humans by killing zombies. Any human killed by a zombie becomes a zombie.

VARIANTS	RULES	TIPS
Infection	Zombies are equipped with Energy Swords. Whoever has the most points after 3 rounds wins.	• Zombies cannot use vehicles or pick up weapons. • Leading players generally start the next round as a zombie. • Humans can cooperate to survive, but they're by no means teammates in a conventional sense. • The last man standing is marked by a waypoint indicator, so there is truly no place for him to hide. • Narrow corridors and confined interior areas are deathtraps for humans. • In Hide and Seek mode, zombies are very tough. However, as humans have Active Camo, they can use stealth tactics to survive.
Save One Bullet	Infection game where there are no weapons to pick up on maps, so ammo is limited for humans.	
Alpha Zombie	Infection game where players who start the round as zombies are more powerful than those they infect.	
Hide and Seek	Zombies are fast, more resistant and have Rocket Launchers. Whoever becomes the last human alive gets 5 bonus points.	

ADJUSTABLE OPTIONS

In Custom Games mode, the player hosting a match is free to modify an impressive number of options to adjust specific rules. However, it's important to have a general appreciation of how such changes can influence the balance of play. Small alterations of default settings are fine, but dozens of changes can make a match confusing to play or, worse still, frustrating and incomprehensible. Unless you're actively seeking to design and develop a special Variant to revolutionize online Halo 3 play, you should remember that "less is more" – players generally find it easier to adapt to and enjoy small, interesting changes than complex revisions of entire rulesets.

To access the Options menu (Fig. 1), simply press ✖ in the Custom Games Lobby once you've selected a Variant. The sheer amount of settings that you can modify is really quite daunting, but – thankfully

– they're all very self-explanatory (and, as you'll notice, a help message details the effect of each parameter at the bottom of the screen).

Generally, the most fun can be had by tweaking a couple of settings to add spice to an established Variant. You could give zombies permanent Active Camo for fraught, fast-paced Infection games, or alternatively increase player movement speed, reduce the gravity level and start everyone with Rocket Launchers and Brute Shots for explosive Slayer battles... the possibilities are endless. Once you've finished fine-tuning your Custom Variant, you can save it for future use (or editing) by pressing ✖ on any page of the Options menu. It will then appear under the name you chose as an additional Variant in the appropriate section of the "Game" menu (Fig. 2).

MULTIPLAYER TACTICS
GENERAL TIPS

Let's start with two fundamentals. Although you may be keen to dive back into the fray after each fight, it pays to stay in cover while your shields recharge, or until you have reloaded your weapons. On the subject of reloading, our stance in multiplayer is exactly the same as Campaign mode: *reload or die*. We really can't overstate how important it is to enter battles with a full clip and a full shield bar.

Watch the Motion Tracker for enemy contacts in your immediate vicinity, but remember that it isn't a standard radar: it only detects opponents that are moving at speed or firing. On maps with multiple floor levels, it will also pick up enemies that are moving above and below your position, which can either cause undue alarm or inspire complacency.

There is no such thing as "kill stealing" in free-for-all games, despite the protestations of certain opponents – it's every man, woman and Sangheili warrior for themselves. In team and objective-oriented matches, the good of the team comes first. Essentially, when you get the chance to put an opponent down, just *do it*.

Don't always hurry to charge into battle. Smart players often profit by surveying the scene and judging the correct moment to strike.

If you crouch as you walk, you will be invisible to enemy Motion Trackers. Naturally, this is only of use in Game Types and Variants that don't reveal your position with a waypoint marker. Crouching while airborne will enable you to slightly extend the duration of a leap, and even reach heights or distances that are not possible with a standard jump.

Melee attacks are a crucial ingredient of fights in multiplayer. The best players have an instinctive appreciation of the ideal moment to step forward during close-range duels and finish off their opponent with a bone-breaking blow. There's no hard and fast strategy, but we strongly recommend that you pay careful attention to how your rivals use them during your first weeks of play. Don't forget that a strike to the back of an opponent is in general instantly lethal.

Learn to recognize and quickly react to audio cues. From the fizzing of a Plasma Grenade to the "whoosh!" of a Rocket Launcher, the insistent alarm that accompanies a Missile Pod lock-on to the distinctive hum of a charged Plasma Pistol, sound effects alert you to dangers before you can see them. Play with the volume too low, and you'll miss these critical prompts.

Wandering more or less aimlessly in free-for-all games tends to be rather ineffective. Until you familiarize yourself well with all maps and their subtleties, you can start by traveling on simple routes or loops that are easy to memorize. This way, you will feel less naked and know better what to expect and how to react accordingly. If you notice that your opponents get used to your patterns, though, be prepared to adapt immediately, or you'll become laughably predictable.

Anything that you throw into a Man Cannon or Gravity Lift will be propelled with a momentum based on that object's mass and trajectory at the point of entry. We suggest various useful applications for this feature in the map-specific tips provided later in this chapter, but there's plenty of scope for experimentation.

Saved Films offer more than the opportunity to behold past glories, or create clips of amusing and impressive events. The Theater is actually a repository for all the potential training reels a player keen to improve their all-round game could ever hope for. While watching a film, switch to one of the leading players, or an individual who excelled in a particular area, and study their behavior. It's often the case that a great performance will be largely due to that person's inherent skill, timing and experience, but there are other occasions when you'll notice a specific technique or trick that you can learn from – and, of course, incorporate into your own repertoire.

Unlike in Halo 2, players in Halo 3 have their reserve weapons clearly visible on their player model. Forewarned being forearmed, having the chance to recognize these can help you to avoid nasty surprises. For example, if you see the distinctive handle of a Gravity Hammer sticking out above an opponent's head, that's a clear indication that sprinting forward to make a melee attack is a bad, *bad* idea.

Get into the habit of using explosive devices in the environment to your advantage. If your quarry is foolish enough to move next to an object with the potential to detonate, you are practically obligated to shoot it in order to start or end a fight with a bang. Similarly, if you espy distant rivals fighting in close proximity to a Power Core, try to cause an explosion that might claim them both.

Memorize the positions where you respawn during your first few weeks of play, especially during free-for-all matches. Knowing where enemies are likely to appear from can help you to avoid unexpected attacks.

Even though first-time players might understandably assume otherwise, objects such as the Oddball, flags in CTF games and the bomb in Assault matches are actually all lethal melee weapons – one hit is generally all it takes to beat an enemy to the ground.

Though you lose the ability to perform ranged attacks, you can still use equipment while carrying objects such as flags and bombs.

BASICS

CAMPAIGN

EXTRAS

MULTIPLAYER

PLAYING CO-OP

MULTIPLAYER
BASICS

GAME TYPES

MULTIPLAYER
TACTICS

MULTIPLAYER
MAPS

FORGE

TEAM TIPS

In team games, don't rush to take vital weapons, equipment or vehicles if you're less than skilled at using them. Here's a hypothetical situation for you. A poor marksman with limited multiplayer experience grabs a Sniper Rifle in a CTF game, and proceeds to fire shots at a distant Banshee before being assassinated by an opponent who steals the weapon. How will the teammates of this individual react? Let's just say that it's safe to assume that they won't suggest that everyone has cake and a bit of a sing-song to celebrate. Seriously: team game etiquette really *matters*. No one worth playing with will resent you for making mistakes, but if you habitually waste key weapons and make life difficult for your allies through selfish or inconsiderate behavior in team games, you'll rapidly find yourself becoming a permanent fixture on numerous "Avoided Players" lists.

Communication is absolutely essential in objective-based games, and helps in all team-oriented matches. It's important to be clear and concise, so use simple descriptive terms to identify areas and specific positions. If you don't know the name of an area, a good suggestion is to refer to it by the name of the nearest weapon spawn point. On Valhalla, for example, "The flag is by the Spartan Laser spawn" tells your team exactly what they need to know, while "The flag is in the middle" does not.

Try to use the things that you find for the good of the team. For example, if you're playing an Assault game and pick up a Bubble Shield, join the attack and deploy it at the bomb arming spot to cover your teammates. When you have a Warthog with a free seat, slow down to offer nearby allies a ride. Above all else, don't waste resources. In objective-based games, everything you do should be for the benefit of the team. If you don't feel comfortable with this concept, you might want to stick to free-for-all Game Types.

If your team doesn't intend to use certain vehicles, it can sometimes be prudent to destroy them to prevent them from falling into enemy hands. Naturally, this is a tactical decision that needs to be approved by everyone – you really won't be popular if you blow up a Warthog that your allies have marked for a specific task or strategy.

Camping enemy spawn points can cause confusion and irritation that will hamper their efforts to plan and execute a cohesive strategy. If you realize you are being targeted in this way, communicate the danger to your teammates and cooperate to neutralize the threat immediately. If you don't, the results can be disastrous. One Territories game on Sandtrap we experienced leaps to mind, where a player racked up over twenty consecutive kills by loitering with a Chopper by the main enemy spawn point, also destroying vehicles as they appeared. We shouldn't need to tell you which team triumphed in *that* round...

Placing an unneeded vehicle on top of a bomb arming spot or flag spawn can be a real irritant for your opponents; you can also park them in front of control panels (such as those found on High Ground and Last Resort). Sometimes, enemies will accidentally climb inside the vehicle rather than grabbing the flag, or may decide to quickly move the obstruction aside. Anything that slows them down gives your team the opportunity to launch a more concerted defensive strike. Of course, if there's no one around to take advantage of this inconvenience, you may simply be handing your rivals the gift of a rapid escape...

In Team Slayer games, don't forget that your wellbeing is of paramount importance, and aim to have a positive kill to death ratio. Every single demise you suffer is a point for the opposing team, so it's extremely unwise to throw your life away in skirmishes that you have little chance of winning.

If you get the impression that you're a late addition to a well-organized group, don't just give up and go fight on your own — you'll be wasting your time. Instead, follow and observe your teammates, and try to identify the tasks that you could accomplish to make a contribution to their overall strategy.

EQUIPMENT TIPS

Unlike standard equipment, the Overshield (red) and Active Camo (blue) are activated instantly once you come into contact with either sphere.

- The Overshield, as its name suggests, provides the gift of an additional layer of shielding, but also offers a very brief period of invulnerability when collected. The extra shield energy will then gradually dissipate, so it's advisable to exploit the advantage it grants by aggressively seeking opponents before its effect ends.

- Active Camo offers the benefit of temporary transparency, though eagle-eyed opponents will still be able to detect your presence by spotting the distinctive (though, admittedly, difficult to track) "distorted air" as you move. Firing weapons will increase your visibility, so it's often more profitable to aim for subtle one-hit melee attacks or grenade tags instead.

All equipment types that appear in multiplayer matches are functionally identical to their counterparts in Campaign mode.

You can safely crouch-walk over deployed Trip Mines, though this is a dangerous trick to use — you're effectively doomed if an opponent spots you while you are creeping past one.

An evil trick to play on your opponents in free-for-all matches is to pick up and plant a Trip Mine in the exact position in which it spawns. Anyone paying attention will notice that the device is armed (there are, after all, distinct audio and visual cues), but it's surprising how often players will suffer a lapse in concentration and simply attempt to collect it. You can also plant Trip Mines around or even on top of vehicles, with amusingly

lethal consequences for anyone who incautiously jumps inside after failing to heed the warning signs.

Remember that the Power Drain has an area of effect that passes through many walls and other barriers. It's not enough to hide — distance is the key if you want to keep your shield intact.

The Grav Lift device isn't merely a tool for vaulting walls — it has applications in combat, too. You can drop one to send an opponent who is running forward to make a melee attack flying over your head, and it's an effective (and really funny) way to deal with onrushing vehicles, too.

The Power Drain device will roll through a Bubble Shield when thrown, but its effect is blocked by the energy walls. Consequently, if a Power Drain is inside a Bubble Shield, everyone outside will be safe from its effect, and vice versa.

VEHICLE TIPS

As in Campaign mode, vehicles generally offer a degree of protection that corresponds with their physical appearance. Therefore, while a pristine Warthog will absorb a high degree of damage from incoming small arms fire, another with a smashed windscreen and broken hood will practically wave the bullets through.

Frag Grenades and Plasma Grenades are excellent tools when you face light vehicles, as a well-timed throw into their path can cause them to roll and crash, spilling the driver and any passengers from their seats. The Mongoose is particularly susceptible to the effects of nearby explosions.

Be aware of the potential hazards in a level before you jump into a vehicle, especially during team games on large maps such as Valhalla and Sandtrap. If there's a chance you could run into an adversary wielding a Spartan Laser or a Missile Pod, it might be advisable to wait for your teammates to deal with the threat before you set out on an ill-fated journey in a valuable Banshee, Warthog or Wraith.

The EMP effect of a charged Plasma Pistol shot is something that all drivers should learn to fear. However, note that the Plasma Pistol only disables the engine, and has no effect on weapons systems. If you halt a Warthog's progress, for instance, bear in mind that there is nothing to stop its turret operator from cutting you to shreds once he or she spots you.

In the hands of an expert pilot, the Banshee can quite easily evade rockets fired by the Missile Pod — with instinctive use of the speed boost function and sideways roll, they become no more than a time-consuming inconvenience. However, the Spartan Laser is utterly devastating. On maps such as Valhalla and Sandtrap, teams that control the Spartan Laser can reasonably expect to control the skies.

Due to its raw speed, mobility and extremely fast respawn rate on most maps, the Mongoose is an excellent choice for journeys in and out of enemy territory.

The easiest way to destroy an enemy Wraith is to board it from behind and plant a grenade. In team games where they appear, wasting a Wraith is a cardinal sin. You should always have a second player operate the turret to deal with infantry, and move forward very cautiously.

If your team is enduring frequent low-level strafing runs by an enemy Banshee (especially the really annoying type where the pilot is essentially running players over), break out a Plasma Pistol or, better still, a Power Drain to knock out their engines.

HALO 3

BASICS

CAMPAIGN

EXTRAS

MULTIPLAYER

PLAYING CO-OP

MULTIPLAYER
BASICS

GAME TYPES

MULTIPLAYER
TACTICS

MULTIPLAYER
MAPS

FORGE

WEAPON TIPS

As soon as you spawn, grab the first weapon you encounter as backup to your Assault Rifle. Even if you set off with the express intention of collecting a particular firearm, it always pays to have a second gun in reserve. Rather than reloading the Assault Rifle when its clip is exhausted in a skirmish, you can switch to your other weapon to finish your adversary off.

Look out for the red dot that appears in the center of the reticle with certain weapons (such as the Battle Rifle). This indicates a guaranteed headshot, which is deadly if your target's shield is down.

There are three techniques involving weapons that you can employ to increase the height of a jump, which may enable you to get on top of ledges and platforms that are otherwise out of reach. The "Brute Shot jump" involves firing the weapon at the ground as you leap to make the force of the detonation propel you skywards; for maximum height (but with added risk), fire twice. The "grenade jump" is a classic technique that all players should be aware of by now – just plant a Frag Grenade or Plasma Grenade in the appropriate position, then leap over it as it explodes to attain great heights. Finally, the "Gravity Hammer jump" is also a good trick. To perform one, look down at the ground, then swing the weapon and jump simultaneously. This can also be used to evade or confuse opponents during combat.

Throwing grenades to soften up opponents before you launch an attack is a highly profitable tactic. The shield damage and momentary disorientation can enable you to seize the advantage against adversaries armed with far superior weapons.

Grenades can also be employed to deter assailants from giving chase, especially when you run through doors, which can provide time for your shield to recharge. Spike Grenades are remarkably efficient in enclosed spaces. Not only will the spikes rebound from nearby surfaces, you can plant them on walls and ceilings to give a pursuing player a nasty shock.

When death is certain, throw a grenade as a valedictory gesture of defiance. If your opponent is weakened by the battle or, even better, you manage to tag them, the pain of your demise will be alleviated by the good cheer inspired by a "Beyond the Grave" kill. Note that the Spike Grenade tends to be marginally easier to aim than the Plasma Grenade.

If you press and hold the zoom button, you will return to the previous zoom level immediately when you remove your thumb. This is an interesting feature when you wield scoped weapons, particularly the Sniper Rifle and Beam Rifle. It's almost certainly too awkward for snipers to line up a shot with the thumbstick depressed, but it's handy if you need to briefly take a closer look at something.

To quickly leave the intermediate zoom level while using a Sniper Rifle or Beam Rifle, simply perform a melee attack to instantly return to the default view.

Shots from the Sniper Rifle can ricochet from certain surfaces. With practice, you can take advantage of this feature to hit enemies that you can't actually see.

If you are confronted by an enemy sniper, concentrate on keeping your adversary "descoped" – that is, shoot them in measured bursts to prevent them from zooming in and making a precision shot.

Feel free to practice "no-scope" kills with the Sniper Rifle and Beam Rifle. It's an art that only an elite few will ever come close to perfecting, but even a basic proficiency can be valuable in matches that involve sniper weapons only.

If you are fighting on smaller maps or inside building interiors, the "plasma punch" can be a devastating technique. Run towards an opponent with a charged shot, then release it and follow up with melee attacks.

Turrets may be powerful, but they make their users extremely slow – and, therefore, ripe targets for grenade sticks and melee attacks.

If you hit an opponent at close range with a Shotgun and they somehow survive the blast, follow up with a melee strike to finish them off. This is quick, saves ammo, and reduces the need to reload.

When you dual wield, try to pick one-handed weapons that complement each other. Usually, this will be a plasma/ballistic combination – such as a Plasma Pistol and a Magnum, or a Spiker and a Plasma Rifle – where one gun is efficient against shields, while the other works well against armor, flesh and bone.

The Needler can be less effective at very close range, as its projectiles don't have time to begin tracking a target.

Always aim for an opponent's feet with the Rocket Launcher. If you miss them, you will still have a good chance of causing death or serious injury with the blast radius, whereas a rocket fired at a target's torso would simply fly past them.

With the new "sword parry" feature, using an Energy Sword against an opponent armed with the same weapon is much more tactical. In a sword versus sword fight, you can now stop a lunging duelist in their tracks and block by pressing the melee button. If your timing is precise, the parry will stun your opponent briefly, offering a window of opportunity for you to run them through with your own lunge.

WEAPON	STRENGTHS	WEAKNESSES
Assault Rifle	• This is the default spawn weapon. • Fast rate of fire, large reserve stock of bullets. • Solid and reliable (though not spectacular) in close to medium range skirmishes. • Very common. • Strong against armor.	• Its clip size never seems to be quite large enough to put an opponent down, so it's judicious to switch to a second weapon to finish, or use a melee attack. • Low accuracy when fired continuously. Use short, controlled bursts. • Weak against shields.
Battle Rifle	• Excellent all-purpose weapon. • Headshots are instantly lethal once an opponent's shield is down. • Works well over medium to long range. • Strong against armor.	• Less effective at close range. • Slower fire rate than the Carbine. Each burst of bullets that misses is of greater consequence than a single misplaced Carbine shot, so the Battle Rifle is more suited for competent marksmen. • Weak against shields.
Beam Rifle	• Headshots are instantly lethal. • Usually has a larger supply of ammunition than the Sniper Rifle. • Expert players insist that it's easier to perform "no-scope" kills with a Beam Rifle.	• Overheats very quickly. • Not practical at close range unless you can perform no-scope kills. • "Contrail" beam reveals your position to attentive players. • Has a very slow respawn
Brute Shot	• Best used over close to medium range. • Accurate barrages are as disorientating as they are damaging. • Blade attachment makes it a viciously efficient melee weapon. • Enables you to perform high jumps to reach otherwise inaccessible heights. • Strong against light vehicles.	• Torturously protracted reload time. • Respawn times vary from map to map, but it's generally rather slow to appear (with Isolation the main exception). • Less effective over open ground – its projectiles are easy to dodge.
Carbine	• Excellent all-purpose weapon. • Headshots are instantly lethal once an opponent's shields are down. • Suited for medium to long range fights, but is perhaps marginally less accurate than the Battle Rifle over long distances. • Very fast fire rate.	• Arguably better than the Battle Rifle when you face a jumping, cavorting opponent at close range, but it's often still advisable to switch to a more appropriate weapon during toe-to-toe firefights.
Energy Sword	• The main "lunge" attack generally leads to an instant kill, but can be parried by other sword users. • Basic melee attacks are very fast. • Energy Sword spawn points tend to be fiercely contested areas, so you'll have to fight hard to earn the right to use it. • Is less immediately apparent on your person when "sheathed", so you can switch weapons and use surprise lunges at any time.	• Has a limited battery supply, as in Campaign mode. • You'll need to put it away and switch to a different weapon while you cross open ground. If an opponent out of range sees you approaching with an Energy Sword, they'll backpedal furiously and shoot you down before you can even get close. Oh, and expect your path to be strewn with grenades, too.
Flamethrower	• Tremendously strong at close range, and very dangerous in confined spaces. • Can be used to "paint" areas with flames. • Although stealth attacks from behind are a threat, very few players will be foolish enough to attempt a frontal assault.	• Very limited range. • Reduces the movement speed of the user. • Your enemies can continue to attack until the flames consume them, so last-ditch grenade throws are a constant peril. • Only a real threat in confined spaces – over open ground, you don't have a hope.
Fuel Rod Gun	• The Fuel Rod Gun doesn't appear as standard on any of Halo 3's maps, though you can add it to custom map configurations. • Devastating over short to medium range. • Excellent against land-based vehicles.	• With the exception of its limited suitability for long-distance exchanges and the potential for accidental suicides in close combat situations, there's very little to criticize about the Fuel Rod Gun. It's a truly outstanding weapon in most scenarios – which is perhaps why Bungie has chosen to omit it from the standard map weapon layouts.
Gravity Hammer	• Wide area of effect – you don't have to hit an opponent directly to hurt them. • Effect penetrates thin barriers. • The force of an impact can send an opponent flying, with obvious applications on maps that feature deadly drops. • A standard melee attack doesn't deplete its battery life and can be performed to dispatch weakened adversaries.	• Highly visible, even when slung over the shoulder – if opponents can see you coming, they'll react accordingly and keep a safe distance. • Much slower than the Energy Sword. Miss, and you may be made to pay the price for your haste. • Naturally, the range limitations that apply with the Energy Sword are almost as pertinent with the Gravity Hammer. Small rooms and winding corridors are the best hunting grounds; in external areas or open floor spaces, you won't last long.
Machine Gun Turret	• Incredibly high rate of fire once it gets up to speed, and its effective range is surprisingly far (though with an obvious incremental hit to accuracy). • It's certainly not short of ammunition.	• It takes a while to reach its full fire rate, which often gives opponents sufficient time to go on the offensive, or duck behind cover. • You're exceptionally slow and vulnerable to grenades when you use it. • It makes a lot of noise, so don't be surprised when you become the center of attention…
Magnum	• Can be dual wielded. • Single headshots are instantly lethal on targets once their shield energy is depleted. • Excellent when combined with a Plasma Pistol or Plasma Rifle.	• Weak against shields. • Definitely a weapon for accomplished players – it's much harder to aim than other precision weapons.
Mauler	• Very powerful at close range, and doubly so when dual wielded. • Fast fire rate – it makes the Shotgun seem almost pedestrian by comparison.	• Accuracy and damage decreases rapidly with distance – at anything other than very close range, it's completely toothless.
Missile Pod	• Has an automatic lock-on feature, and its missiles track targets inexorably until they hit something, or run out of fuel. • Acts as a great Banshee deterrent – even if the pilot manages to dodge the missiles, you're still taking them out of the game while they perform evasive maneuvers.	• Small ammo supply. • Very slow respawn time on most default maps where it appears. • The usual turret drawbacks apply. • Excellent against vehicles, but you'll need to pick your targets carefully. The more distant they are, the more likely it is that your rocket will simply hit the terrain and explode harmlessly. • Great damage against infantry, but it's very hard to aim – and, emergencies aside, a great waste.
Needler	• Utterly deadly over close to medium range. Everyone, irrespective of the weapons at their disposal, has ample reason to fear the Needler. • Positioned in intriguingly close proximity to key power weapons on a few maps. You'll often find that the smart money is on the soldier with the Needler to triumph.	• If an opponent is too far away (or even too close) for the needles to start tracking, you'll probably inflict more damage by shouting at people. • It's a very trivial weakness, but the Needler is unsuited to setting off explosive devices.
Plasma Pistol	• Can be dual wielded. • Charged shots disable shields immediately. • Experienced players will fully appreciate how effective it can be when combined with a Battle Rifle, Carbine or Magnum; newcomers to the Halo series should take the time to learn. • Overcharge shots also disable vehicle engines for a short period of time on impact.	• Laughably ineffective as a weapon in its own right – its primary fire mode just isn't cut out for the rigors of multiplayer combat. • It can take a great deal of practice until you can regularly hit opponents or vehicles with charged shots. • While you hold a charged shot in place, the Plasma Pistol's battery level will steadily drain. • Its incessant humming during an overcharge provides ample warning of your intentions to anyone within the immediate vicinity.

WEAPON	STRENGTHS	WEAKNESSES
Plasma Rifle	• Can be dual wielded – ideally with a ballistic weapon for maximum effect. • Excellent against shields. • Very fast fire rate. • Respawns quickly on maps where it appears.	• Weak against armor. • Prone to rapidly overheating if fired continuously – use measured bursts to avoid this. • Its range isn't too bad, but accuracy is always an issue with the Plasma Rifle.
Plasma Turret	• Doesn't appear on any maps by default, but can be added to custom weapon layouts. • Its attributes are very similar to the Machine Gun Turret, but it's better at stripping shields.	• Again, it's very similar to the Machine Gun Turret. However, it's less effective against armor, and lacks accuracy over medium distances.
Rocket Launcher	• Direct hits invariably lead to an instant kill. • Large blast radius makes it effective at taking out vehicles, groups of enemies, and jumping targets.	• Rockets are easy to dodge over medium to long range. • Painfully slow reload time. • As many Halo 2 players will testify, the blast radius is both a blessing and a curse – even great players occasionally fall afoul of the rocket's prodigious splash damage after shooting at a nearby assailant, or after accidentally hitting intervening scenery.
Sentinel Beam	• The Sentinel Beam doesn't appear on the launch maps by default. • Great at stripping shields quickly.	• Weak against armor. • Prone to overheating.
Shotgun	• As you might expect, the Shotgun is utterly brutal at close range. • You can interrupt the reloading process at any time once the first cartridge is in the chamber.	• Slow reload time. • Poor range. • Experienced players know to backpedal if faced by an opponent with a Shotgun. It's sometimes beneficial to keep it hidden until you draw close.
SMG	• Can be dual wielded • Has an extremely high rate of fire, and a respectably large clip size. • Respawns quickly on the maps where it appears. • Strong against armor.	• Only effective at close range. • Suffers from high recoil when used on its own, but much more so when dual wielded. • Weak against shields.
Sniper Rifle	• Headshots are instantly lethal. • Can make four shots in rapid succession, which is impossible with the Beam Rifle.	• Very slow reload time. • Next to useless at close range unless you can perform no-scope kills. • White contrail reveals your position to attentive players. • Long respawn time on all default maps.
Spartan Laser	• A direct hit is an instant kill. • You can cancel the firing process at any time before the shot is made, with no battery penalty. • Effective over long distances. • It's the most accurate anti-vehicular weapon in the game. It inspires a special brand of terror in Banshee pilots – they will often not even hear or see the shot coming.	• Due to its sheer novelty and raw power, ownership of the Spartan Laser is contested vigorously, so be prepared for a furious fight to gain possession of it. • It's painfully slow to fire, especially when you're dodging bullets as you take aim, and its battery life expires in a flash. Or, to be precise, five of them.
Spiker	• Can be dual wielded, and is incredibly powerful over short distances if you have a pair. • Has a venomous fire rate, and a healthy clip size.	• The decaying trajectory and relatively slow speed of the spikes make it a weapon that is only suited to enclosed spaces, where you can surprise enemies within its functional range.

PLAYING CO-OP

MULTIPLAYER BASICS

GAME TYPES

MULTIPLAYER TACTICS

MULTIPLAYER MAPS

FORGE

UNLOCKING ARMOR

If you want to underline your credentials as a Halo 3 expert during multiplayer matches, you'll need to take the time to customize your appearance. There are numerous different armor "sets" for both Spartan and Elite body types, and these can be mix-and-matched to create a wide variety of distinct combinations. A handful of these are available from the very first time you play, but others can only be selected once you have fulfilled specific requirements. The tables here show how many of these can be unlocked but, at Bungie's request, we don't reveal them all. Once you complete this part of your collection, rest assured that there are still more to find...

	SET	PIECE	UNLOCK CONDITION
SPARTAN	EVA	Body	Complete Tsavo Highway on Normal, Heroic or Legendary
		Shoulders	Complete The Ark on Normal, Heroic or Legendary
		Head	Complete Campaign mode on Normal
	EOD	Body	Complete Tsavo Highway on Legendary
		Shoulders	Complete The Ark on Legendary
		Head	Complete Campaign mode on Legendary
	Security	Shoulders	Earn 750 Gamerscore points
		Head	Earn 1000 Gamerscore points
	Scout	Body	Unlock "Too Close to the Sun" Achievement
		Shoulders	Unlock "We're in for some Chop" Achievement
		Head	Unlock "Used Car Salesman" Achievement
	Mark V	Head	Unlock "UNSC Spartan" Achievement
	ODST	Head	Unlock "Spartan Graduate" Achievement
	Rogue	Head	Unlock "Spartan Officer" Achievement

	SET	PIECE	UNLOCK CONDITION
ELITE	Flight	Body	Complete Tsavo Highway on Heroic or Legendary
		Shoulders	Complete The Ark on Heroic or Legendary
		Head	Complete Campaign mode on Heroic
	Ascetic	Body	Unlock "Up Close and Personal" Achievement
		Shoulders	Unlock "Overkill" Achievement
		Head	Unlock "Steppin' Razor" Achievement
	Commando	Body	Unlock "Triple Kill" Achievement
		Shoulders	Unlock "Killing Frenzy" Achievement
		Head	Complete "Overkill" Achievement

MULTIPLAYER MAPS

Introduction

Over the following 44 pages, we take a detailed look at each of the 11 multiplayer maps featured in Halo 3. With annotated maps designed to help you find your way around and locate the best weapons, and a wide variety of tips (many contributed by Bungie), absorbing the information offered in this section is the perfect way to kick-start your online career.

Note: While the information provided for each map was correct at the time of going to press, be warned that Bungie may choose to change item locations or types at any time.

HALO 3

BASICS

CAMPAIGN

EXTRAS

MULTIPLAYER

PLAYING CO-OP

MULTIPLAYER
BASICS

GAME TYPES

MULTIPLAYER
TACTICS

**MULTIPLAYER
MAPS**

FORGE

1 Each map is annotated with the positions of weapons, equipment, vehicles, and other points of interest. If you can't recognize a symbol, keep the back cover foldout open for easy reference.

2 Maps have been carefully prepared to provide the best possible overview of the playing areas. There's really no substitute for actual playing experience, but they will be especially useful for new players seeking to familiarize themselves with each map as quickly as possible.

3 If a map features multiple floors that can't be shown on a single map, they are shown separately.

4 Given the behind-the-scenes calculations that govern the speed at which weapons, equipment and vehicles respawn, it would be misleading to provide lists of supposedly "definitive" figures. If a Battle Rifle is ostensibly set to reappear after 30 seconds there's actually no guarantee that it will do so every time. Taking that into consideration, we've instead opted to offer a simple visual system that gives a clear indication of how regularly a weapon will reappear. If you're wondering how the colored bars translate into actual times, the table below contains the illumination you seek.

Respawn Times	Bars
180 seconds +	
120-179 seconds	
90-119 seconds	
60-89 seconds	
30-59 seconds	
Less than 30 seconds	

5 This information provided by Bungie gives a general idea of the styles of play and participant numbers that every map is broadly suited to.

6 For each map, we offer a quick list of the most highly coveted weapons, vehicles and equipment types, especially during free-for-all matches.

CONSTRUCT

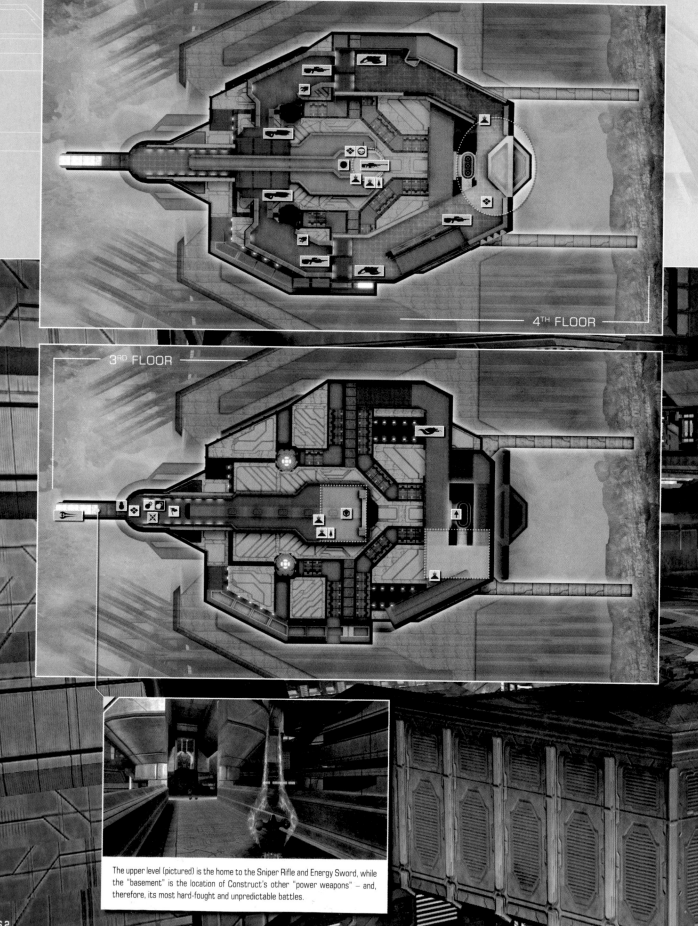

4TH FLOOR

3RD FLOOR

The upper level (pictured) is the home to the Sniper Rifle and Energy Sword, while the "basement" is the location of Construct's other "power weapons" — and, therefore, its most hard-fought and unpredictable battles.

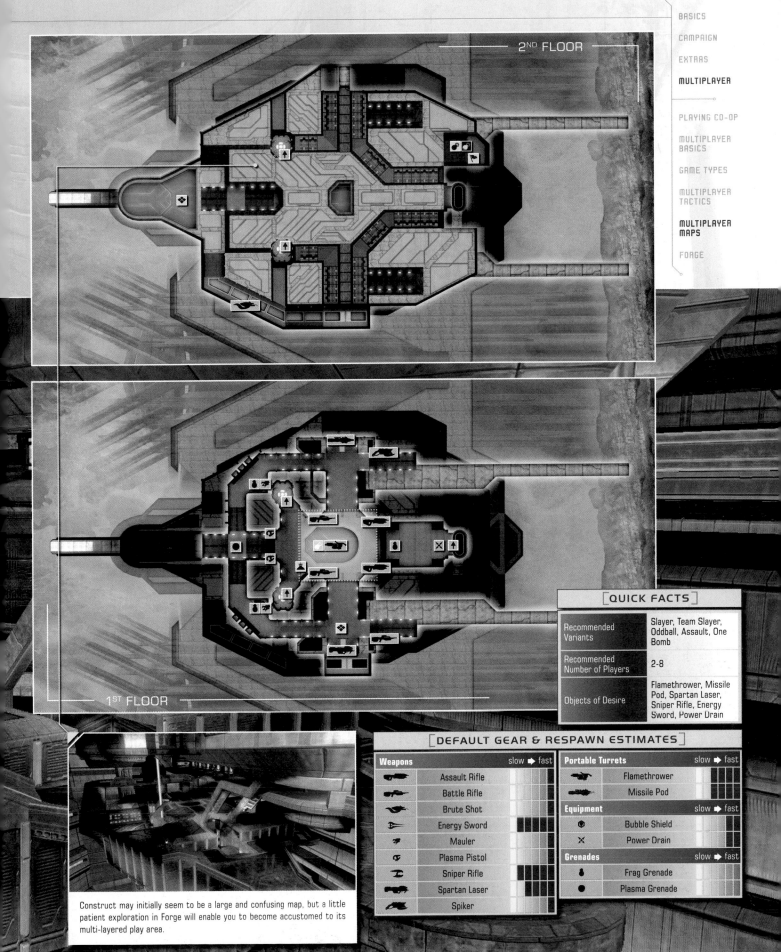

BASICS

CAMPAIGN

EXTRAS

MULTIPLAYER

PLAYING CO-OP

MULTIPLAYER BASICS

GAME TYPES

MULTIPLAYER TACTICS

MULTIPLAYER MAPS

FORGE

2ND FLOOR

1ST FLOOR

[QUICK FACTS]

Recommended Variants	Slayer, Team Slayer, Oddball, Assault, One Bomb
Recommended Number of Players	2-8
Objects of Desire	Flamethrower, Missile Pod, Spartan Laser, Sniper Rifle, Energy Sword, Power Drain

Construct may initially seem to be a large and confusing map, but a little patient exploration in Forge will enable you to become accustomed to its multi-layered play area.

[DEFAULT GEAR & RESPAWN ESTIMATES]

Weapons		slow ➡ fast
	Assault Rifle	
	Battle Rifle	
	Brute Shot	
	Energy Sword	
	Mauler	
	Plasma Pistol	
	Sniper Rifle	
	Spartan Laser	
	Spiker	

Portable Turrets		slow ➡ fast
	Flamethrower	
	Missile Pod	

Equipment		slow ➡ fast
	Bubble Shield	
	Power Drain	

Grenades		slow ➡ fast
	Frag Grenade	
	Plasma Grenade	

CONSTRUCT

General Tips

The Gravity Lifts aren't just a means of moving to higher platforms — they're also valuable escape routes. However, remember that opponents will sometimes throw grenades to follow you, so try to vacate the landing area as soon as you hit the floor.

Gravity Lifts on Construct are different than others found in multiplayer. Most lifts function like elevators — you enter and exit from the same side. For these lifts, however, you enter one way, and exit the opposite way, so you don't need to turn around.

Beware of the lift exits — they are excellent camping spots! If you're partial to a certain amount of lurking in these areas, note that you can actually stick players traveling upwards with Plasma Grenades.

Having two Plasma Pistols and a pair of Power Drains, Construct is a map where EMP damage is an almost constant threat. If either should deplete your shields, you can usually be sure that a barrage of bullets or a precision headshot is imminent. It pays to have a grenade at the ready; taking your assailant with you is suitable consolation.

The Plasma Pistol/Battle Rifle combo is one that all experienced players will love and loathe in equal measure, and it's a common feature of battles that take place here (Fig. 1). When you hear the distinctive drone of an overcharge, consider it a vital (and often life-saving) prompt to be ready to dodge, duck or jump accordingly.

One of the two Power Drain units is located on the bottom floor, just outside the main Gravity Lift. If you can collect it as you run into the elevator, it enables you to pull a nasty surprise on any opponents that are giving chase. Turn around as you land, throw it back down the shaft, then get out of the way before the effect hits you. Your former hunter, both weakened and disoriented, will be a cinch to dispatch (Fig. 2).

0 1

0 2

BASICS

CAMPAIGN

EXTRAS

MULTIPLAYER

PLAYING CO-OP

MULTIPLAYER
BASICS

GAME TYPES

MULTIPLAYER
TACTICS

**MULTIPLAYER
MAPS**

FORGE

03

04

The main central platform leaves combatants exposed from almost every angle — you need to keep moving at all times while traveling across it. For that reason, many players will gravitate towards the upper or lower levels.

Shoot the volatile Power Cores to weaken nearby enemies, and don't linger in areas where they are positioned on walls (Fig. 3).

The two metal beams that extend diagonally from the middle level to support the far end of the floor above look steep, but you can actually run up them. This makes them a great short-cut to the Energy Sword spawn point. They're also very handy for launching ambushes on players fighting or camping above, but be warned that you're clearly visible from below (Fig. 4).

On the top level, there is a barrier with glass walls. Above this, there are two small ledges to either side that you can snipe from. However, the process of reaching them is almost prohibitively complicated — other than getting up there to say that you have, there's no real advantage in doing so during a match.

You really can't trust your Motion Tracker during games on Construct. As it will also pick up movement on the bottom floor while you are on the top floor, you can never be sure if approaching contacts are going to be agents of your imminent demise, or just two Spartans bickering over the Missile Pod in the basement area. A threatening blip on the Motion Tracker is cause for vigilance, granted, but you'll need to rely heavily on your knowledge of the level and the way people tend to play it.

The basement area is home to an almost obscene array of weapons. However, there's a definite ebb and flow to the carnage that takes place there. Even in busy free-for-all games that feature many players, there are occasional moments of relative calm as people seeking power weapons grow tired of frequent deaths, and opt to explore the upper floors instead.

EPITAPH

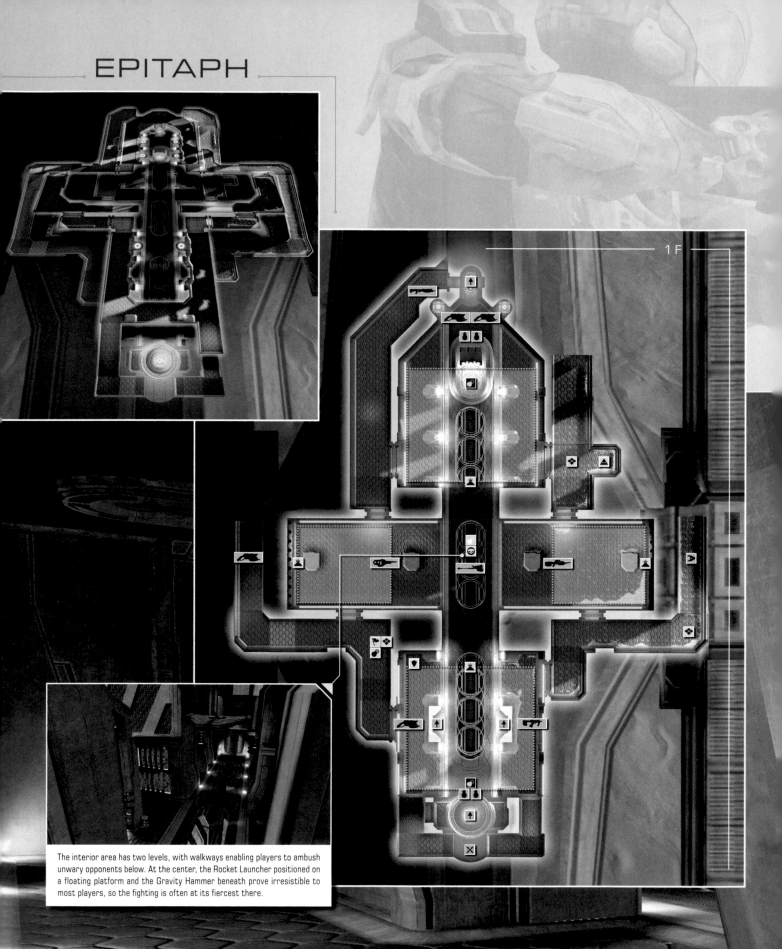

The interior area has two levels, with walkways enabling players to ambush unwary opponents below. At the center, the Rocket Launcher positioned on a floating platform and the Gravity Hammer beneath prove irresistible to most players, so the fighting is often at its fiercest there.

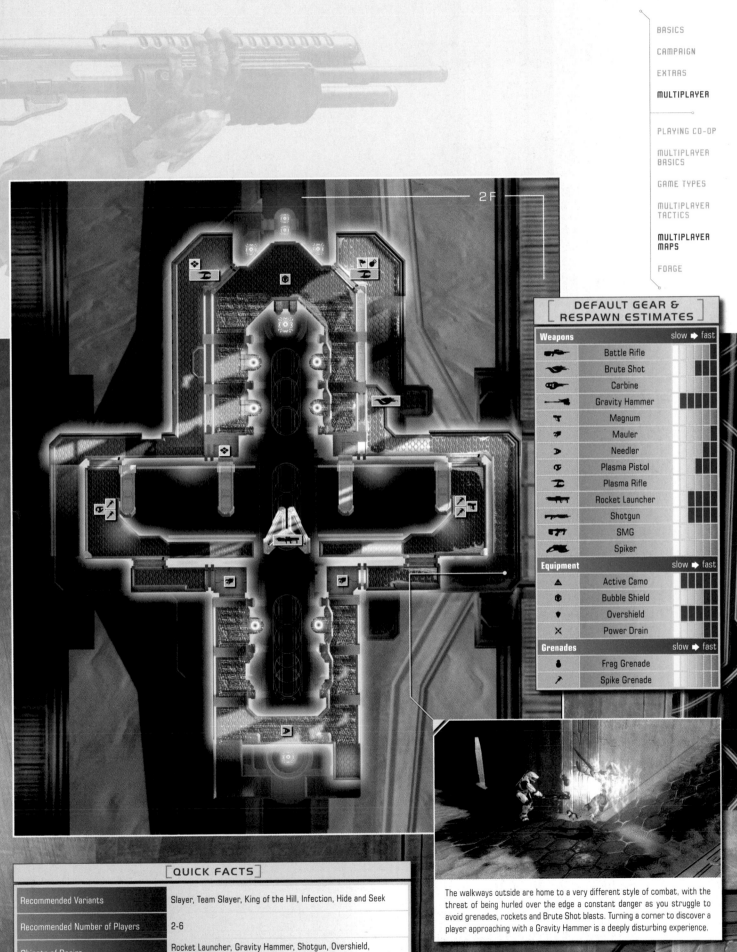

HALƏ3

BASICS

CAMPAIGN

EXTRAS

MULTIPLAYER

PLAYING CO-OP

MULTIPLAYER BASICS

GAME TYPES

MULTIPLAYER TACTICS

MULTIPLAYER MAPS

FORGE

2F

DEFAULT GEAR & RESPAWN ESTIMATES

Weapons	slow ➡ fast
Battle Rifle	
Brute Shot	
Carbine	
Gravity Hammer	
Magnum	
Mauler	
Needler	
Plasma Pistol	
Plasma Rifle	
Rocket Launcher	
Shotgun	
SMG	
Spiker	

Equipment	slow ➡ fast
Active Camo	
Bubble Shield	
Overshield	
Power Drain	

Grenades	slow ➡ fast
Frag Grenade	
Spike Grenade	

The walkways outside are home to a very different style of combat, with the threat of being hurled over the edge a constant danger as you struggle to avoid grenades, rockets and Brute Shot blasts. Turning a corner to discover a player approaching with a Gravity Hammer is a deeply disturbing experience.

[QUICK FACTS]

Recommended Variants	Slayer, Team Slayer, King of the Hill, Infection, Hide and Seek
Recommended Number of Players	2-6
Objects of Desire	Rocket Launcher, Gravity Hammer, Shotgun, Overshield, Active Camo

EPITAPH

General Tips

The power weapons that everyone will flock towards are the Gravity Hammer and Rocket Launcher, but don't forget about the Shotgun and Brute Shot – they're both just as powerful in their own unique ways, and they're less likely to be surrounded by a bickering rabble.

A Power Drain lies behind the Gravity Lift that propels players to the Rocket Launcher platform. It won't land on the platform if you throw it into the lift, but it will travel over it – which is enough for the passing device to strip your target's shields (Fig. 1).

On the other side of this Gravity Lift, there is a Needler. This is a great weapon to have during the early-game rush for the Rocket Launcher and Gravity Hammer. If you can arrive unfashionably early, you will be able to devastate enemies squabbling over the ostensibly more desirable weapons with controlled bursts of pink mist.

The Rocket Launcher platform is not fixed – it sways, rocks and may even flip if hit by bullets or explosions (Fig. 2).

The Gravity Hammer is positioned in the very centre of the building, but you're better off taking it somewhere where you are less exposed. The walkways outside are a particularly good stalking ground. Note that there is an Overshield power-up very close to the Gravity Hammer spawn point. If you pick it up on the way, you'll have a potentially commanding advantage over your rivals.

Beware of enemies "door camping" outside – you'll die more than a few deaths at the hands of opponents loitering out of sight beyond the shield barriers, especially when they wield powerful melee weapons.

HALO 3

BASICS

CAMPAIGN

EXTRAS

MULTIPLAYER

PLAYING ONLINE

MULTIPLAYER
BASICS

GAME TYPES

MULTIPLAYER
TACTICS

MULTIPLAYER
MAPS

FORGE

As with all levels that feature energy shields over doorways, try to avoid getting involved in cat-and-mouse battles with opponents on the other side. They're actually quite time-consuming, and there's always a huge risk that someone else will pick you (or, frustratingly, your opponent) off while you're distracted.

Grenades are deadly on the outside walkways. Many players are in the habit of jumping in an attempt to minimize blast damage (or simply to avoid bullets), and they can be thrown over the edge by the explosion (Fig. 3).

If you're the climbing type, you'll be pleased to hear that there are some interesting points you can reach inside the main building. Firstly, you can jump on top of the buttresses either side of the Rocket Launcher platform. This is both a good escape route, and an interesting camping spot – you can drop down at the back and be out through a door very quickly if needs be. Note that you can reach the furthermost buttress via the tiny ledge on the wall (there are actually a few of these), and even make your way to a small platform in the far corner. Of course, you're an easy target for anyone that spots you up there, but it's a potentially interesting place to be (Fig. 4).

The Shotgun spawn point (on the lower level of the outside walkways, to the far north of the building) is an excellent position for defending a VIP. Enemies can drop down from the upper walkway, and attack via the doors, but the back exit is completely secure – it's a Gravity Lift, which (with a certain pleasing irony) leads to the Bubble Shield spawn point. If you position your VIP

next to it, the curvature of the walkway will protect him or her from enemy bullets and grenades, and there's a ready-made escape route should the defending force be overpowered.

0 3

0 4

GUARDIAN

2F

[QUICK FACTS]

Recommended Variants	Slayer, Team Slayer, Oddball, King of the Hill, Land Grab
Recommended Number of Players	2-6
Objects of Desire	Sniper Rifle, Gravity Hammer, Shotgun, Overshield, Active Camo

Don't let its compact size fool you – this is a map where the relatively small playing area belies the complexity and varied nature of the combat that takes place there.

HALO 3

BASICS

CAMPAIGN

EXTRAS

MULTIPLAYER

PLAYING CO-OP

MULTIPLAYER
BASICS

GAME TYPES

MULTIPLAYER
TACTICS

**MULTIPLAYER
MAPS**

FORGE

1F

The bottom corridor features a Sniper Rifle and a Gravity Hammer, two weapons that can dominate skirmishes on Guardian.

[DEFAULT GEAR & RESPAWN ESTIMATES]

Weapons		slow ➡ fast
	Assault Rifle	
	Battle Rifle	
	Brute Shot	▮▮▮▮
	Carbine	
	Gravity Hammer	▮▮▮▮
	Magnum	
	Mauler	▮▮▮
	Needler	▮▮▮
	Plasma Pistol	▮▮▮
	Plasma Rifle	
	Shotgun	▮▮▮▮
	SMG	
	Sniper Rifle	▮▮▮▮
	Spiker	
Equipment		slow ➡ fast
⚠	Active Camo	▮▮▮
⬡	Bubble Shield	▮▮▮
✳	Flare	▮▮
♥	Overshield	▮▮▮
Grenades		slow ➡ fast
▮	Frag Grenade	
●	Plasma Grenade	

GUARDIAN

General Tips

The Bubble Shield spawn point on top of the tree stump is an extremely interesting position. If you activate the device on top of the root, anyone who wants to attack you must leap over to your location, which makes them a ripe target for a melee attack as they land. For this reason, you should regard this area as a key waypoint in your attempt to outfox the pursuing horde during Oddball games (Fig. 1).

The Gravity Hammer is positioned at the centre of the map, on the lower level. Intriguingly, though, the Sniper Rifle – this map's other principle power weapon – is situated further along the very same corridor. This sets up some interesting early match confrontations, so the lower level is definitely not a place for the faint of heart to frequent.

When you first start playing on Guardian – or even, if you're sensible, beforehand – you should make it a priority to learn where each fixed Gravity Lift leads to. This is a small map, but that doesn't mean that you won't get lost.

Get the Gravity Hammer away from the lower corridor as soon as you can. As you should know, it's best used in areas where you can surprise people as they round corners, so it's better to blaze a trail towards the indoor area.

You can smack opponents over the edge of the map with the Gravity Hammer if they incautiously stand by a ledge on the outside walkway (Fig. 2). This is especially easy when they are jumping at the time.

0 1

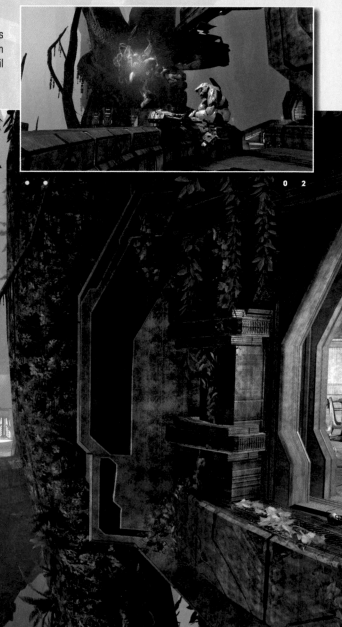

0 2

HALO 3

BASICS

CAMPAIGN

EXTRAS

MULTIPLAYER

PLAYING CO-OP

MULTIPLAYER
BASICS

GAME TYPES

MULTIPLAYER
TACTICS

MULTIPLAYER
MAPS

FORGE

If an enemy thinks they are safe behind the glass where the Gravity Hammer spawns, teach them otherwise – if you swing the hammer in their direction, its effects will pass through such barriers with ease (Fig. 3).

The only real sniping spot on this map is the ledge just beyond the Needler spawn point (Fig. 4). However, there are a few drawbacks to this position. Firstly, you'll often need to destroy the Fusion Core before you can safely establish yourself there, which draws unwelcome attention; secondly, you're constantly exposed to people sneaking up from behind. Last, but by no means least, there is a Gravity Lift on the far lower side of the map that lands right here. Snipers really don't have an easy life on Guardian. On the plus side, this is a great map to practice your "no scope" shooting skills.

The Shotgun is situated at the end of a dead-end corridor, which is a design choice that can make life difficult. If someone passing at the other end of the corridor spots you before you can close the gap, you're an easy target – unless, of course, you immediately switch to your backup weapon. You'd be surprised by how many players will simply run forward while shooting the Shotgun, to minimal effect...

The center of the map is something of a death trap, given the lack of cover and exposed location. Try to avoid it as much as possible.

At the top of the big Gravity Lift there are two small openings in the floor on either side of the landing area. If you have an opponent in hot pursuit, you can quickly drop down to the bottom level to confuse them.

0   3

0   4

The Flare can come in handy when you play One Flag CTF on this level. Throw it into the flag room to cause confusion, then run in and grab your prize. While your opponents need to see you to shoot you, you can simply sprint in with the appropriate button held to automatically pick up the flag. It should go without saying that it is a good idea to practice this offline before you try it in a competitive environment.

Active Camo is a ninja's best friend on this map. Combine it with a Gravity Hammer, dual Maulers or a Shotgun for maximum effect.

INTERIOR

I

II

BASE

[QUICK FACTS]

Recommended Variants	Slayer, One Flag, One Bomb, Escort, Hide and Seek, Territories
Recommended Number of Players	4-12
Objects of Desire	Spartan Laser, Sniper Rifle, Rocket Launcher, Machine Gun Turret, Ghost

[DEFAULT GEAR & RESPAWN ESTIMATES]

Weapons	slow ⟶ fast
Battle Rifle	
Brute Shot	
Carbine	
Mauler	
Needler	
Plasma Pistol	
Rocket Launcher	
Shotgun	
SMG	
Sniper Rifle	
Spartan Laser	
Spiker	

Portable Turrets	slow ⟶ fast
Machine Gun Turret	

Equipment	slow ⟶ fast
Active Camo	
Bubble Shield	
Grav Lift	
Overshield	
Power Drain	

Grenades	slow ⟶ fast
Frag Grenade	
Spike Grenade	

Vehicles	slow ⟶ fast
Ghost	
Mongoose	

BASICS

CAMPAIGN

EXTRAS

MULTIPLAYER

PLAYING CO-OP

MULTIPLAYER
BASICS

GAME TYPES

MULTIPLAYER
TACTICS

**MULTIPLAYER
MAPS**

FORGE

In objective-based games where the front gate is initially locked, you can use the control panel here to open it.

The Spartan Laser spawn point is often one of the most fiercely contested areas of real estate on High Ground, especially during free-for-all Game Types.

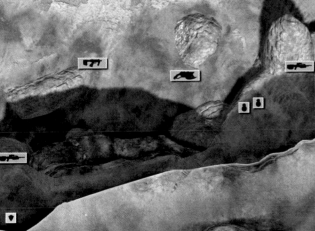

BEACH

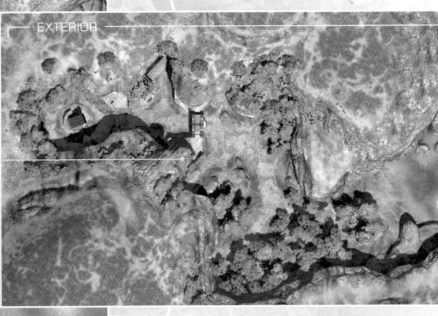

EXTERIOR

I TOWER: INTERMEDIATE FLOOR

II BUNKER

Beach Area

The base area has three principal points of ingress: the main gate (which may be closed at first), the bunker on the left (via the hole in the wall and the trapdoor above it), and the broken wall section on the right.

The pipe provides a direct route into the base, but is the easiest entry point for a defending team to guard.

The beach is a happy hunting ground if you favor stalking newly spawned players, but don't forget that other combatants will be equally inclined to prey on the vulnerable.

Beware of snipers in the beach area, especially down by the water's edge and on the upper rock ledge.

The Ghost is a particularly powerful tool for sniper suppression (though less so if the sniper is positioned on the rock ledge, of course).

tactic best suited for free-for-all games only, though – indiscriminate use of explosives will not make you particularly popular in team-based matches.

To blow open the trapdoor above the bunker, you need to either shoot at it or hit it with a grenade. In team-based games, there is a less noisy way to open it if a stealthy approach is your objective: simply drop a Bubble Shield on top of it.

In Territories games, you can temporarily prevent your opponents from using the trapdoor entrance to the bunker by dropping a Grav Lift beneath the opening, which may gift you a few valuable extra seconds. If you encounter this trick, you can try to destroy it from above, but watch out – clever players will throw a Spike Grenade at the floor to greet your imminent arrival...

When you attack the base in objective-based games, you can take advantage of the Ghost to provide an armed escort for Mongoose raiding parties. However, both Ghost and Mongoose drivers should be extremely wary in this area – it's very easy to stick either vehicle with Spike Grenades.

If you are defending the base, consider sending a Ghost driver out to destroy the opposing team's vehicles as they appear, and to terrorize their spawn area, hampering any attempt to organize a structured attack.

When you attack the base, securing and deploying the Grav Lift to reach the Spartan Laser spawn point or the gate controls is important, but it's vital that you coordinate with your teammates before you place it. The defending team will aim to destroy the device immediately.

If you hear combat as you pass the Spartan Laser spawn point, you can sometimes score easy kills by throwing grenades up there. This is a

With a little practice, it's possible to climb certain trees on the hill area, walk to the end of a branch, and crouch to hide in the leaves. There are two trees in particular where this can be a fruitful tactic. The first is the tree opposite the main gateway. The cover here is reasonable, though the element of surprise is lost the moment an opponent knows you are there. The most interesting tree, however, is the one nearest to the Grav Lift spawn point (Fig. 1). If you carefully run to the end of the branch pointing in the direction of the ocean, only players with eagle eyes, outstanding luck, or remarkable prescience will be able to see you. Unfortunately, the leaves that conceal you also greatly reduce your view of the battlefield. However, a gifted sniper will appreciate the gaps in the foliage that provide views of the cave entrance, the Rocket Launcher spawn point and, to a lesser extent, the Spartan Laser spawn point.

In Assault games, the team attacking the base can benefit by stopping to pick up the Bubble Shield, which can be deployed over the arming spot to protect the player with the bomb.

HALO 3

BASICS

CAMPAIGN

EXTRAS

MULTIPLAYER

PLAYING CO-OP

MULTIPLAYER
BASICS

GAME TYPES

MULTIPLAYER
TACTICS

MULTIPLAYER
MAPS

FORGE

Base Area

You can jump from the broken wall to reach the roof above the base flag spawn point (Fig. 2). This provides an excellent view of the entrance to the pipe room, the main gate and, of course, the flag below.

The top of the missile launcher at the back of the base is also a good sniping spot, providing a clear view of the main gate.

The turret on top of the gateway enables defending teams to devastate incoming vehicles, guard the Rocket Launcher spawn point, and to encourage opposing teams to channel their attacks via the two caves, which slows them down. That said, the turret operator can be picked off with ease by a sniper. Attacking teams should make it a priority to destroy this gun emplacement immediately, and ideally turn the turret against the base occupants.

and above the pipe is especially good for free-for-all games (Fig. 3) – even people entering the room may fail to notice you, and anyone emerging from the pipe will be oblivious to your presence. The other one enables you to fire (or throw grenades) at enemies as they walk through the pipe, which makes it a better choice while defending the base in objective-oriented games.

If you are defending an objective point, the Power Drain is an effective way to break up concerted attacks, or to prevent your opponents from escaping with the flag in a vehicle via the main gate. Don't waste it frivolously!

There is a small camouflaged ledge just over the wall from the Spartan Laser spawn point. It's a good avenue of retreat in the heated battles that take place in this area (less knowledgeable players may assume you have jumped to the ground below), and is also a great position for launching surprise attacks.

As every fraction of a second counts in the rush to secure the Spartan Laser in certain Game Types, base-side soldiers can reach the spawn point by jumping to it from the metal platform above the gateway.

In the room that contains the pipe exit inside the base, there are two thin metal supports that extend from the far wall. You can jump on these and use them as ambush points. The one behind

In the same room, there is another hiding spot behind the pipe. You can sometimes escape pursuing foes if you can conceal yourself here, gaining vital seconds for a shield recharge, or you can lie in wait for oblivious enemies to pass by before leaping out to strike.

Remember that anyone traveling through the pipe will be crouch-walking as they move, and therefore invisible to radar.

The Brute Shots located in the base are highly effective against the Mongoose, which makes them vital tools in CTF games. A furious, well-aimed barrage will at very least weaken (and potentially dismount) both driver and passenger, which makes it very hard for the opposing team to escape with your flag.

Despite the buzz saw report of Assault Rifles and pounding Brute Shot detonations, the outdoor area is a surprisingly tranquil environment. There are plenty of positions that offer cover, while the spot near the "goo chute" that leads to the underground level is frequently favored by snipers.

HALO 3

BASICS

CAMPAIGN

EXTRAS

MULTIPLAYER

PLAYING CO-OP

MULTIPLAYER
BASICS

GAME TYPES

MULTIPLAYER
TACTICS

**MULTIPLAYER
MAPS**

FORGE

DEFAULT GEAR & RESPAWN ESTIMATES

Weapons	slow ➡ fast	Equipment	slow ➡ fast
Assault Rifle		Flare	
Battle Rifle		Regenerator	
Brute Shot		**Grenades**	slow ➡ fast
Needler		Frag Grenade	
Rocket Launcher		Spike Grenade	
Shotgun		**Vehicles**	slow ➡ fast
Sniper Rifle		Ghost	
Spiker		Mongoose	

QUICK FACTS

Recommended Variants	Team Slayer, Multi Flag, Assault, Infection, VIP
Recommended Number of Players	2-10
Objects of Desire	Rocket Launcher, Ghost, Sniper Rifle

UNDERGROUND

The underground area is home to both bases, and is distinguished by the evidence of advanced Flood infestation. Don't be alarmed – the fleshy sacs on the walls will not spawn Infection Forms if hit by stray bullets.

ISOLATION

Outdoors

Each bunker has a Mongoose waiting outside. You'll obviously use these to reach key weapons swiftly once a round starts, but don't be too quick to casually abandon them. The Mongooses on Isolation have a longer respawn time than on other maps, so it's better to take them back to your base area, or have someone ready to collect one for another purpose.

Don't miss the two Brute Shots positioned to the left and right of the Ghost spawn point — tucked away in corners, it's easy to pass them by.

Gaining ownership of the Ghost is a massive benefit in team-based games. Though it is vulnerable to the Brute Shot and Rocket Launcher, it's a powerful fast-response vehicle (try outrunning a Ghost while carrying a flag back to your base, or fending one off with a Sniper Rifle), and makes the process of defending your bunker much, much easier.

The Sniper Rifle is positioned at the south end of the map, just beside a Needler. The north end of the map is the best sniping spot — not only does it offer an excellent view of the garden area, you can also escape down the hole leading to the lower level. (In CTF or Assault games, some may prefer to take the Sniper Rifle back to their team's bunker to make pot-shots through the windows, which is something you should always be prepared for.)

The Shotgun can be found resting against the structure to the north of the map, and is an excellent tool for base defense in CTF and Assault matches.

Much like those on High Ground, you can climb the trees in the upper garden area (Fig. 1). The cover they offer depends on your position (the ends of the branches are best) and armor color (bad luck if you're on the Red Team). If you practice offline, trying each tree out in turn, you may find some handy camping spots that offer a good view of some key positions.

0 1

If you're feeling ambitious at the start of a round, you can try for the "double" — grab the Sniper Rifle, then drop through the hole and pick up the Rocket Launcher. Odds are that you'll encounter the business end of a Ghost straight away, though…

HALO 3

BASICS

CAMPAIGN

EXTRAS

MULTIPLAYER

PLAYING CO-OP

MULTIPLAYER
BASICS

GAME TYPES

MULTIPLAYER
TACTICS

**MULTIPLAYER
MAPS**

FORGE

Underground

The layout of both bases is identical. They each have four entrances: two at the side, one behind (which leads to the upper garden area) and an opening in the ceiling that enables friend or foe alike to drop down from above. In objective-based games, it's common sense to position someone to guard this weak spot.

A Rocket Launcher sits between both bases, and is obviously a very powerful weapon in the enclosed spaces of the underground level. In objective-based games, however, picking it up is easier said than done — not only do you need to worry about potential rivals getting there first, you also have to contend with enemies firing from their bunker. Your team can potentially help you by throwing a Regenerator through the window, though this takes careful coordination. Additionally, there's also the not insignificant matter of a Ghost that spawns just along the corridor...

Both base areas contain (and are surrounded by) a variety of weapons, but the key assets on this map – the Ghost, Sniper Rifle, Needler, Shotgun and Rocket Launcher – are all scattered around the map. The start of every team-based round usually features a ferocious scramble to secure the best of these. It's important to find a balance if you have a flag or bomb arming site to defend, though. For example, if too many soldiers go out to secure weaponry and vehicles, your team can fall afoul of a quick and dirty attack designed to overwhelm the handful of defenders left behind to guard the base. Equally, an overly-cautious strategy can leave you in the undesirable situation where your opponents gain control of the best weapons.

The hole next to the Sniper Rifle/Needler spawn point drops you almost directly on top of the Rocket Launcher spawn point. You can surprise people in the bunker areas (or anyone attempting to take possession of the Rocket Launcher) by dropping down with a Needler (Fig. 2).

0 2

You will find two Spike Grenades above the south hole. You can throw them down at passing enemies, especially if the Rocket Launcher is still there.

There is a Flare not far away from the hole at the north of the map. If you've been conducting a reign of terror with a Sniper Rifle from this position, and the locals are accumulating with the Halo 3 equivalent of pitchforks, torches and murderous intent, you can activate it to assist a hasty retreat through the hole leading to the lower level. This trick can also work well in Oddball and VIP matches.

Though suitable for a variety of Game Types, Isolation is frequently the stage for CTF and Assault matches. In these, the two bunker rooms play host to flags and bombs, but also plenty of sniping through the facing windows.

More so than on any other map, the Brute Shot is a key weapon on Isolation. There are four on the default map, all within easy sprinting distance of both bases (the positional symmetry means that two are effectively allocated per team). Furthermore, all Brute Shots have a fast respawn time, so expect to encounter them (or, more specifically, the grenades they fire) on a regular basis.

[QUICK FACTS]

Recommended Variants	Team Slayer, One Flag, Territories, One Bomb, Escort, Infection
Recommended Number of Players	4-12
Objects of Desire	Spartan Laser, Sniper Rifle, Active Camo, Power Drain, Warthog, Ghost

BEACH

I

WIND WHEEL

CAMP FROMAN

II

BASE

HALO 3

BASICS

CAMPAIGN

EXTRAS

MULTIPLAYER

PLAYING CO-OP

MULTIPLAYER
BASICS

GAME TYPES

MULTIPLAYER
TACTICS

**MULTIPLAYER
MAPS**

FORGE

I INTERIOR

The main vehicle entrances to the base are blocked by barriers. You can use the terminal inside to drop these for the rest of the round in objective-based games.

The bridge that leads to the Wind Wheel can be lowered to create another route of attack in Assault and CTF games.

II UPPER FLOOR

DEFAULT GEAR & RESPAWN ESTIMATES

Weapons		slow ➡ fast
	Assault Rifle	
	Battle Rifle	
	Brute Shot	
	Magnum	
	Needler	
	Plasma Pistol	
	Shotgun	
	SMG	
	Sniper Rifle	
	Spartan Laser	
	Spiker	

Portable Turrets		slow ➡ fast
	Machine Gun Turret	

Equipment		slow ➡ fast
	Active Camo	
	Bubble Shield	
	Grav Lift	
	Power Drain	
	Radar Jammer	

Grenades		slow ➡ fast
	Frag Grenade	
	Spike Grenade	

Vehicles		slow ➡ fast
	Ghost	
	Mongoose	
	Warthog	

LAST RESORT

Base Area

The inside of the Wind Wheel can be an interesting spot to set up camp with a Spartan Laser or Sniper Rifle, but only for accomplished marksmen — compensating for the movement of the wheel while aiming will be beyond the abilities of many players.

The turrets on the upper walkway can be used to defend the Base from incoming vehicles. One gives an excellent view of the point where your opponents will attempt to jump vehicles through the Wind Wheel, while the other turret has a clear view of the route that takes your opponents past Camp Froman. However, you're extremely vulnerable to sniper fire while you man the turrets in their fixed positions. Depending on the circumstances, it may be better to detach them from their bases and move to a less exposed area.

In objective-based games, the team defending the Base should aim to secure the Sniper Rifle at Camp Froman and the Shotgun at the back of the Wind Wheel immediately.

If you're in a hurry, you can knock the Shotgun to the ground from its spawn point by throwing a grenade at it.

There is a Needler close to the Spartan Laser spawn point, which sets up some extremely interesting confrontations. In the rush to secure the Spartan Laser in certain Game Types, a smart player will generally opt to collect the Needler first, then take the Spartan Laser by force.

The Grav Lift offers just enough height to reach the central catwalk where the turrets are located (Fig. 1). This is an easy way to get upstairs quickly, and can come in handy for gaining an equal footing with any would-be Spartan Laser users.

There are several entrances to the Base, and even the biggest team will struggle to defend them all. You may find that, strategically, it makes more sense to have a couple of floating "reaction forces" charged with defending a general area, rather than spreading your team too thinly in an attempt to post a soldier on every point of ingress.

In Assault games, the recess beside the staircase is a good place to lurk when you are defending the bomb arming site.

The defending team has access to a Radar Jammer. Using it will confuse and alarm an attack force, but this cuts both ways — you can create disarray among your own ranks, too. Unless you are playing in an established team with a well-drilled defensive strategy, it's better to throw it in the direction of the Wind Wheel.

Though it may seem like the best option, you don't always need to jump on board a Warthog to make an escape with the enemy flag. If the vehicle has a competent driver and an experienced gunner, they can instead run rampage inside the base, creating a distraction that enables a flag carrier to (somewhat unexpectedly) escape on foot.

HALO 3

BASICS

CAMPAIGN

EXTRAS

MULTIPLAYER

PLAYING CO-OP

MULTIPLAYER
BASICS

GAME TYPES

MULTIPLAYER
TACTICS

**MULTIPLAYER
MAPS**

FORGE

In objective-based games with a large number of players, the defending team should consider sending a small detachment to control Camp Froman, using it as a first line of defense.

Conversely, if you can control Camp Froman as the attacking team, you can have a sniper set up shop on the catwalk. From there, your marksman will be able to see into the base, and cause havoc before his teammates begin a concerted assault.

It's a tricky jump, but you can also hop on top of the trees beside Camp Froman. Your view of the ground below is restricted, but it's a good ambush spot in certain Game Types. There's also a little patch of grass in the corner below that you can use for the same purpose.

There are lots of Fusion Cores with fast respawn times on this map, so always be ready to shoot one to weaken a passing enemy, or even push one over a ledge to hit an opponent traveling below.

In Territories games, Territory #4 can be one of the most important. If you can manage to secure it early enough, you'll also gain control of a pivotal respawn point, one that offers more rapid access to #2, #3 and #5. The only problem with Territory #4 is that it's very exposed to snipers, so take a Bubble Shield along when you make the attempt to capture it.

0 2

Beach Area

Aim to grab a Battle Rifle as soon as you can after you spawn — there's a plentiful supply, and you're virtually naked without one.

Jumping a vehicle through the Wind Wheel is the quickest route to the Base, but it's extremely risky if an opponent is manning the nearest turret. It can also be a tricky jump for inexperienced drivers — it's surprising how many times players manage to crash disastrously even when not under direct fire.

If you're a lousy sniper with 20 minutes to spare, you can start a solo game and hone your marksmanship skills on the seagulls at the beach area — it's genuinely good practice for actual combat situations.

The top of the broken arch on the beach (and above the sea wall) is a good sniping spot (Fig. 2). You can get up there via the beach, or by jumping up from the sea wall.

It's possible to grenade jump into the high opening at the far end of the sea wall. This can be a good trick to have in your repertoire if you need to make a last-ditch attempt to stop an enemy flag carrier.

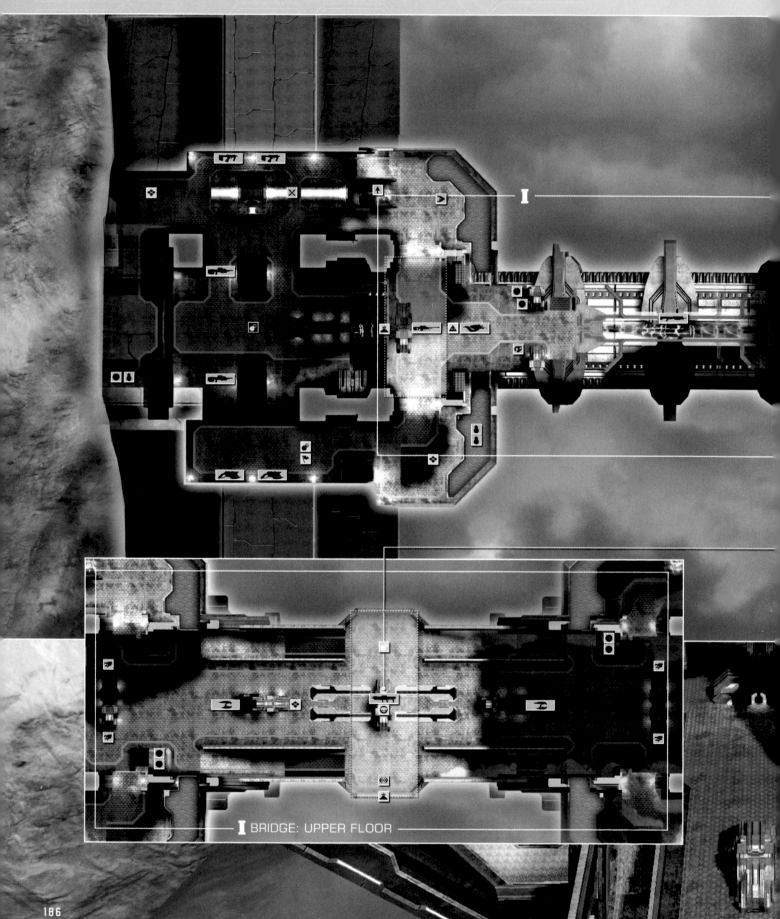

I BRIDGE: UPPER FLOOR

BASICS

CAMPAIGN

EXTRAS

MULTIPLAYER

PLAYING CO-OP

MULTIPLAYER
BASICS

GAME TYPES

MULTIPLAYER
TACTICS

**MULTIPLAYER
MAPS**

FORGE

[QUICK FACTS]

Recommended Variants	Team Slayer, One Flag, Multi Flag, Assault, One Bomb, VIP
Recommended Number of Players	2-8
Objects of Desire	Rocket Launcher, Sniper Rifle, Shotgun, Power Drain, Active Camo, Overshield, Brute Shot

[DEFAULT GEAR & RESPAWN ESTIMATES]

Weapons	slow ➡ fast
Battle Rifle	
Brute Shot	
Mauler	
Needler	
Plasma Pistol	
Plasma Rifle	
Rocket Launcher	
Shotgun	
SMG	
Sniper Rifle	
Spiker	

Equipment	slow ➡ fast
Active Camo	
Bubble Shield	
Overshield	
Power Drain	
Radar Jammer	

Grenades	slow ➡ fast
Frag Grenade	
Plasma Grenade	

Gain control of the two levels of the bridge in objective-based games, and you'll have the upper hand. The top section is home to the fiercest combat (especially when the Rocket Launcher is in play), while the smaller walkway underneath is the site of many tense stand-offs.

As you'll soon notice, both "base" areas have a distinct color scheme — one base has a distinct blue tint (pictured above), while the other has a yellow hue. For easy reference, we're going to refer to them as "Blue Base" and "Yellow Base".

Bridge Tips

The Rocket Launcher can be found at the very centre of the top bridge, which – naturally – is the site of particularly messy early-match battles, with flare-ups occurring whenever the weapon respawns. There is a Fusion Core on either side of the platform it rests on. Anyone standing over the Rocket Launcher when one of these explodes will lose practically all of their shield energy, so the first person to jump up often pays for their enthusiasm (Fig. 1). Further complicating matters is the presence of a Radar Jammer right next to this position. If someone sets it off, everyone will be jumping at shadows.

The Shotgun is positioned at the centre of the lower bridge. It's great for base defense, so try to pick it up whenever you can. However, the fight to gain control of it can be deadly. If you are the first to make a dash for it, you might become an easy target for a Plasma Grenade thrown by a more cautious (and, some might argue, wiser) opponent.

The battle to gain control of the bridge's upper level often determines the outcome of many CTF and Assault games. Push your opponents back, and you'll gain access to the ramps leading down to the lower level; you'll also secure control of the Rocket Launcher spawn point. In One Flag and One Bomb variants especially, it's essential that defending teams allocate sufficient manpower to control this area.

On the far ends of the main bridge, you can walk on the barriers situated at either side to jump directly to the platforms beyond.

The lower bridge is the quickest route into your opponent's base... if you can survive the short journey. Being very narrow at the center, and with no cover once an assailant commits to moving over it, it's very easy to defend. The presence of a Plasma Pistol and Plasma Grenades at either end perhaps indicates what works best here – either blow enemies from the narrow walkway, or even panic them into falling off the edge. Two players hiding behind cover could potentially hold this position against a much larger force. The main danger, though, is that you can be overwhelmed should opponents run down the nearby slopes from the upper level.

Base Tips

Each base has a Sniper Rifle on either side of the lower bridge level. In objective-based games, it's generally best to use this to defend against opponents attacking via the Man Cannon, occasionally helping out on the lower bridge when required. Broadly speaking, it's inadvisable for a sniper to set up shop on the upper bridge – there's just too much cover for opponents to hide behind.

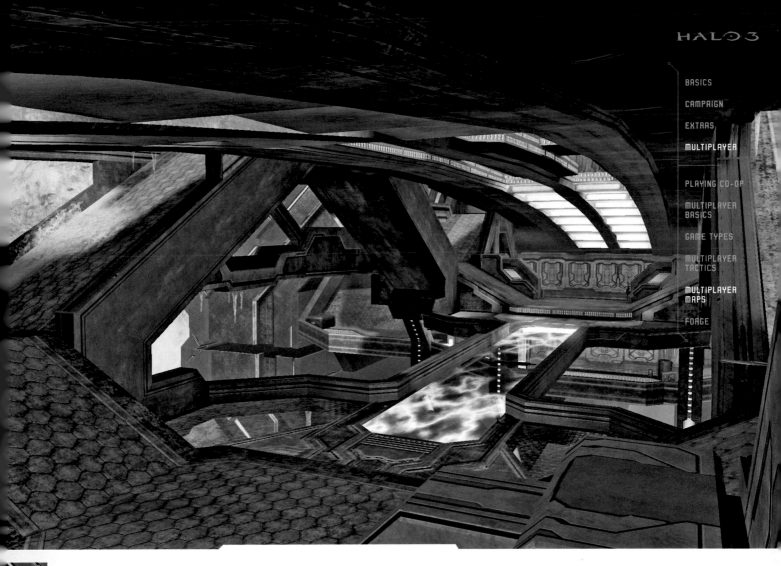

HALO 3

BASICS

CAMPAIGN

EXTRAS

MULTIPLAYER

PLAYING CO-OP

MULTIPLAYER
BASICS

GAME TYPES

MULTIPLAYER
TACTICS

MULTIPLAYER
MAPS

FORGE

Blue Base is home to the Overshield, while Yellow Base has Active Camo in the equivalent position. There's a Brute Shot next to both power-ups, so the decision to visit this low corridor in Team Slayer games can be fatal if an opponent gets there first.

The Man Cannons offer the quickest route into the opposing base, but are — as a rule — very easy to defend. Anyone flying through the air is a simple target for someone with a Sniper Rifle or Battle Rifle, and the landing spot — right on top of the Needler spawn point — can be strewn with grenades by defenders in anticipation of a group's arrival.

The Blue Base has a Bubble Shield positioned right in front of the Man Cannon. If you throw this into the Man Cannon just before you take off, it provides cover for your entire flight (Fig. 2), and helps you to establish a "beach head" on landing. Naturally, this is a strategy that takes a little coordination, and also a certain amount of luck — skilled opponents will attempt to destroy the Bubble Shield by planting a grenade at the position where it lands.

The Yellow Base has a Power Drain positioned near to the Man Cannon instead of a Bubble Shield. This can be used in one of two ways. The first is to toss it through the Man Cannon to damage the shields of opponents flying towards the landing spot — it will usually reduce them to approximately one third. The second (and less satisfying) option is to throw it at the landing position just before they touch down.

Though Yellow Base soldiers guarding the Man Cannon in objective-based games will be itching to throw the Power Drain through the gravity device, it can actually be more profitably employed by players fighting to get an upper hand on the bridge.

If equipment items hit players as they fly through the Man Cannon, the collision can reduce their momentum, causing them to fall to their deaths.

In CTF games, it is possible to drop the flag in the Man Cannon for a teammate to collect on the other side if needs be. You can even turn this into an actual strategy by sacrificing yourself to slow the advance of any opponents giving chase. You may not get the kudos of the actual flag capture, but your team will love you all the more.

If you throw Frag Grenades into the Man Cannon in such a way that they hit the ground before they take off, they will explode at a low point in their flight arc. With practice, you can learn how to time these throws to damage incoming enemies. Similarly, if an opponent attempts to escape you by jumping into a Man Cannon, you're practically obliged to bid them *bon voyage* by throwing a couple of grenades in to keep them company.

SANDTRAP

EXTERIOR

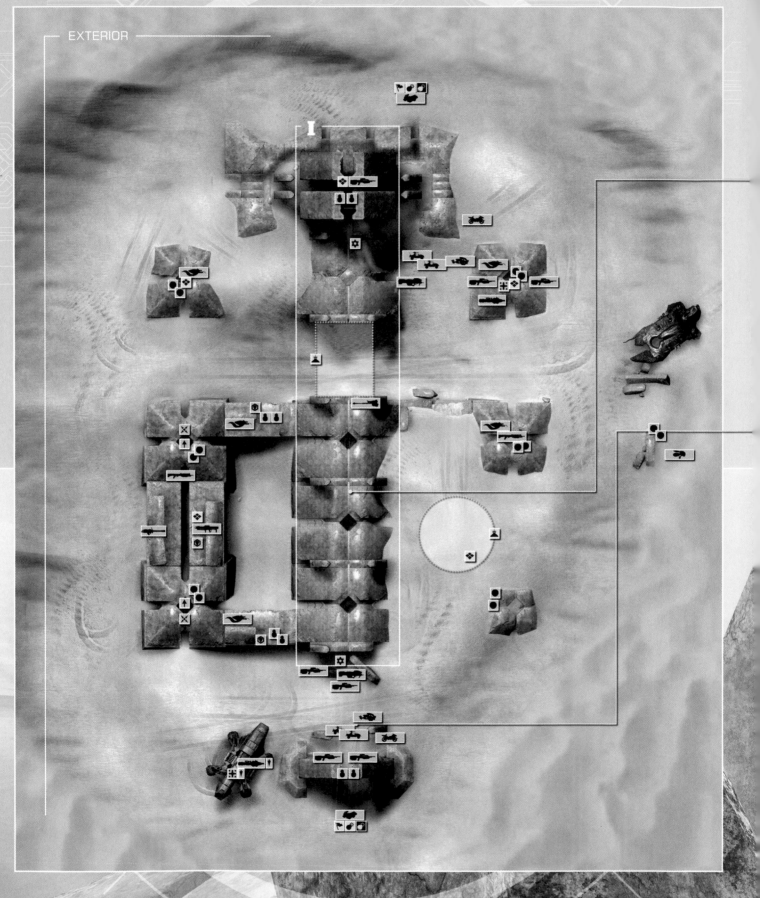

BASICS

CAMPAIGN

EXTRAS

MULTIPLAYER

PLAYING CO-OP

MULTIPLAYER
BASICS

GAME TYPES

MULTIPLAYER
TACTICS

**MULTIPLAYER
MAPS**

FORGE

The tops of the ancient buildings offer an excellent view of the battlefield, and are typically frequented by snipers preying on soldiers foolish enough to cross the map on foot.

The vehicles that spawn on both halves of the map are a precious resource, and one that teams should endeavor to defend in objective-based games. Having your side's quota destroyed by a marauding Chopper can turn the tide of the battle in the favor of your opponents.

[**QUICK FACTS**]

Recommended Variants	Team Slayer, King of the Hill, One Flag, Territories, One Bomb
Recommended Number of Players	6-16
Objects of Desire	Banshee, Chopper, Rocket Launcher, Missile Pod, Spartan Laser, Gravity Hammer, Sniper Rifle

[**DEFAULT GEAR & RESPAWN ESTIMATES**]

Weapons	slow ➡ fast
Battle Rifle	
Brute Shot	
Gravity Hammer	
Rocket Launcher	
Shotgun	
Sniper Rifle	
Spartan Laser	

Portable Turrets	slow ➡ fast
Machine Gun Turret	
Missile Pod	

Equipment	slow ➡ fast
Bubble Shield	
Grav Lift	
Power Drain	
Regenerator	
Trip Mine	

Grenades	slow ➡ fast
Frag Grenade	
Plasma Grenade	

Vehicles	slow ➡ fast
Banshee	
Chopper	
Elephant	
Mongoose	
Warthog	

INTERIOR

SANDTRAP

General Tips

The Sandtrap map is home to a unique vehicle: the Elephant. This indestructible Behemoth-class troop transport is equipped with an unbreakable Machine Gun Turret, and may have an additional (though destroyable) turret in certain Game Types. In CTF and Assault games, flags, bombs and bomb arming points are all positioned on the Elephant itself, making it a unique moving base.

The Elephant driver is completely covered from attack from the front and sides, but is – of course – completely vulnerable to attacks from behind the cabin (Fig. 1). For this reason, the driver's teammates should always be quick to warn him or her when enemies jump on board.

The inclusion of the Elephant adds an additional strategic layer to certain Game Types, particularly Assault and CTF. If you move it, you increase the distance between a major spawn point for your team (friendly faces will regularly appear back from their brief sojourn in purgatory when it is under allied control), and your supply of vehicles. That said, against better organized opponents, there's a danger that they may move their Elephant closer in an attempt to overpower you, so it's sometimes a necessary step.

You can also steal the opposing team's Elephant and bring it closer to your own in CTF and Assault matches, but this is just as likely to be a tactical *faux pas* of the highest order as it is a strategic masterstroke.

The single Banshee on this map can cause havoc if left unchecked, and there's usually a vicious battle to secure it in all Game Types where it appears. The pilot doesn't have complete control of the skies, though – the presence of Missile Pods and Spartan Lasers means that winning the violent race to get on board is a pyrrhic victory that ends with an abrupt explosion not long after takeoff. For this reason, some teams prefer to simply destroy it, then move on. However, there's a definite benefit to having members of an opposing team distracted by the need to destroy a Banshee. Who said that tactics were ever easy?

HALO 3

BASICS

CAMPAIGN

EXTRAS

MULTIPLAYER

PLAYING CO-OP

MULTIPLAYER
BASICS

GAME TYPES

MULTIPLAYER
TACTICS

**MULTIPLAYER
MAPS**

FORGE

Looking after and making good use of your vehicles is the key to succeeding in team-based games. Sending a Chopper to camp the position where your enemy's vehicles spawn can be a highly effective strategy, particularly in Territories sessions.

While you can move outside the perimeter of the map, the sand there is littered with explosive mines — you won't survive for long if you move more than a few strides past the boundary markers.

In a team-based Oddball game, if you can get your carrier into a fast vehicle, you can drive around in the minefield indefinitely (Fig. 2). The principle dangers out there are Banshees and Missile Pods — plus, of course, anything that might cause you to slow down.

The killzone that surrounds the map does not start immediately at the dune ledges. There is room enough for a vehicle to drive along the edges of the map. Players who have their attention focused on the playable area will often fail to see a vehicle driving there.

Remember that it's not just the Chopper's cannons that you need to worry about — if it boosts before it hits another light vehicle, the results are rarely pretty.

The wreckage of the crashed Phantom can actually be a very good camping spot.

If you can collect one during the journey, you can throw a Power Drain onto an enemy Elephant to weaken your opponents before you attack.

When there's no immediate danger from Missile Pods, you can use a Banshee to ferry a teammate armed with a Sniper Rifle to

the highest towers (Fig. 3). Riding on top of a Banshee is tricky, but eminently possible if the pilot doesn't make any sharp turns or rapid bursts of speed.

The ideal choice of weapon is governed by your position on the map. A Battle Rifle is a requisite throughout, of course, but it pays to have something with more punch at close range when you move through the tunnels that run throughout the buildings.

Watch out for enemies wielding the Gravity Hammer inside the tunnels — there are literally dozens of potential ambush spots.

Try not to cover open ground on foot if you can avoid it — you'll be easy prey for snipers and patrolling Warthogs and Choppers. Vehicles spawn quickly on this map, so grab a ride whenever you can.

SNOWBOUND

INTERIOR

[QUICK FACTS]

Recommended Variants	Slayer, Team Slayer, King of the Hill, One Flag, Land Grab
Recommended Number of Players	2-8
Objects of Desire	Spartan Laser, Beam Rifle, Shotgun, Overshield, Active Camo

HALO3

BASICS

CAMPAIGN

EXTRAS

MULTIPLAYER

PLAYING CO-OP

MULTIPLAYER
BASICS

GAME TYPES

MULTIPLAYER
TACTICS

**MULTIPLAYER
MAPS**

FORGE

The map edges are deadly. Walk over the perimeter, and the automated defense system will open fire immediately.

The roofs of the two bases provide the best view of the battlefield, but this works both ways — your opponents will have an equally clear sight of you. As the Spartan Laser spawns in one base, and the Beam Rifle in the other, we refer to the buildings as the Spartan Laser Base and Beam Rifle Base in the tips that follow, for ease of reference.

DEFAULT GEAR & RESPAWN ESTIMATES

Weapons	slow ➡ fast
Battle Rifle	
Beam Rifle	
Brute Shot	
Carbine	
Mauler	
Needler	
Plasma Rifle	
Shotgun	
Spartan Laser	
Spiker	

Equipment	slow ➡ fast
Active Camo	
Bubble Shield	
Overshield	
Power Drain	

Grenades	slow ➡ fast
Frag Grenade	
Plasma Grenade	

Vehicles	slow ➡ fast
Ghost	

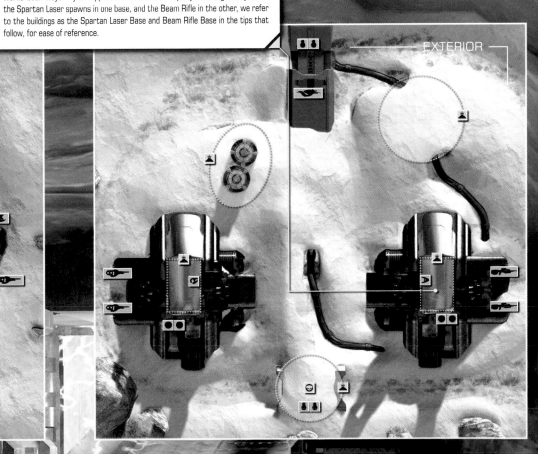

EXTERIOR

SNOWBOUND

Exterior

Pick your battles wisely in the outside area. If you begin firing at a distant opponent who can easily duck behind cover, you will waste ammo and draw attention to yourself. With dangers such as the Beam Rifle, Spartan Laser and Ghost to worry about, it's better to keep a low profile until you are sure you can secure a kill.

The Spartan Laser and Beam Rifle, the principle "power weapons" on this map, can enable skilled players to dominate the outside area. In free-for-all games, many combatants will rush for these spawn points in the hope of securing one of them as soon as the match begins. The fracas that ensues has the feel of a lottery, so you'll often be better served by focusing your attention elsewhere or, if you really *need* either weapon, by arriving fashionably late to pick off a weakened survivor.

There is a Needler on top of the Spartan Laser Base. An especially cunning player could aim to grab it, then lie in wait for other players to emerge from the room below.

If you get your hands on a Beam Rifle, it's worth swinging by the Active Camo spawn point to see if it is available.

When you spawn outside, it's essential that you grab a Carbine or a Battle Rifle straight away. The Assault Rifle will be of little help to you if a marksman attacks from medium or long range.

Grabbing the Ghost when it spawns (or stealing it from another player) can be a great way to secure a few "easy" kills, but opponents will often hear you long before they see you. Additionally, you are an easy target for an opponent wielding the Spartan Laser.

Guardian turrets only start firing once you are a few steps beyond the perimeter. Therefore, you can actually use them as cover when you fight on the open snowfield (Fig. 1).

Beyond the Spartan Laser Base, you can stand on a ledge just over the perimeter. It's safe to stay here, though — an invisible boundary wall prevents you from moving far enough to invoke the ire of the Guardian turrets. This is a good sniping spot, and you can also escape here with the Oddball.

If you're close to the perimeter, carrying the Oddball and under attack, make a dash over the boundary before you die. The Oddball will be reset to its original position.

You can reach a high point on either tower, but we can think of no conceivable benefit derived by doing so — given the fuss and careful preparations necessary to achieve it, your time could be better spent

HALO 3

BASICS

CAMPAIGN

EXTRAS

MULTIPLAYER

PLAYING CO-OP

MULTIPLAYER
BASICS

GAME TYPES

MULTIPLAYER
TACTICS

**MULTIPLAYER
MAPS**

FORGE

actually killing opponents. You'll need a willing assistant to stand on, and either a grenade jump from their head (which necessitates the mutual sacrifice of a Betrayal) or a double Brute Shot jump to get up there. Don't press too far forward on the stick, or you'll simply shoot straight over; it takes a delicate touch to land safely. Now, after all that, you did remember to bring a Beam Rifle along, didn't you?

If you espy opponents battling in the distance, it's often worth pitching a Frag Grenade in their general direction in an attempt to steal a kill. However, remember that grenades will not bounce if they land on snow. It sounds obvious, but it's easy to forget.

Interior

The energy shields covering the main entrances to the underground areas admit passage to you and your opponents, but block weapons fire, explosions and vehicles.

The shield walls blocking the majority of entrances are great escape routes in either direction, but try not to get caught up in "cat and mouse" exchanges with an opponent on the opposite side. No matter how fierce your mutual desire to win the duel may be, other players will have little respect for your battle of wills — and you're an easy target for a Plasma Grenade or melee attack while your attention is so narrowly focused.

When you have the Oddball, hide next to a shield door. As you are equipped with a supremely powerful melee weapon , you can simply hit opponents to kill them as they attempt to walk through. The best way to counter this is to aim to tag the Oddball carrier with a grenade. They may kill you, but you'll have the satisfaction of taking them with you...

When inside either base, you can actually look up and see enemies moving above through the transparent ceiling.

The Shotgun spawns at the main entrance to the room that connects the two bases. In the close confines of the basement floor, this weapon rules supreme.

The Brute Shot may be located outside, but it is ill-suited to long

or even medium range battles unless you're a supremely good marksman. You may find that it's much more effective in the close confines of the underground rooms, where you can finish battles with a swipe of its viciously sharp blade attachment. That said, it can be a very useful tool if you manage to surprise an opponent armed with a Spartan Laser or Beam Rifle, or driving a Ghost.

Arm yourself with a dual-wield combo (or, perhaps better still, a Shotgun or a Brute Shot) if you intend to wage war in the narrow corridors of the underground area.

You can't drive the Ghost through the shields, of course, but you can gain access to the basement area via the pipe tunnel . This isn't necessarily a wise strategy, though — there's not a great deal to do down there, and you're an easy target for grenades.

Look out for the panels on either side of the Shotgun spawn point, just inside the basement entrance. These explode if shot or caught up in an explosion (Fig. 2). This is a good way to take down a rival making a break for the nearby weapon.

0   2

Both main "base" rooms feature a screen that you can hide behind. Very occasionally, you will find that you can catch inattentive opponents out this way. You can also jump onto the purple beams that extend from the left and right of the screen. You can't climb very high but, again, the split-second that it takes for many opponents to notice you can be sufficient to give you enough time to make a decisive first strike. (Well, as long as they enter the room via the door you are facing, of course...)

THE PIT

BOTTOM FLOOR RAMP

[QUICK FACTS]

Recommended Variants	Team Slayer, One Flag, Multi Flag, Assault, One Bomb, VIP
Recommended Number of Players	4-10
Objects of Desire	Rocket Launcher, Energy Sword, Sniper Rifle, Machine Gun Turret, Active Camo, Overshield

BASICS

CAMPAIGN

EXTRAS

MULTIPLAYER

PLAYING CO-OP

MULTIPLAYER
BASICS

GAME TYPES

MULTIPLAYER
TACTICS

**MULTIPLAYER
MAPS**

FORGE

DEFAULT GEAR & RESPAWN ESTIMATES

Weapons		slow → fast
Assault Rifle		
Battle Rifle		
Brute Shot		
Energy Sword		
Magnum		
Mauler		
Needler		

		slow → fast
Plasma Pistol		
Plasma Rifle		
Rocket Launcher		
Shotgun		
SMG		
Sniper Rifle		
Spiker		

Portable Turrets	slow → fast
Machine Gun Turret	

Equipment		slow → fast
Active Camo		
Overshield		
Power Drain		
Regenerator		

Grenades		slow → fast
Frag Grenade		
Plasma Grenade		

Both base areas are effectively identical, and are home to a fairly solid range of weapons. The Machine Gun Turrets and Sniper Rifles are key weapons for defending objectives.

There are numerous routes through the center of the map, which plays host to some of The Pit's most furiously contested and unpredictable battles.

INTERIOR

THE PIT

General tips

As a glance at the previous double-page spread should reveal, the weapon placements on this map are broadly symmetrical. Anything that spawns in one base should also appear in the other, which makes fighting your way into enemy territory a little easier.

As The Pit's architecture means that you are often vulnerable to sudden ambushes and long-range sniping, it pays to collect a Battle Rifle in addition to something more suitable for toe-to-toe exchanges.

It's possible — though, with the exception of low-gravity Custom Games, almost prohibitively awkward — to get up to the second floor of the main building in both bases. You'll either need to make a grenade jump from a teammate's head, perform a Brute Shot jump (two shots are required, so practice offline), or form a human pyramid with a group of organized allies. The latter technique, as you can imagine, has obvious applications during VIP or team-based Oddball games. It's also the best sniping position on the entire map (Fig. 1).

0 1

The Energy Sword spawn room (also known as the Ops Center) can be a good place to hide in Oddball matches (Fig. 2). However, there are small holes in the wall that enable opponents to throw grenades through to flush you out. Be ready for this when it happens.

0 2

The Energy Sword room is something of a choke point on this map. As the Spartan-sticker has a lower respawn time than most power weapons, there's usually a fair amount of traffic in the region. The inclusion of a Power Drain and two Maulers nearby makes for some varied fights. You may be first to arrive at the sword, but that's no guarantee that you'll get to keep it for long.

There are plenty of Plasma Grenades on this map, so have one at the ready when you approach common haunts for Energy Sword users. Even if they catch you with a lunge, you can stick them with a grenade at the same time to make it their last in a while…

HALO3

BASICS

CAMPAIGN

EXTRAS

MULTIPLAYER

PLAYING CO-OP

MULTIPLAYER
BASICS

GAME TYPES

MULTIPLAYER
TACTICS

**MULTIPLAYER
MAPS**

FORGE

0 3

0 4

Don't waste the Regenerators on meaningless battles in Assault matches — they're very precious tools when it comes to arming a bomb.

You can find two Plasma Pistols and two Magnums at the center of The Pit, which is rare — Halo 3's multiplayer maps tend to separate these weapons. This dual-wield combo is unbelievably powerful against single opponents... but only on the proviso that you hit them with the initial charged shot. If you miss, you're done for. In congested areas, it's just not practical — if you face more than one enemy, you'll probably be dead before you can overcharge the Plasma Pistol. It's better, then, to stalk paths less traveled in search of stragglers separated from the main herd.

The two Machine Gun Turrets on either base are obviously very tempting, but the operator is an easy target for an enemy sniper. In free-tor-all games you should simply wrench it from its housing and set off for a suitable location to mount ambushes (the Sniper Rifle spawn point can be a profitable choice – Fig. 3). In objective-based games, a player armed with the turret can provide valuable support to a team assaulting the opposing base, or making a fleet-footed return with the enemy flag.

The Rocket Launcher is a much sought-after weapon on this map, and it spawns in a long, tight corridor. It's a good idea to throw grenades to spook potential rivals approaching from the other side. Another sensible way to handle skirmishes in this hallway is to grab the nearby Needler on the way there, and spray anyone unfortunate enough to be trapped in the close confines (Fig. 4). There's very little they can do other than hop, curse and sputter if you catch them halfway towards the Rocket Launcher spawn point.

Returning the flag isn't easy on this map, as the quickest way back isn't always the safest. A route that can be surprisingly successful, though, is to take the long road along the lowest part of the map, past where the Overshield spawns. Due to the absence of specific weapons there, the opposing team will often neglect to station someone to guard the area.

LAKE BASE

LAKE BASE: INTERIOR

HALO 3

BASICS

CAMPAIGN

EXTRAS

MULTIPLAYER

PLAYING CO-OP

MULTIPLAYER
BASICS

GAME TYPES

MULTIPLAYER
TACTICS

**MULTIPLAYER
MAPS**

FORGE

The center of the Valhalla map is where some of its fiercest skirmishes take place. Many of these involve the constant battle to gain control of the Spartan Laser, but it's also the area where rival vehicles clash en route to their respective objectives.

Both bases are identical, and are the location of Valhalla's most powerful vehicles and weapons. The "Man Cannons", gravity lifts angled for a broadly horizontal trajectory, enable players to reach the central portion of the map rapidly – though the predictable flight arc contributes a degree of risk if there are snipers lurking within range.

WATERFALL BASE

II

II WATERFALL BASE: INTERIOR

[QUICK FACTS]

Recommended Variants	One Flag, Multi Flag, Assault, One Bomb, Team Slayer, Territories, VIP
Recommended Number of Players	6-16
Objects of Desire	Banshee, Wraith, Spartan Laser, Sniper Rifle

[DEFAULT GEAR & RESPAWN ESTIMATES]

Weapons	slow ➡ fast
Battle Rifle	
Brute Shot	
Plasma Pistol	
Shotgun	
SMG	
Sniper Rifle	
Spartan Laser	
Spiker	

Portable Turrets	slow ➡ fast
Machine Gun Turret	
Missile Pod	

Equipment	slow ➡ fast
Bubble Shield	
Power Drain	
Regenerator	

Grenades	slow ➡ fast
Frag Grenade	
Plasma Grenade	

Vehicles	slow ➡ fast
Banshee	
Mongoose	
Warthog	
Wraith	

203

General Tips

The Plasma Grenades and Battle Rifles in both bases have extremely short respawn times. Unless a particularly urgent event requires your immediate attention, it's generally worthwhile to wait for them to appear before you move on.

Anything that can fit into a Man Cannon is subject to its effect. Grenades, equipment, vehicles, Fusion Cores: whatever enters the blue energy waves will be propelled over a distance determined by that object's weight and angle of entry. Here are a few interesting ideas that you should consider.

- For fast Mongoose deployment, setting off via the main central Man Cannon is by far the quickest way to reach the center of the map. If you hit the blue energy waves at the correct angle and at high speed, you have a better chance of landing on your wheels (rather than your head) when you hit the ground. At the start of team-based games, this strategy is frequently used by both teams in the mad rush to secure the Spartan Laser.

- There is a Fusion Core on the surface just above the central Man Cannon on both bases. You can either shoot this to injure opponents as they attempt to escape, or push it into the Man Cannon. The chances of actually hitting anything are slim, but you'll holler with delight if you ever secure a kill this way.

- Similarly, you can fire grenades with the Man Cannon. However, you should note that Frag Grenades will explode in midair if they hit a surface beforehand. If you're aiming for a hundred-to-one shot attempt to kill a fleeing foe, a Plasma Grenade is the better choice.

- In Custom Games where Trip Mines have been added to the mix, positioning them at approximate landing spots can be amusingly effective. If you do this in team-based games, though, it's prudent to warn your allies beforehand.

- If you've grabbed the enemy flag in CTF games, but realize you have no chance of surviving the short run to the Man Cannon, try throwing it in to the device as a dying gesture. (This can actually be a useful strategy: if you have a second team waiting with a vehicle for the flag to land, you can even plan to turn and fight in an attempt to slow down the enemy pursuit.)

If you face numerous foes arriving at the arming spot or flag in Assault and CTF games, the Power Drain situated in both bases is a great way to disrupt large-scale attacks. Hold your nerve, wait until they can almost touch their objective, then deploy it. You know what to do next...

Under the rock arch near the Waterfall Base, there is a rock that you can stand on (Fig. 1). Due to the dim light, it can be hard for opponents to spot you there, which makes it an excellent position for ambushes.

The Missile Pod positioned in each base acts principally as a Banshee deterrent in team games. If you employ it against ground-based vehicles, pick your shots carefully, and don't waste missiles on distant targets.

0 1

HALO 3

BASICS

CAMPAIGN

EXTRAS

MULTIPLAYER

PLAYING CO-OP

MULTIPLAYER
BASICS

GAME TYPES

MULTIPLAYER
TACTICS

**MULTIPLAYER
MAPS**

FORGE

The team that takes control of the Spartan Laser gains an immediate advantage if they know how to make the most of it. You can either plan to take it back to your base to augment your defense if required, or immediately set out to destroy your opponent's vehicles. Whichever choice you make, it's pretty wasteful to fire it at pedestrians or Mongooses.

The sole Machine Gun Turret on Valhalla has an unusually short respawn time, and can play a big part in the battle to gain supremacy in the center of the map. The trick is to get it to a position where your reduced mobility is less of an issue.

The slope at the front of each of the bases can be climbed for the most direct route to the enemy flag or bomb arming site. You can even drive a Mongoose up this slope. As a rule, it's better to run or drive up the left-hand side – lest you forget, there is often a Fusion Core to the right of the central Man Cannon.

On the left-hand side of the Lake Base (facing into the map), there is a great camping spot behind the rock that leans against the cliff wall. For snipers, it has a lot going for it – namely a view of the Spartan Laser spawn point, as well as a reasonably clear view of the ground in front of the base. The icing on the cake is that it offers an escape route at the back.

In objective games, running across the map to reach your opponent's base (unless you have a specific reason for doing so) can be very time-consuming.

In Oddball games, you can hide in the interior area of either base by jumping on the sloped walls. From this position, opponents following the waypoint indicator will often assume that you are actually on the upper base level, which might grant you a few extra seconds.

0 2

Vehicle Tips

The Banshee is often a dominant force on this map. In objective-based games, it's absolutely vital that you don't waste yours – there's a long wait until another one spawns. In the hands of a capable pilot, it's a powerful tool for base defense. The further towards your opponent's base you move, the shorter your potential lifespan; however, if used purely to patrol and control the area around your base, you may find that your attacks falter without its support.

In the rush to reach the Spartan Laser in team games, try using the Banshee to make "airborne insertions".

It's always worth attempting to hijack other enemy vehicles (with the exception of the plentiful Mongoose) if you get the opportunity to do so. If you can take control of the opposing team's Banshee or Wraith (Fig. 2), you gain a big short-term advantage. Additionally, if someone tries to run you down with a low-flying Banshee and is foolish enough to miss, it's practically an obligation that you make them pay by stealing their wings.

In One Flag or One Bomb games, the defending team can block entrances to their base with vehicles. This won't stop a determined opponent from getting through, of course, but it will slow them down.

FORGE

The Forge is a powerful, easy-to-use real-time object editor that enables you to customize Halo 3's multiplayer maps in a wide variety of ways. Better still, this feature can be a uniquely social experience if you wish: you can have a handful of players adjusting the map while others (up to eight participants) actually play. The applications of the tools it puts at your disposal, as you'll soon realize, are pretty much endless.

You can access the Forge from the Main Menu, and then adjust the Network setting in the Forge Lobby if you intend to invite friends for collaborative editing via a LAN or Xbox LIVE. As a party leader, you can press ⊗ to adjust a selection of settings before you start your session, such as deciding who will be entitled to enter Edit Mode, or defining the attributes of participants (if you play in a large party, you could choose to make editors invulnerable to facilitate harassment-free creativity). You can save your Options configuration by pressing ⊗ if you like. When ready, select Start Forge to begin.

On the map itself, you control your character normally. If you are in a party, players will be split into teams and can fight as if they were in Team Slayer mode. You can change teams by pressing 🄻🄱 or 🅁🄱 in the Forge Lobby, or from the pause menu. The ingenuity of this feature is that it enables parties to stick together and enjoy themselves while a map is adjusted in meaningful ways, or fine tuned to encourage a particular style of play.

As a first-time editor, note that you can press ⏵ to visit the pause menu where there's a useful Forge page in addition to the usual Settings menus. The Forge page is where you can save edited maps for future use in the Custom Games Lobby and, more importantly for now, it also provides a list of controls for Edit Mode (Fig. 1).

When you're ready, press up on ✛ to enter Edit Mode. To help you get started, we've put together the following list of important controls.

Movement: You control your character more or less as if you were piloting a Banshee without the influence of gravity. Additionally, you can move vertically (🄻🄱 to fly down and 🅁🄱 to fly up), and speed up your rate of motion by holding 🄻🅃.

Manipulating Objects: When you aim at an object you can interact with, your "hand" icon will turn green. Press Ⓐ to grab it: you are then free to move it around as you please, manipulate it (hold 🅁🅃) and, of course, drop it (press Ⓐ again). To delete an item, press Ⓨ while aiming at it.

HALO3

BASICS

CAMPAIGN

EXTRAS

MULTIPLAYER

PLAYING CO-OP

MULTIPLAYER
BASICS

GAME TYPES

MULTIPLAYER
TACTICS

MULTIPLAYER
MAPS

FORGE

0 2

0 3

Item Menu: Press ⓧ to display the Item Menu.

- If you open the Item Menu without pointing at an item, you will have access to a number of special pages (press 🅛🅑 or 🅡🅑 to flick between them). Each page contains a category of items (weapons, vehicles, equipment, and so forth) that you can add to the map as you see fit by pressing 🅐. There are only two restrictions that you must take into account. Firstly, each item has a "cost" (the figure on the right-hand side of the menu) that is subtracted from an overall Budget that you cannot exceed. Secondly, most items can only be placed a certain number of times. Once you reach the maximum total, you will not be able to add more until you delete others. The remaining quantity that you can spawn appears to the left of each item in the menu.

- If you enter the Item Menu while pointing at an item, you will be shown its properties (such as its respawn rate, availability at start of each game, et al.) and be given the option to alter these.

- If you press ⓧ when the Item Menu is open, you will call up the Budget Summary. This reveals, among other things, how many items of the selected type are allowed on the map at any one time. If you increase the maximum number allowed on the map, you will be able to spawn in more objects of that type. However, that space is reserved and paid for in advance, so you'll need to weigh up whether you can afford it or not.

- Don't forget that you can interact with other players in unique ways while editing, dropping powerful weapons for beleaguered friends to use in times of crisis – or, for that matter, capriciously removing them to amuse yourself and others. Seeing the vehicle you're driving around in vanish from under you is quite an experience. You should also note that spawning extremely heavy objects to drop on top of players never, *ever* ceases to be funny...

While you can't modify landscapes or architecture in the Forge, the simple act of placing a few new weapons or vehicles on a map can completely change the flow and feel of the combat that takes place there. Editing maps, then, is all about striking a balance between the urge to place cool objects everywhere, and understanding what will make your creation fun to play.

There are certain limits to the number and nature of objects that you can place on each map. For example, you won't be able to introduce Scorpions to Valhalla, or Hornets to Snowbound – many locales are not suitable for certain vehicles, so you'll find that they do not appear in the Item Menu. Another restriction is the Budget system, as every item that you add (or that is already in place) has a cost which is subtracted from this total. As a consequence, a default map only leaves you with reasonable room for maneuver.

As you'll find, the best maps are often the product of a restrained, considered approach to item placement. Add too many weapons, especially the more powerful models, and you'll notice that games can become chaotic, disjointed and arbitrary. This is why the Bungie team will debate, for example, the placement of a Sniper Rifle or Wraith for weeks on end during the development process. It may seem like a trivial detail on first inspection, but these things genuinely *matter*.

That said, feel free to ignore the previous paragraph completely, and create maps crafted with as much freeform lunacy as you and your available budget can conjure up (Fig. 2). The Piggyback team certainly doesn't expect to win any design awards or to top Fileshare download charts with its insanely crude "Fusion Core Fracas" map (Fig. 3), but it's the taking part that counts, after all.

If you're extremely keen to craft amazing new Custom Variants to take the Halo 3 world by storm, feel free to drop by the forums at **www.bungie.net** to seek advice, inspiration, and like-minded potential collaborators.

[MULTIPLAYER TRAINING IN THE FORGE]

Not only is the Forge a highly powerful and flexible editing tool, it's also a useful playground if you want to experiment with all the items at your disposal in multiplayer Halo 3. As a fringe benefit, it's additionally a great way to learn the exact layout of each map, as the editor function enables you to fly anywhere you like within the confines of the level boundaries. If you're especially adventurous, you can activate features such as invincibility,

infinite grenades and unlimited ammo. Suitably kitted-out and protected from harm, you can then practice tricky grenade jumps, hone your extreme Warthog driving skills, or amuse yourself by seeing what happens if you boost a Ghost at full speed into a pair of unstable Fusion Cores. The latter might seem like a trivial waste of time, but accidents *do* happen – and forewarned is, after all, forearmed...

INDEX

If you are looking for specific information, this alphabetical listing is just what you need. Simply search for the keyword you're wondering about, and turn to the relevant page number, which refers directly to the corresponding explanation in the guide.

Depending on how far you have already progressed in the game, be aware that the index may lead you to potential spoilers. To avoid any such premature revelations, all index entries that link to the Extras chapter are written in red. You should avoid opening this chapter at all costs until you have played through the entire Campaign at least once.

TERM	PAGE
A Achievements	128-129
Allies	140
Alpha Zombie (Variant)	153
Anti-Aircraft Wraith	063, 140
Ark (Mission 6)	072-083
Armor	159
Assault (Game Type)	152
Assault (Variant)	152
Assault Rifle	021, 136-137, 158
Attrition Bomb (Variant)	152
Attrition CTF (Variant)	151
Audio	015
Auto Look Centering	009
Auto Turret	082, 134
B Banshee	139
Basics	006-015
Battle Rifle	021, 136-137, 158
Beam Rifle	021, 136-137, 158
Berserk Brute	131
Bestiary	130-133
Black Eye (Skull)	115
Brute	020, 130-131
Brute Captain	030, 131
Brute Chieftain	030, 130-131
Brute Minor	131
Brute Shot	021, 136-137, 158
Brute Stalker	082, 131
Bubble Shield	031, 134
Budget (Forge)	207
Built-in Game Types	151-153
Button Configuration	008
Button Layout	009
C Campaign	016-109
Campaign menu	009
Campaign Meta-game	117-127
Campaign Scoring	117-127
Capture the Flag (CTF) (Game Type)	151
Carbine	021, 136-137, 158
Carnage Report	150, 117
Carrier Form	070, 133
Catch (Skull)	115
Checkpoint	010, 015
Chieftain	030, 130-131
Chopper	052, 141
Cloaking	082, 134
Combat Form	070, 133
Commands	008
Construct Map	162-163
Controls	008

TERM	PAGE
Cooling Time (Weapons)	136
Co-op	144, 145
Cortana (Mission 8)	096-103
Cortana (Scoring Tips)	126
Covenant (Mission 7)	084-095
Cover	113
Crazy King (Variant)	152
Crosshair	010
Crouch Behavior	009
Crow's Nest (Scoring Tips)	120
Crow's Nest (Mission 2)	032-043
Custom Games	146, 153
Custom Games Lobby	146
Custom Variant	153
D Deployable Cover	043, 134
Difficulty Level	009, 013
Difficulty Multiplier Scoring	117, 118
Drone	043, 132
Dual Wielding	014
Duel (Variant)	151
E Editor (Forge)	206-207
Eliminatio (Variant)	151
Elite (Armor)	159
Elites	071
Enemies	020, 130-133
Enemy Classes	117
Enemy Vehicle Classes	117
Energy Shield	010, 013
Energy Sword	070, 136-137, 158
Enlisted Rating	148
Epitaph Map	166-167
Equipment	010, 015, 134
Equipment Tips (Multiplayer)	156
Escort (Variant)	153
EXP (Experience Points)	148-149
Experience Points (EXP)	148-149
Extras	110-141
F Famine (Skull)	116
Field Promotions	149
File Share	011
Film Clip	012
Flag Rally (Variant)	152
Flamethrower	071, 136-137, 158
Flare	134
Floodgate (Mission 5)	064-071
Floodgate (Scoring Tips)	123
Fog (Skull)	115
Foreword	004-005
Forge	206-207
Forge Lobby	206

TERM	PAGE
Frag Grenade	021, 136-137
Fuel Rod Gun	053, 136-137, 158
G Game Controls	008-009
Game Types (Multiplayer)	151-153
Gamerscore	128-129
Gamertag	147
General Tips (Multiplayer)	154
Ghost	063, 140
Giant (Enemy Vehicle Classes)	117
Grade	148-149
Grav Lift	043, 134
Gravity Hammer	030, 136-137, 158
Grenades	010, 21, 134-135
Grunt	020, 131
Guardian Map	170-171
H Halo (Mission 9)	104-109
Halo (Scoring Tips)	127
Headshot	113
Heavy (Enemy Vehicle Classes)	117
Hero (Enemy Classes)	117
Hide and Seek (Variant)	153
High Ground Map	174-175
Hornet	095, 139
How to Play	006-015
Hunter	062, 132
I Incendiary Grenade	083, 135
Infantry (Enemy Classes)	117
Infection (Game Type)	153
Infection (Variant)	153
Infection Form	070, 133
Influential VIP (Variant)	153
Inventory	134-135
Invincibility	063, 136-137
Iron (Skull)	115
Isolation Map	178-179
J Jackal	020, 132
Juggernaut (Game Type)	152
Juggernaut (Variant)	152
Jump Pack Brute	043, 131
K K/D Spread	150
Kamikaze Grunt	030
King of the Hill (Game Type)	152
L Land Grab (Variant)	152
Last Resort Map	182-183
Leader (Enemy Classes)	117
Legendary Primer	112-113
Light (Enemy Vehicle Classes)	117
Look Inversion	009
Look Sensitivity	009
Lowball (Variant)	151
M Machine Gun Turret	042, 136-137, 158
Mad Dash (Variant)	152
Magnum	021, 136-137, 158
Main Menu	009
Manipulating Objects	206
Map Editing	206-207
Maps (Multiplayer)	160-206
Matchmaking	146
Matchmaking Lobby	146
Mauler	083, 136-137, 158

TERM	PAGE
Medals	149-150
Media	011-012
Melee Attack	014
Menus	009
Meta-game	117-127
Military Title	148
Missile Pod	063, 136-137, 158
Mission 1 (Sierra 117)	022-031
Mission 2 (Crow's Nest)	032-043
Mission 3 (Tsavo Highway)	044-053
Mission 4 (The Storm)	054-063
Mission 5 (Floodgate)	064-071
Mission 6 (The Ark)	072-083
Mission 7 (The Covenant)	084-095
Mission 8 (Cortana)	096-103
Mission 9 (Halo)	104-109
Mongoose	062, 139
Mosh Pit (Variant)	152
Motion Tracker	010
Movement	013
Multi Flag (Variant)	151
Multiplayer	142-207
Multiplayer Maps	160-205
Multiplayer Maps Introduction	160-161
Multiplayer Respawn Times	162-205
Multiplayer Tactics	154-159
Mythic (Skull)	116

TERM	PAGE
N Narrows Map	186-187
Needler	021, 136-137, 158
Neutral Bomb (Variant)	152
Ninjaball (Variant)	151
Ninjanaut (Variant)	152
O Oddball (Game Type)	151
Oddball (Variant)	151
Officer Rating	149
One Bomb (Variant)	152
One Flag (Variant)	151
One Sided VIP (Variant)	153
Onscreen Display (Campaign)	010
Onscreen Display (Multiplayer)	147
Options (Custom Games)	153
P Pause Menu	009
Penalties Scoring	117, 118
Pit	198-199
Plasma Grenade	021, 134
Plasma Pistol	021, 136-137, 158
Plasma Rifle	042, 136-137, 159
Plasma Turret	042, 136-137, 159
Playlist (Multiplayer)	146
Power Drain	043, 134
Primary Weapon	010
Prowler	141
Pure Form	071, 133
Q Quick Start	018
R Radar	010
Radar Jammer	042, 134
Rally Point	009
Ranged (Pure Form)	071, 133
Ranked Playlists	146
Rating	148-149
Recommendations (Skulls)	118

TERM	PAGE
Regenerator	043, 134
Reload Time (Weapons)	136
Reserve Weapon	010
Respawn Times (Multiplayer)	162-205
Rocket Launcher	063, 136-137, 159
Rocketball (Variant)	151
Rockets (Variant)	151
S Sandtrap Map	190-191
Save One Bullet (Variant)	153
Scarab	060-061
Score System	117-127
Scores & Multipliers	118
Scoring	117-127
Scoring Mechanics	117
Scorpion	082, 138
Screenshot	012
Sentinel	133
Sentinel Beam	083, 136-137, 159
Service Tag	147
Shade Turret	053, 141
Shields	010, 013
Shotgun	021, 136-137, 159
Sierra 117 (Mission 1)	022-031
Sierra 117 (Scoring Tips)	119
Skill	148-149
Skull Multipliers Scoring	117, 118
Skulls	114-116
Slayer (Game Type)	151
Slayer (Variant)	151
SMG	042, 136-137, 159
Sniper Rifle	021, 136-137, 159
Snowbound Map	194-195
Social Playlists	146
Spartan (Armor)	159
Spartan Laser	095, 136-137, 159
Specialist (Enemy Classes)	117
Spike Grenade	042, 135
Spiker	031, 136-137, 159
Stalker (Pure Form)	071, 133
Standard (Enemy Vehicle Classes)	117
Stick Layout	009
Storm (Mission 4)	054-063
Strategies & Tips Campaign Scoring	118
Strengths (Weapons)	137, 158
Style Multipliers Scoring	117, 118
T Tank (Pure Form)	071, 133
Tank Flag (Variant)	151
Team King (Variant)	152
Team Oddball (Variant)	151
Team Slayer (Variant)	151
Team Tips (Multiplayer)	155
Territories (Game Type)	152
Territories (Variant)	152
The Ark (Mission 6)	072-083
The Covenant (Mission 7)	084-095
The Covenant (Scoring Tips)	125
The Pit Map	198-199
The Storm (Mission 4)	054-063
The Storm (Scoring Tips)	122
Theater	012
Thunderstorm (Skull)	116

TERM	PAGE
Tilt (Skull)	116
Time Bonus Scoring	117
Tough Luck (Skull)	115
Trip Mine	053, 134
Tsavo Highway (Mission 3)	044-053
Tsavo Highway (Scoring Tips)	121
Turret	136-137, 158-159
U Unlockable armor	159
User Instructions	018-019
V Valhalla Map	202-203
Variants	151-153
Vehicle Tips (Multiplayer)	156
Vehicles	015, 138-141
Veto	146
VIP (Game Type)	153
VIP (Variant)	153
W Warthog	052, 138
Waypoint Indicator	010, 147
Weaknesses (Weapons)	137, 158
Weapon Guide (Multiplayer)	158
Weapon Tips (Multiplayer)	157
Weapons	014, 021, 134-137, 158
Weapons Strengths/ Weaknesses	137, 158
Wraith	052, 140